Accountabilities

Accountabilities

FIVE PUBLIC SERVICES

Patricia Day ◆ Rudolf Klein

TAVISTOCK PUBLICATIONS

London and New York

First published in 1987 by
Tavistock Publications Ltd
11 New Fetter Lane, London
EC4P 4EE

Published in the USA by
Tavistock Publications
in association with Methuen, Inc.
29 West 35th Street,
New York NY 10001

© 1987 Patricia Day and Rudolf
Klein

Typeset by Cambrian
Typesetters, Frimley, Surrey
Printed in Great Britain by
Richard Clay (The Chaucer
Press)

*British Library Cataloguing in
Publication Data*

Day, Patricia
  Accountabilities: five public
services.
  1. Corporations, Government
  —Great Britain
  I. Title   II. Klein, Rudolf,
  1930–
  354.4109'2   HD4147

  ISBN 0–422–79340–X
  ISBN 0–4222–79350–7 Pbk

CONTENTS

Introduction

Accountability is one of the fashionable words of our time. Over the past decades, new institutions and new techniques have been developed in the service of accountability, ranging from the National Audit Office to a gaggle of ombudsmen. Accountability is not merely seen as a crucial link in the chain between governors and governed: effective democracy, it is argued, implies a system which ensures that the former are accountable to the latter. Equally accountability is increasingly seen as a means of stretching scarce resources: if better value for money is to be achieved in the public sector, it is argued, then once again an effective system of accountability is needed.

This preoccupation with the institutions and techniques of accountability mirrors wider concerns. The modern Welfare State is also the service-delivery State. Its development has compounded the problems of making those who deliver services answerable both to those who finance them and those who use them. The growth of professionalism and expertise has led to the privatization of accountability, in so far as professionals and experts claim that only their peers can judge their conduct and performance. Furthermore, as the systems of service delivery have become more complex, so it has become more difficult to assign responsibility.

Existing links of accountability have become overloaded or broken; hence the search for new ones. Yet if there is a great deal of interest in accountability, there is also a great deal of confusion about what this chameleon word means. This book therefore represents an attempt to clarify the concept by exploring the perceptions and practice of accountability in a variety of settings in the public sector. And, although our concern is with accountability in the context of British institutions and services, the hope is that our analysis will also have resonance in other countries. For to the extent that the problems of accountability reflect the wider problems posed by big government and the reliance on expertise and professionalism, the British case is far from unique.

Our starting-point is that accountability is all about the construction of an agreed language or currency of discourse about conduct and performance, and the criteria that should be used in assessing them. It is a social and political process. It is about perceptions and power. It can therefore be expected to vary in different contexts, depending on the nature of the policy arena and the power of the different organizational actors. So, for example, there has been much discussion recently about the accountability of doctors and of policemen. If accountability is thought to be problematic in such very different services as the National Health Service and the police service, what have surgeons got in common with police officers?

To answer questions such as these, our book reports on a study financed by the Economic and Social Research Council of the way in which members of different public authorities define and carry out their role in the process of accountability. It compares and contrasts their role in National Health Service authorities, police authorities, regional water authorities, local authority education and social service committees. These were chosen not only because they represent a mix of directly elected and nominated members, but also because they deliver very different kinds of services and employ labour forces which vary greatly in terms of their professional status, organizational power, and expertise. They therefore allow us to explore the range of problems encountered in trying to translate the concept of accountability, in its various meanings, into effective reality: problems of organizational resistance and complexity, professional power, uncertainty about objectives and lack of knowledge about the relationship between service inputs, processes, and outputs.

The book represents a study of the perceptions and practice of accountability in one set of authorities, limited in its geographical setting, at one point in time. We do not therefore claim that our findings represent a definitive picture of how members of different authorities and committees go about their task. Our aim in carrying out our study was both more limited and more ambitious. It was to use our case studies, not to reach specific conclusions about how existing institutions work (which may well vary with changing political and financial environments) but to generate general insights into the kinds of problems encountered in trying to give meaning to that elusive concept: accountability.

The study was made possible by the 114 members of different authorities who gave us their time. We are grateful for their co-operation but must leave them nameless since our interviews were carried out on the understanding that the study would not identify the participants. Equally we are grateful to the officers of the various authorities who agreed to be interviewed and also helped us with the collection of background documents and information.

The development of our ideas was greatly helped by the comments of our colleagues at the Centre for the Analysis of Social Policy. Sylvia Hodges organized us and our interviews: the study owes much to her. Eve Gonty typed successive drafts, and we owe much to her skill and patience. Lastly we are most grateful for the patience of our publisher for allowing us to exceed successive deadlines.

1

The career of a concept

'Every idle word that men shall speak, they shall give account thereof in the day of judgement:'

(St Matthew xii. 36)

Accountability begins with individuals in simple societies. It ends with institutions in complex societies. It starts with telling stories and adding up. It ends with justification and explanation. The concern of this book is with the problems of accountability in societies grappling with the problems of complexity, of remoteness, and of specialization in the twentieth century. But to explore the way in which the notion has grown, and taken root in the language of everyday discourse about politics and administration in Britain today, means going back 2,000 years and more.

At its simplest, accountability is about the face-to-face relationship of individuals. Even if we do not think that we have to give an account of ourselves at the last judgement, by answering for our conduct or giving an explanation for what we have done, we may feel accountable for our daily actions either to others or to our own sense of what is right or appropriate: super-ego can take the place of super-God. In the first instance, when we talk about accountability in the context of social life, it implies that our actions are open to inspection and can challenge scrutiny. In the second instance, when we talk about accountability in a religious or ethical sense, it implies that our actions can be set against a certain set of rules or expectations about right conduct. Lastly accountability is about keeping our financial books in order: whenever we call for *le compte* in a French restaurant, we are going back to one of the roots of the word.

It is these various related but subtly shifting meanings of the concept that are caught in the dictionary definitions of the word. To account is to answer for the discharge of a duty or for conduct. It is to provide a reckoning. It is to give a satisfactory reason for or to explain. It is to acknowledge responsibility for one's actions. Indeed accountability and responsibility are often held to be synonymous: a reminder that one cannot be accountable *to* anyone, unless one also has responsibility *for* doing something.

But even simple accountability between individuals implies a social framework.[1] Psychological and social norms precede organizational and institutional requirements. Accountability implies both a shared set of expectations and a common currency of justifications. There has to be agreement about the context, the reason why one actor owes explanation to another since it is precisely this sense of obligation which translates the giving of accounts into accountability. Equally there has to be agreement about the language of justification, what constitutes good reason for explaining conduct.

If there is no such agreement, as when a delinquent is called upon to explain his or her behaviour, we talk not about accountability, but about excuses, apologies, or pretexts.[2] Conversely when there is agreement, as in the rendering of financial accounts, there is usually consensus both about context and criteria. The language of arithmetic is not in dispute, although there may still be arguments about why, for example, a given job took twice as long as agreed in the first place, and was therefore twice as expensive: here the giving of 'good' reasons may have the same characteristics as a delinquent trying to find suitable excuses, apologies, or pretexts.

In short, accountability, even at its simplest in the relationship between individuals, presupposes agreement both about what constitutes an acceptable performance and about the language of justification to be used by actors in defending their conduct. Furthermore, it implies a definition of the relationship between actors. To talk about accountability is to define who can call for an account, and who owes a duty of explanation. Both points are central to the theme of this book – accountability in the context of public services in Britain today – and the next section therefore turns to the development of political notions of accountability.

Origins of political accountability

Political accountability begins when individuals are given responsibility for carrying out tasks on behalf of their fellow citizens. The division of civic labour, the delegation of particular roles to individual citizens, creates the demand for political as distinct from personal accountability. So we find that the 'hallmark of the Athenian state', perhaps the first truly political society of which we have any record, 'was its concern for the accountability of its officials'.[3] For the men of Athens 'to have officials accountable was the key to responsible government: unaccountability meant lawlessness'. Indeed, it was precisely lack of accountability which, in the eyes of Athenians, characterized tyrants like Xerxes, the Persian despot.

Accountability in Athens was direct, continuous, and comprehensive. Ten times a year, the officials charged with carrying out the administration had to report on their conduct in office to the Assembly of the citizens. If they failed to carry a vote of confidence, if their explanation was judged to be inadequate, they faced a trial by jury of their fellow citizens. Even if they survived this ordeal, as many did not, all officials were required to submit a review of their performance at the end of their terms of office. Nor was this all. At any time, Athenian officials might find themselves impeached. This was a particular occupational hazard for generals and ambassadors. An unsuccessful battle or embassy might mean trial, and if convicted, death or exile. Demosthenes maintained that every Athenian general was tried for his life two or three times in his career and that the danger of being sentenced to death by the city's courts was greater than the risk of dying in battle.

To start our analysis of the career of the concept of political accountability with ancient Athens is to stress its origins in a particular view of what constitutes democratic society. Who says democracy, it is tempting to say, also says accountability. It is a tradition of political thought which sees the defining characteristic of democracy as stemming not merely from the election of those who are given delegated power to run society's affairs – Athenian officials were elected – but from their continuing obligation to explain and justify their conduct in public. Revocability may give an extra edge to accountability, as does the prospect of a trial for one's life, but it is not the same thing. From this perspective, it is precisely day-by-day accountability, in which the rulers explain and justify their actions directly to the ruled, which distinguishes a democratic society from an elective tyranny.

To start with ancient Athens is not only to underline the link between current notions of accountability and a particular view of what constitutes a democratic society, but also to emphasize that the ideas were born in a particular kind of society: a very simple society, in terms of its social and industrial structure, with a culturally homogeneous body of citizens within a heterogeneous population. It was a society in which political accountability for those citizens still could have many of the characteristics of individual accountability; its face-to-face nature, its immediacy, and the existence, despite violent disagreements on specific policy issues, of a shared context and shared criteria for judging good conduct or performance.

The problems of political accountability in modern societies, and the ambiguities of the concept in today's environment, stem precisely from the fact that while our ideas were born in relatively simple societies, they have developed in societies which have become increasingly complex over the centuries. It is this increasing complexity, marked by the division of labour and the growth and professionalization of expertise which explains why the concept of accountability, like that of democracy itself, has become an ever-more complex and difficult notion to apply in practice. In the remainder of this chapter we shall explore in a schematic form the implications of growing complexity and specialization for political accountability. But before doing so, we must first turn to a different tradition of thinking about account-ability; in terms not of political responsiveness but of good estate management. For many of the modern problems of accountability hinge on the extent to which it is possible to devise institutions and mechanisms which will marry up these two traditions.

Audit and stewardship

*'There was a certain rich man, which had a steward; and the
same was accused unto him that he had wasted his goods. And he
called him, and said unto him, How is it that I hear this of thee?
Give account of thy stewardship.'*

(St Luke xvi. 1–2)

Accountability is not only about political responsibility, but also
about financial responsibility: the verification of financial accounts
to check on whether the appropriate funds have come in and
whether the outgoing money has been spent properly. This
concept of accountability as verification is neither historically nor
logically linked to ideas about political accountability seen as
answerability to the people. But it is linked to notions of
government seen as the management of an estate, where the task
of running affairs is delegated to stewards who are required to
answer for the way in which they have exercised their responsibilities, whether to the *demos* or to the king. Presumably even a
tyrant like Xerxes called his servants to account for the way in which
they raised the levies for his armies and how they spent the money.

Financial accountability in its origins can be distinguished from
political accountability by the fact that it is a neutral, technical
exercise. It is about keeping true and accurate accounts in a realm
where there is agreement about the currency: money. In contrast,
political accountability is about giving persuasive accounts in a
realm where there may be disagreement about the currency: the
criteria for judging actions or policies to be right or justified. The
former involves book-keeping and adding up; the latter involves
dialogue and debate about what should be included in the balance
sheet.

Not surprisingly, therefore, institutionalized accountability, or
audit, developed independently of political accountability. In
Normanton's phrase, 'The state auditor, professional or elected,
was one of the first of all administrative technicians', to be found
both in the Greek city states and in the Egyptian kingdoms.[4] For if
financial accountability is independent of political accountability,
the reverse does not seem to follow. Aristotle wrote:[5]

'Some officials handle large sums of public money: it is therefore necessary to have other officials to receive and examine the accounts. These inspectors must administer no funds themselves. Different cities call them examiners, auditors, scrutineers and public advocates.'

In short, neutral expertise would appear to be a necessary input into the processes of political accountability. If making the governors accountable to the governed requires information from neutral experts even in a simple, face-to-face society like ancient Athens, then clearly the need becomes all the greater in complex societies where actions and events are ever more remote from the citizens and ever less amenable to assessment by direct personal experience. Moreover, the growing division of labour, and the development of professional claims to monopolies of expertise, not only reinforce the need to harness managerial accountability to political accountability, but also create demands for extending the scope of audit: financial accountability in the strict sense is, as we shall discover, no longer adequate.

For, if accountability is about reciprocity between individuals in face-to-face settings, and as such is a good thing in its own right, it is about the distribution of authority in complex political or organizational settings. The ability to call people to account defines the locus of authority in any given society. In a democratic society, political accountability is an assertion that all authority derives from the people, just as in a monarchic society, accountability is an assertion that all authority flows from the king. But the notion of authority as the *right* to call people to account needs to be complemented by the notion of power as the *ability* to call people to account, through the exercise of control over performance: the key link in the chain of accountability. If the Athenian assembly could not control its officers, or if Xerxes could not control his stewards, in the crucial sense of knowing what they were doing, then calling them to account becomes largely a meaningless concept. Legitimate authority does not necessarily convert into effective power; effective power, whether legitimate or not, in turn requires effective control for accountability.

If this was a central problem even in simple societies then it is compounded in complex societies. For such societies are distinguished by two characteristics. The first is the lengthening hierarchy of command in government. The second is the increasing specialization in both society and government. The next section, therefore, examines the implications of these two characteristics for concepts of accountability in the modern world, the problems that stem from the fact that accounts, seen as explanations of what happened, are themselves becoming ever more complex.

From simple to complex models of accountability

In Athens, as we have seen, the model of accountability was simple and direct. The line of political accountability ran directly from the Assembly, that is the whole body of citizens, to those with delegated authority to carry out the civic function (see *Figure 1-A*). The audit was the servant of the Assembly. If we leap ahead more than 1,000 years, simplicity is again the key characteristic of accountability in medieval England, but it is financial or managerial accountability divorced from any ideas of political democracy. The king was accountable only to God for his actions. But by the twelfth century a division of labour and specialization had developed among his servants. As the beginnings of a bureaucratic structure of government became evident, so a rudimentary system of fiscal accountability began to emerge.[6] The treasurer was charged with keeping the accounts of income; the constable was responsible for keeping the accounts of the king's household expenditure. Barons, sitting in the Court of the Exchequer, in turn held both officials and those who owed the king payments to account in what was, in effect, a judicial trial.

Accountability in this context had two main characteristics. It represented an attempt by the king to achieve control over the way in which his estate, that is the realm, was managed. In other words, the division of labour presented by the development of a very unsophisticated form of bureaucracy immediately creates the need for a machinery of control over those charged with carrying out the king's business, to make them answerable for the way in which they perform their task. Equally accountability in this context was seen as a form of judicial adjudication, in which neutrals – the Barons of the Exchequer – were meant to ensure

Figure 1 *Models of accountability*

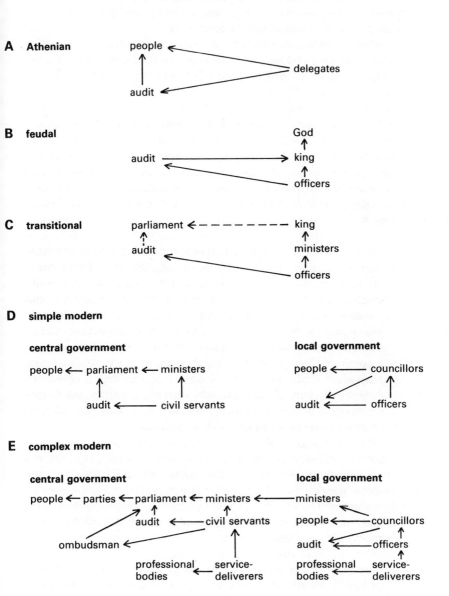

that due process had been followed. Accountability was defined in terms of making the king's officers responsible not only for fiscal propriety, but also for acting according to the law in the way they raised and spent money (see *Figure 1-B*).

From the sixteenth century onwards, if not earlier, the constitutional history of England is largely about whether parliament could substitute itself for God by holding the king or his ministers accountable (see *Figure 1-C*). The battle over the centuries was whether parliament could assert its control over expenditure, by making sure that the money it voted was not only spent appropriately – that funds voted for one purpose were not devoted to another – but also properly, without waste or corruption. Already by the seventeenth century, Locke had developed a contractarian theory of government, in which accountability was the crucial link in the chain between the executive and the legislature:[7]

'The executive power placed anywhere but in a person that has also a share in the legislative, is visibly subordinate and accountable to it, and may be at pleasure changed and displaced. . . . Of other ministerial and subordinate powers in a commonwealth, we need not speak, they being so multiplied with infinite variety in the different customs and constitutions of distinct commonwealths, that it is impossible to give a particular account of them. Only thus much is necessary to our present purpose, we may take notice of them, that they have no manner of authority, any of them, beyond what is by positive grant and commission delegated to them, and are all of them accountable to some other power in the commonwealth.'

By the nineteenth century John Stuart Mill had further developed these notions to form what essentially remains the modern notion of political accountability in a representative democracy.[8] This hinges on the concept of ministerial accountability, seen as the ability of parliament to call the executive to account for its actions:

'Instead of the function of governing, for which it is radically unfit, the proper office of a representative assembly is to watch and control the government; to throw the light of publicity on its acts; to compel a full exposition and justification of all of them which any one considers questionable; to censure them if found condemnable, and, if the men who compose the government abuse their trust, or fulfil it in a manner which conflicts with the deliberate sense of the nation, to expel them from office.'

Ministers, Mill recognized, will not as a rule have 'adequate, and what may be called professional, knowledge of the department' over which they are called to preside. 'Professional advisers must therefore be provided', Mill concluded – in recognition of the growing specialization both within society and within government. From this it follows that there has to be a clear hierarchy of responsibility, so that it is apparent who is to be answerable for what:

'As a general rule, every executive function, whether superior or subordinate, should be the appointed duty of some given individual. It should be apparent to all the world who did everything, and through whose default anything was left undone. Responsibility is null when nobody knows who is responsible. Nor, even when real, can it be divided without being weakened. To maintain it at its highest, there must be one person who receives the whole praise of what is well done, the whole blame of what is ill.'

These quotations from Mill help to underline some of the recurring themes in any discussion about accountability. There is the emphasis on accountability seen as 'exposition and justification'. There is, too, the echo of the Athenian interpretation of accountability as the immediate visibility of actions, so that it 'should be apparent to all the world who did everything'.

The development of a constitutional theory of political accountability went hand in hand with the development of the machinery of fiscal accountability. Even as early as the thirteenth century, parliament had sought to examine the accounts and the attempts continued in the succeeding centuries, meeting the objection from Henry IV that 'Kings do not render accounts'.[9] But appropriately the first successful and systematic assertion of parliament's right to examine the accounts followed the 'Glorious Revolution' of 1688, whose prophet was Locke. After the revolution the Commons felt that they 'might claim a more extensive function, as naturally derived from their power of opening and closing the public purse, that of investigating the wisdom, faithfulness and economy with which their grants had been expended'.[10] There followed legislation to set up 'commissioners of accounts' with a roving mission to enquire into the government's accounts.

For a century or so after the Glorious Revolution, parliament sporadically and fitfully tried to assert a grip over government spending by setting up a variety of temporary commissions and committees. However, the next major development in the system of financial accountability was the result of a pre-emptive strike by the prime minister of the day, Lord North. By setting up a statutory Commission for Examining the Public Accounts in 1780, he sought to isolate 'the question of economy, as a technical and an administrative question from the hotter issues of parliamentary reform and the influence of the Crown'.[11] The creation of the commission was notable not merely for its appeal to neutral, independent expertise in the process of accountability; previous *ad hoc* parliamentary commissions and committees had been essentially political instruments. But it also marked an expansion of the notion of financial accountability itself from the balancing of books to the management of resources, from economy to efficiency. The commissioners were concerned both with the avoidance of waste and the management of the government's business. Their reports represent an attempt to create an efficient bureaucracy by setting down organizational rules for the proper conduct of government business. So, for example, they argued that there should be a clear hierarchy of accountability and a clear allocation of responsibilities. Officers who had previously been licensed bankers for the public were now to be its 'instruments', publicly accountable for their handling of receipts and expenditures.

In the event, however, a somewhat narrower concept of accountability was to be triumphantly institutionalized by Gladstone's Exchequer and Audit Department Act, 1866. This represented a victory both for the concept of disinterested expertise as the tool of parliament and for Gladstone's own restricted view of the role of government. The Act created the office of the comptroller and auditor-general. Although appointed by the treasury, he was responsible only to the House of Commons and reported to its Public Accounts Committee.[12] It gave parliament an effective tool of control over how the government spent its money, and thus for calling ministers to account for their fiscal stewardship. But the emphasis on financial regularity, as distinct from the wider notion of efficient administration, represented Gladstone's own preoccupation with 'economy'. He saw it as his duty to cut down a number of public servants and to save 'candle-ends and cheeseparings in the cause of the country'.[13] So, for example, when leading a diplomatic mission to Corfu he instructed his officials to 'scratch out the address on the parchment label of the despatch bags and to use the same label in returning the bag to the colonial office in London'. For him, financial accountability was an instrument for promoting economy, just as it was an instrument for promoting control for the House of Commons.

The irony of this development of an institutionalized form of parliamentary accountability was that it came just as the concept of the government's role which it embodied was becoming an anachronism. The Gladstonian reform can, at the risk of some oversimplification, be seen as putting financial accountability into the service of political accountability and thus neatly completing the circle of accountability from officials to ministers, from ministers to parliament, and from parliament to the people (see *Figure 1-D*): a necessary, if not sufficient, condition for the kind of representative democracy prescribed by Mill (although, as yet, a great many of the people were not enfranchised). But it also reflected the minimalist view of the government's functions and, consequently, a relatively simple concept of accountability just as the role of the government was expanding and becoming more complex; for example, parliamentary accountability was not linked to the emergent local government system. The tax collection State, in which it made sense to put exclusive emphasis on economy, was moving towards the service-delivery State, whose ever expanding, ever more complex activities created new problems of accountability.

Accountability in the service delivery State

Just as Gladstone was celebrating the candle-ends State, the service delivery State was in the process of emerging. It was a development which was increasingly to call into question over the following century the adequacy of the institutions of political accountability which were forged during the triumphal emergence of representative government in the middle of the nineteenth century. For if the emergence of representative government looked forward to a full-blown parliamentary democracy, the institutions of accountability looked backward to the era of minimal government.

At the beginning of the 1860s, when parliament finally succeeded in asserting its control over expenditure, government spending was £88 million.[14] By the turn of the century this figure had more than trebled and was launched on a steep upward path. If this dramatic rise represented in part increased military expenditure, it also reflected the growing involvement of government, at both central and local levels, in providing services like education and health which were to become the foundations of the Welfare State.

What is significant about this development, as far as accountability is concerned, is that it marked not just a transformation in the scale and complexity of State activities: the creation of new links of accountability between central and local government and of a new tier in the hierarchy of administration below that of the traditional officials or bureaucrats, the tier of service deliverers (see *Figure 1-E*). But it also marked a transformation in the kinds of activities being undertaken: the creation of an army of 'experts' or embryo professionals. The Welfare State, as it was to emerge, was also the Professional State. The significance of this development for the concept of accountability was twofold. First, the experts derived their claim to authority not so much from delegation (as in the Athenian model) as from their own special knowledge and skills, so breaking the main link in the traditional chain of political accountability. Second, the criteria of accountability derived from the notion of good stewardship proved to be increasingly difficult to apply to the new activities of the State.

Some of these problems were already beginning to emerge by the middle of the nineteenth century. They can be illustrated by the development of the New Poor Law system. This represented, as contemporaries showed by their hostility, a challenge to traditional concepts of political accountability as answerability to local ratepayers. Indeed, the whole system was based on the assumption that local citizens were incompetent to run the system, and that their involvement was synonymous with self-interest and corruption. The administration of the Poor Law, the 1834 Report argued, should be in the hands of 'permanent and salaried officials'.[15] Those, in turn, should be 'well-qualified'. Such a body of officials would, furthermore, be selected so as not to be biased by 'local interests or partialities'. Lastly, and perhaps most importantly, their work would be supervised by a central Board of Commissioners charged with inspecting and auditing the work of local administrators and with trying to achieve 'uniformity'. The report argued:

'The Commissioners would act upon the widest information, under the direct control of the Legislature, and the supervision of the public, and under no liability to pecuniary or private bias, partiality or intimidation. They would have the immediate advantage of having well-defined objects assigned to them, powerful means at their disposal, and clear rules for their guidance.'

The Chadwickian vision of administrative rationality embodied in the New Poor Law system marks the half-way house in the development of the concept of accountability in what was to become the Welfare State. It represented an attempt to assimilate accountability in service delivery to the bureaucratic model: the designation of 'well-defined objects' and 'clear rules' whose implementation could then be monitored, by means of inspection and audit, in a hierarchic administrative structure. Parliament would set the 'objects' and define the 'rules', while a set of neutral, independent experts (the commissioners) would provide the information required by the legislature to complete the circle of political accountability. As in the case of parliamentary control of expenditure, managerial accountability would be put into the service of political accountability.

The vision was never to be fully attained. The reasons for this failure are complex, but two continue to be particularly relevant for any discussion of accountability in contemporary Britain. The first is that the Chadwickian vision provoked a debate about the location of accountability. So far in this chapter the discussion has centred on the role of parliament. But the growth of services and the division of responsibility for them between local and central government also raises questions about possible conflicts between different lines of accountability. If responsibility is the other side of the coin of accountability, if the two would seem to be logically indivisible, then local provision of services would appear to imply accountability to the local body of citizens, just as national provision would seem to imply accountability to the national body of citizens. But if responsibility for setting objectives and defining rules is national, if the aim is to achieve a 'uniform' pattern of service delivery, while responsibility for providing services is local, where then does the accountability lie? Is the concept of accountability divisible? The problem was to be compounded during the course of the twentieth century by the growing dependence of local government on the centre for finance, but it is already revealed by the tensions that became apparent during the implementation of the New Poor Law reforms.

The other reason for the failure of the Chadwickian vision, central to any discussion of accountability today, was that its faith in controlling services through defining their aims was betrayed by the ability of those actually running the Poor Law system at the local level to substitute their own objectives and rules. The system of audit and inspection, proposed by the 1834 Report, assumed that it would be possible to eliminate the discretion of the service providers. But the stones on which the objectives and rules were written turned out to be friable, as their interpretation was challenged by practice. In short, any concept of accountability in service provision based on a notion of the hierarchic delegation of clearly defined tasks, whose achievements the providers can then be answerable for, would seem to run up against the phenomenon of 'street-level bureaucracy': the ability of those at the point of delivery to control the information which feeds into the hierarchy of accountability and further, to define their own policies and actions.[16] The bureaucratic model of accountability does not fit easily into the service delivery State because of the ability of the providers to subvert control.

Compounding the problems of accountability in the service-delivery State is the growth of professionalism in the twentieth century. For this introduces yet another dimension into the concept of accountability, so breaking the chain. Central to the notion of professionalism is the assertion that what defines a professional is precisely the fact that he or she is accountable only to his or her peers. It is the profession as a body which sets the objectives and rules which govern the performance of individual members. Professions, from this perspective, can be seen as a species of QUANGOs – quasi non-governmental organizations – which are collectively granted monopoly rights of practice in return for policing the competence of their members. The creation of a profession can be seen, it has been argued in the context of the medical profession, as a contract between public and profession, by which the public go to the profession for medical treatment because the profession has made sure that it will provide 'satisfactory treatment'.[17] But of course it is the profession which defines what is 'satisfactory treatment'.

The case of medicine is perhaps the most highly developed example of a self-regulating profession. But it is an example which has inspired other service-providers: a point which is further elaborated in Chapter 3. At this stage of the argument it is sufficient to note that the combination of the service delivery State and the growth of notions of professionalism among service-deliverers introduces a new element into the debate about accountability. Professional accountability is not integrated into the system of political or managerial accountability. It effectively breaks down the circle of accountability. It is incompatible with the concept of accountability as a series of linkages leading from the people to those with delegated responsibilities via parliament and the managerial hierarchy since it brings on stage a set of actors who see themselves answerable to their peers, rather than to the *demos*. And it marks the final breakdown of the attempts to reconcile our traditional notions of accountability, as they were forged in ancient Athens, with the realities of complex modern societies in the twentieth century, and helps to explain the contemporary search for alternative ways of giving new life to the old vision.

Accountability and participation

The search began with the post-1945 creation of the Welfare State. The democratization of social provision led – paradoxically, it might seem at first sight – to demands for the political democratization of social provision. The paradox is more apparent than real, for the Welfare State was the embodiment of the service-delivery State. It represented the triumph of managerialism and professionalism: the ultimate division of labour, with responsibility delegated to an ever expanding army of specialists whose authority derived from their own expertise. The reaction set in early, although it was not until the 1970s that the critical voices joined in a fortissimo chorus.

Already in 1952 Richard Crossman put what, two decades later, was to become the standard critique from a Socialist stance.[18] No effort, he pointed out, had been made to 'encourage popular participation in the Welfare state'. Furthermore, he argued, 'We are a nation deeply imbued with a sense of social status and inhibited by an oligarchic tradition, which makes responsibility the privilege of the educated minority, and irresponsibility the negative freedom of the half-educated masses. The leaders – and this applies at least as much in the Labour movement as outside it – profoundly distrust active democracy.' To translate Crossman's vocabulary of democracy into our own language of accountability, the governors were not answerable to the governed, and the crucial link in the chain of accountability was therefore missing. The answer, Crossman concluded, was to increase 'even at the cost of "efficiency", the citizen's right to participate in the control, not only of government and industry, but of the party for which he votes, and of the trade union whose card he carries'.

So was set the theme which was to emerge strongly two decades later: the call to move back to the Athenian notion of democracy as direct involvement by citizens in decision-making. In turn, this notion of democracy as active participation implies a return to the Athenian concept of accountability. It resurrects the concept of accountability seen as direct answerability to the people. It is a call for short-circuiting the complex structure of accountability, which itself reflects the growing complexity of government, and returning to something like the face-to-face, direct answerability of the original, simple model, with those carrying out tasks on behalf of the people being directly answerable to the people. It was a call which reflected not only dissatisfaction with the structure of accountability but also a challenge to the claims of expertise as such and to the existing division of labour. It involves an attempt to make the expert directly accountable to the people rather than to the peer group, to reclaim authority from the expert.

The debate of the 1970s once again emphasizes that to define lines and directions of accountability is also to define the distribution of power. Lack of accountability – the inability to *make* someone answerable for their actions – is synonymous with the lack of power. Conversely to be unaccountable is to be all-powerful. The point is well caught in the Memorandum of Dissent to the Report of the Royal Commission on the Constitution by Lord Crowther-Hunt and Professor A. T. Peacock.[19] Having diagnosed a growing 'sense of powerlessness', they conclude:

'It is therefore crucial to the health of the body politic that we should provide the institutional changes required to counter today's widespread and justifiable belief that the country is becoming less democratic, that we the people have not enough to say in, and influence on governments, that we have too little power in the face of government and that government has become too centralised and congested. If we believe in democracy, this must involve seeking to involve more people in the government and policy process. . . . It must mean, too, providing adequate means for the redress of individual grievances against government and the service it provides. And in the interests of more efficient and more responsible decision-making, we must also seek to devise means of lightening the load on our central institutions of government.'

The quotation is significant for the way in which it illuminates various dimensions of the concept of accountability although the word itself is not used. It suggests that we should be concerned, not only with *missing* links but also with *overloaded* or *ineffective* links, a point which will be developed in the following chapter which examines in detail the contemporary debate about the institutions of accountability. It also emphasizes the importance of seeing not only accountability in terms of answerability for policy or performance, but also governmental actions and processes as they affect the individual citizens: the redress of individual grievances is an important component of the concept of accountability. If following the rules in the handling of financial accounts is a basic feature in traditional concepts of managerial accountability, then following due legal and administrative process in the handling of individual cases or claims by citizens is yet another.

If more direct involvement by the people is a necessary condition for a return to something approaching the Athenian concept of direct accountability, it is not a sufficient one. The other theme that emerges from the debate of the past ten years is the emphasis on accountability seen as openness. Effective scrutiny implies effective access to information. How can any body be made accountable without publicity?[20] The following quotation from David Owen illustrates the point:[21]

'There is a corporatist tendency to stress the need for secrecy to safeguard citizens' rights generally, but to be shockingly insensitive to a particular or individual case. If we are to develop a more responsive form of political activity, all our institutions will need to become more accountable and their size will have to be reduced, for the larger an institution, the less democratic and the more bureaucratically top-heavy it is likely to be. Clearly, institutions must range from the small school to the giant coal industry, but we need a new, more vigilant approach to guard against the tendency for the upper level of any institution gradually to accumulate power at the expense of lower levels. Each of the three major concentrations of power within the State, the civil service, the trade unions and large-scale industry, whether in private or state hands, will need to adopt a more open attitude to information if power is to be effectively controlled.'

Accountability seen as making the process of decision-making open and visible to the individual citizen is a widespread contemporary theme. Thus Tony Benn has argued that 'open government' is essential if we want to 'democratise our society', though only a first step in reinforcing the existing links in the chain of accountability by making ministers and officials accountable to parliament, ministers accountable to the parliamentary party, members of parliament accountable to their constituency parties, and so on down the line.[22] And the Conservative government has made it legislatively mandatory for local authorities to publish more information about their performance, although in this case the hope that more information about spending would lead to demands for less expenditure was perhaps as important as concern about strengthening accountability through information.

In part, this concern with accountability stems, as the above quotation from David Owen suggests, from a fear that corporatist tendencies within society have privatized what in the past were public decisions, and have consequently made them invisible and immune from scrutiny. To the extent that governments engage in policy-making through dialogue with corporate interest groups, whether trade unions or private industry, so the traditional political channels of accountability are bypassed. Furthermore, to the extent that governments delegate decision-making authority and public functions to semi-autonomous bodies, like universities or the BBC, so once again new problems of accountability are created.[23] The growth of QUANGOs among which, as we have suggested, many of the Welfare State professions should be counted, implies the growth of activities where there are no appropriate links within the existing system of accountability: a system which still reflects many of the nineteenth-century assumptions about the nature and scope of the State.

Accountability and the rule of law

'That order did not come from God. Justice,
That dwells with the gods below, knows no such law.
I did not think your edicts strong enough
To overrule the unwritten unalterable laws
Of God and heaven, you being only a man.'
(Sophocles, *Antigone*, trans. E. F. Watling, 1947,
Harmondsworth, Penguin)

Perhaps it is because of the growing perception of the inadequacies in the existing system of political and managerial accountability that there has, over the past few decades, been increasing interest in another, far older way of looking at the concept: that of seeing accountability in terms of being answerable, not *to* the people, but *for* proper conduct, defined not by *demos*, not by political processes but by the 'unwritten, unalterable laws'. It is accountability seen, very much as in the context of face-to-face encounters between individuals, as moral propriety; as being answerable for following a certain set of moral precepts or rules of conduct. It is a concept of accountability which not only is different from notions of political or managerial accountability but also may, indeed, cut across them in so far as actions arising from political imperatives offend against the more fundamental rules of human conduct, as in the case of Creon's order to Antigone.

Some such notion seems to be implicit in the contemporary debate about the role of law and of the courts in holding government to account. This emerges clearly from the following pronouncement made by Lord Diplock in 1981:[24]

'It is not, in my view, a sufficient answer to say that judicial review of the actions of officers or departments of central government is unnecessary because they are accountable to Parliament for the way in which they carry out their functions. They are accountable to Parliament for what they do so far as regards efficiency and policy, and Parliament is the only judge; they are responsible to a court of justice for the lawfulness of what they do, and of that the court is the only judge.'

Accountability seen as answerability to the courts for the lawfulness of action has two components. First, and most basically, it can be seen as the legal counterpart of fiscal accountability: as a means of carrying out a legal audit, as it were, on the way in which ministers and their officials carry out their tasks to ensure administrative regularity. The object is to ensure that ministers and their officials do not exceed their legal authority, and that the way in which they have reached their decisions follows the rules of natural justice. Second, and more ambitiously, it can be seen as a way of making political power accountable in the larger sense of controlling whether or not the actions of the government uphold or offend against certain basic human rights.

It is the restrictive, technical definition of legal accountability, seen as judicial review of administrative process, which is implicit in Lord Diplock's observations, quoted above. It is the larger, more ambitious definition of legal accountability, seen as a judicial defence of basic human rights, which seems implicit in the pronouncement of another Law Lord. In a lecture given in 1984 Lord Scarman argued that the creation of the Welfare State and the assumption of responsibility for economic management by governments had created a new situation for which the existing machinery of accountability is inadequate.[25]

'The education, health and well-being of our people largely depend upon the success with which our public administrators fulfil tasks of management, supervision and day-to-day administration. These tasks have confronted the citizen with the public administrator, and the citizen has not always liked what he has seen. He has become too often, in the lawyer's language, a man aggrieved. He has sought in Parliament and the courts redress for his grievances: but with no great success. Parliament can sack a Minister, but not a civil servant. The courts have, literally, no more than a peripheral role: they cannot make decisions as to the substance or quality of an administrative decision: they are limited to a review of its legality, i.e. whether the decision is within the powers conferred by the relevant statute.'

The question prompted by this situation, Lord Scarman concluded, is whether we should not accept that 'public accountability would mean more than responsbility to Ministers who are themselves responsible to Parliament for the acts of their departments? . . . Is there a case for a written constitution imposing checks and balances upon the exercise of legislative and executive powers?' In short, there may be an argument for a written constitution, embodying the fundamental rules of public action, which would allow governments to be called to account and for their actions to be tested on criteria independent of political processes. Political accountability, from this perspective, must be subordinate to and constrained by accountability for the observance of certain 'unalterable laws'. Otherwise, the outcome is 'elective dictatorship'.[26]

So, in a sense, the career of the concept of accountability has come full circle. If accountability in individual terms began its career as a notion of conformity to certain rules of conduct, it continued its career in collective terms as conformity to the will of the *demos*. Now, a different concept of accountability is emerging from the shadows of the contemporary debate: accountability as action in conformity with the public interest and the public good, as defined not by shifting political processes or ideologies but by enduring precepts or an over-arching value system.[27] Growing complexity has generated a demand for a return to a simpler definition of accountability.

Dimensions of accountability

If the concept of accountability is as old as discourse about the nature of civic society and man's place in it, the word itself has passed into the ordinary language of political discussion only relatively recently. It is this which helps to explain why accountability, as it is used today, tends to be such a slippery, ambiguous term. Its various meanings, reflecting changing usages and contexts over time, tend to be conflated in what has become a fashionably 'good' word, often with confusing results. This chapter therefore concludes by setting out, on the basis of the discussion so far, the various dimensions and attributes of accountability. In doing so, we shall move one step nearer to examining the specific problems of accountability in large-scale public services which provide the main theme for this book.

The initial distinction in any framework of analysis must be, as we have already suggested, that between political and managerial accountability.[28] Political accountability is about those with delegated authority being answerable for their actions to the people, whether directly in simple societies or indirectly in complex societies. Here the criteria of judgement are, themselves, contestable and reasons, justification, and explanation have to be provided. The main issue in complex societies is whether the *linkages* between action and explanation are in place and, if in place, adequate to the task in hand: whether the channels of communication are operating and whether the sanctions are sufficient to compel a justification if needed. A secondary set of issues involves questions about the openness of the process and the existence and availability of the information needed to assess actions.

In contrast, managerial accountability is about making those with delegated authority answerable for carrying out agreed tasks according to agreed criteria of performance. This technical process can, though it need not, be carried out by neutral, impartial experts. In turn, managerial accountability has a number of dimensions. Conventionally a distinction is drawn between fiscal, process, and programme accountability,[29] or between regularity, efficiency, and effectiveness audit.[30]

Fiscal/regularity accountability is about making sure that money has been spent as agreed, according to the appropriate rules; legal accountability can be seen as a counterpart to this, in so far as it is concerned to make sure that the procedures and rules of decision-making have been observed.

Process/efficiency accountability is about making sure that a given course of action has been carried out, and that value for money has been achieved in the use of resources.

Programme/effectiveness accountability is about making sure that a given course of action or investment of resources has achieved its intended result.

These dimensions of managerial accountability can also be conceptualized as being concerned with inputs, outputs, and outcomes. Thus fiscal/regularity is about checking that the appropriate inputs, whether of resources or administration, have gone into the policy or service-delivery machine. Process/efficiency accountability is about checking that the appropriate outputs have been produced, and that the ratio between inputs and outputs ('efficiency') is the most favourable possible. But programme/effectiveness accountability is about the ultimate question of whether the intended outcomes have been produced, whether the desired impact has been made.

Putting together the political and managerial notions of accountability in their various dimensions might suggest a simple, hierarchical model. At the top is political accountability which sets the policy objectives and generates the criteria used in the neutral technical process of managerial accountability, running from the relatively simple fiscal/regularity accountability to the more complex programme/effectiveness accountability, from inputs to outcomes.

But this model is based on a number of assumptions and it is precisely these assumptions which make the whole concept of accountability problematic in the modern world. The first is that the institutional and organizational links between political accountability and managerial accountability exist and are effective: that the processes do in fact mesh. The second is that the political processes do in fact generate precise, clear-cut objectives and criteria necessary if managerial accountability is to be a neutral exercise in the application of value-free techniques. The third is that the organization structure is such that the managers accountable to the politicians can answer for the actions and performance of the service deliverers.

In fact, as our discussion has already indicated, all three assumptions are questionable. First, the links between the political and managerial systems of accountability, forged in the nineteenth century, are ill-adapted to the twentieth-century service delivery State. The result is a perception of 'overload' and demands for the creation of new links. Second, it is apparent that political processes do not necessarily generate the kind of clear-cut objectives and criteria required if audit is to be a neutral, value-free exercise: the dividing line between political and managerial accountability is, inevitably, blurred as objectives and criteria are generated at all levels in the hierarchy. The results are demands for opening up the system as a whole to public scrutiny, and creating a more complex (but not necessarily hierarchical) system of accountability. Third, and compounding the arguments both for better links and for a more complex system of accountability, the organizational structure of many public programmes – such as, for example, the health service – is characterized by the fact that some service-deliverers do not fit into a vertical or hierarchical model of accountability; they are an instance of horizontal accountability to their peers.[31]

Lastly, and more generally, the imagery of accountability needs to be elaborated and made more sophisticated. To talk only of links in the system of accountability, to set out a taxonomy of different kinds of accountability, is to risk confining any analysis in a mechanistic, verbal strait-jacket, to imply by the choice of words used that the effectiveness of a system of accountability can be evaluated in terms of the appropriate connections being made and the appropriate techniques used. Equally important, our analysis would suggest, is to examine the dynamics of the system which means looking at the quality of the information flowing down the various pipes (to vary the imagery) and the associated ability to translate nominal control into real control: the extent to which public actions are consequently open to scrutiny by individual citizens. These then are the issues which provide our analytical threads through the maze of the contemporary arguments about the machinery of accountability, to which we turn in the following chapter.

REFERENCES

1 For the literature on accountability in personal relationships, see G. R. Semin and A. S. R. Manstead (1983) *The Accountability of Conduct*. London: Academic Press. H. Garfinkel (1967) *Studies in Ethnomethodology*. Englewood Cliffs, NJ: Prentice-Hall. P. Marsh, E. Rosser, and R. Harre (1978) *The Rules of Disorder*. London: Routledge & Kegan Paul; M. B. Scott and S. M. Lyman (1968) Accounts. *American Sociology Review* 33: 46–62.
2 E. Goffman (1971) *Relations in Public – Micro-studies of Public Order*. Harmondsworth: Penguin.
3 J. T. Roberts (1982) *Accountability in Athenian Government*. Madison, Wisc.: University of Wisconsin Press. A. H. M. Jones (1957) *Athenian Democracy*. Oxford: Basil Blackwell.
4 E. L. Normanton (1966) *The Accountability and Audit of Governments*. Manchester: Manchester University Press: 13.
5 Quoted in E. L. Normanton (1966) *The Accountability and Audit of Governments*. Manchester: Manchester University Press.
6 J. E. A. Jolliffe (1937) *The Constitutional History of Medieval England*. London: A. & C. Black.
7 J. Locke, An Essay Concerning the True, Original Extent and End of

Civil Government. In Sir E. Barker (ed.) (1947) *Social Contract.* Oxford: Oxford University Press: 128.

8 J. S. Mill (1962) *Representative Government.* Everyman's Library. London: Dent: 332.

9 B. Chubb (1952) *The Control of Public Expenditure.* Oxford: Clarendon Press: 16.

10 H. Hallam, *The Constitutional History of England.* Quoted in B. Chubb (1952) *The Control of Public Expenditure.* Oxford: Clarendon Press: 17.

11 J. Torrance (1978) Social Class and Bureaucratic Innovation. *Past and Present* 78, February: 56–81.

12 H. Roseveare (1969) *The Treasury.* London: Allen Lane. See also B. Chubb (1952) *The Control of Public Expenditure.* Oxford: Clarendon Press.

13 J. Morley (1908) *Life of Gladstone*, vol. 1. London: Lloyd: 520–22.

14 A. T. Peacock and J. Wiseman (1961) *The Growth of Public Expenditure in the United Kingdom.* Oxford: Oxford University Press.

15 S. G. and E. O. A. Checkland (eds) (1974) *The Poor Law Report of 1833.* Harmondsworth: Penguin.

16 M. Lipsky (1980) *Street-Level Bureaucracy.* New York: Russell Sage Foundation.

17 A. W. Merrison (Chairman) (1975) *Report of the Committee of Inquiry into the Regulation of the Medical Profession.* London: HMSO Cmnd 6018.

18 R. H. S. Crossman (1952) Towards a Philosophy of Socialism. In R. H. S. Crossman (ed.) *New Fabian Essays.* London: Turnstile Press: 28–9.

19 Royal Commission on The Constitution (1973) *Memorandum of Dissent.* London: HMSO Cmnd 5460–1: para. 79.

20 B. Crick (1972) *Political Theory and Political Practice.* London: Allen Lane: 155.

21 D. Owen (1981) *Face the Future.* Harmondsworth: Penguin: 44.

22 T. Benn (1979) *Arguments for Socialism.* London: Jonathan Cape: 172–73.

23 B. L. R. Smith and D. C. Hague (eds) (1971) *The Dilemma of Accountability in Modern Government.* London: Macmillan: D. C. Hague, W. J. M. Mackenzie, and A. Barker (1975) *Public Policy and Private Interests.* London: Macmillan.

24 H. W. R. Wade (1982) *Administrative Law*, fifth edn. Oxford: Clarendon Press: 30–1.

25 Lord Scarman (1984) The Shifting State. Keynote address to the Royal Institute of Public Administration Conference, University of Aston, 14 September, mimeo.

26 Lord Hailsham (1976) *Elective Dictatorship*. London: BBC Publications.
27 F. R. Ridley (1975) Responsibility and the Official: Forms and Ambiguities. *Government and Opposition* 10, 4, Autumn: 444–72.
28 N. Johnson (1974) Defining Accountability. *Public Administration Bulletin* 17, December: 3–13.
29 D. Robinson (1971) Government Contracting for Academic Research: Accountability in the American Experience. In B. L. R. Smith and D. C. Hague (eds) *The Dilemma of Accountability in Modern Government*. London: Macmillan. See also J. D. Stewart (1984) The Role of Information in Public Accountability. In A. Hopwood and C. Tomkins (eds) *Issues in Public Sector Accounting*. Oxford: Philip Allan.
30 Chancellor of the Exchequer (1980) *The Role of the Comptroller and Auditor-General*. London: HMSO Cmnd 7845: para. 10.
31 D. C. Hague, W. J. M. Mackenzie, and A. Barker (1975) *Public Policy and Private Interests*. London: Macmillan: 357.

2

Expertise in accountability: institutions and techniques

Given a sufficiently comprehensive definition of the concept, the problem of accountability can all too easily become *the* problem of how to reconcile democracy with growing governmental complexity in modern societies. If accountability is about answerability, responsiveness, openness, efficient estate management, not to mention participation and obedience to eternal laws (and the previous chapter suggests that the chameleon word does indeed encompass all these meanings), then it is hardly surprising that the concept has provided the bass accompaniment to the continuing political debate about the government of Britain: a debate provoked by increasing awareness of economic decline which has called into question almost every existing institution from parliament to local government, and which has launched an avalanche of Royal Commission and other reports and led to an epidemic of institutional innovations and experiments over the past two decades.

This chapter analyses this debate in so far as it illuminates the way in which the problem of accountability has been conceptualized, and how different ways of conceptualizing the word have led to different kinds of policy proposals and institutional innovations. The two main conceptual dimensions of the word identified in the previous chapter – political and managerial accountability – are used to sift and organize the mountain of words generated by the debate. For our aim in all this is not to provide a summary of this debate, let alone to plod through it chronologically, but selectively to identify the main assumptions about the nature of accountability underlying the discussion as a first step towards questioning the adequacy and realism of those assumptions and thereby setting our own research agenda: the subject of the next chapter.

The debate starts with concern about overloaded or fractured linkages. If we think of accountability as a system (see *Figure 1-E* in previous chapter), then clearly there is a risk of breakdown or collapse if the lines or linkages are blocked or fail to function. And it is indeed this concern which dominated much of the discussion about parliamentary and constitutional reform throughout the 1960s and 1970s. The discussion started with the contention, soon to harden into a general consensus, that the complexities of modern government had subverted the constitutional system of accountability. The assumption that civil servants were accountable to ministers and that ministers, in turn, were accountable to parliament no longer matched reality, it was argued.[1] If the links had not actually fractured, they were no longer effective. From this contention flowed, in turn, a variety of proposals for changing or improving the existing system or inventing new mechanisms or tools of accountability; and both the arguments about the nature of the 'crisis of accountability'[2] and the institutional innovations which flowed from the argument help to deepen our understanding of the concept itself.

The doctrine of ministerial responsibility has two related, and mutually dependent, aspects. First, it implies that ministers are responsible (or accountable) *to* parliament for what their departments do. Second, it implies that ministers are responsible (or accountable) *for* the actions of all their departmental officials. It therefore links our two dimensions of accountability, and allows us to explore the relationship between them. Ministerial accountability to parliament is political accountability *par excellence*. It is all about explaining and justifying conduct, in the Athenian tradition. Ministerial accountability for the actions of their officials, however, is about managerial accountability. It is all about the way in which ministers control the actions and performance of their subordinates. The real difficulty comes (and this was the starting-point of the reassessment of the doctrine of ministerial responsibility) when administrative life parts company from constitutional doctrine, and government departments become too large and too complex for ministers to accept personal responsibility for what is done in their name by their civil servants. For how is it possible to be accountable *to* parliament for actions *for* which the minister cannot be held personally responsible, given the number of decisions taken in his or her name?

The answer given to this question by the development of constitutional practice over the past thirty years suggests that it may be useful to add a further dimension to the notion of accountability: that of sanctions or their absence. In the case of ministerial responsibility, the notion of accountability has been adapted to mean that ministers have a duty to explain or justify and answer questions about the activities of their departments. But such explanation does not involve any sense of the minister being on trial, in the sense that the Athenian generals were on trial for their conduct of battles. In short, the minister's neck is not on the block, since it is assumed that it was not his hand which took the offending action. Nor, for that matter, is that of the civil servant directly responsible, since the assumption is that he or she acted in the name of the minister, and is therefore accountable only to that minister. So, as we saw in the previous chapter, to be accountable is often held to be synonymous with being answerable: the example of ministerial responsibility suggests that there may be an important difference, if only of shading, in the implications that the two words carry. If accountability in the strict and strong sense carries with it the implication of ultimate sanctions, that ministers will be impeached if their explanations do not carry conviction, then the softer notion of answerability does not necessarily have this overtone.

But the reinterpretation of the doctrine of ministerial responsibility created in turn a new and major problem if parliament was to continue to be seen as the crucial link in the chain of accountability running from the growing army of civil servants and service-deliverers to the public. The nature of this problem was summed up in 1969 by a Conservative politician, Ian Gilmour, as follows:[3]

'A minister is still answerable to parliament for the actions of his department. This is the valuable and genuine part of the doctrine. But parliamentarily that is all it now means or entails. The then Home Secretary, Sir David Maxwell Fyfe, laid down in 1954 that "where an official makes a mistake or causes some delay, but not in an important issue of policy . . . the Minister acknowledges the mistake, and he accepts the responsibility, although he is not personally involved. He states that he will take corrective action in the Department." In plain English, to accept the responsibility for something means to take the blame; but since on Sir David's hypothesis the minister announces that he is going to take corrective action "in the department" there is the clear implication that he is not taking the blame but blaming someone else. "The Minister", Sir David went on, "is not bound to approve of action of which he did not know, or of which he disapproves. But of course he remains constitutionally responsible to Parliament for the fact that something has gone wrong, and he alone can tell Parliament what has occurred and render an account of his stewardship." In this context the phrase "constitutionally responsible to Parliament" evidently means that the Minister is the man who tells parliament that he was not responsible for the mistake.'

The result was, Gilmour concluded, that 'Ministerial responsibility thus protects the Civil Service from Parliament without endangering the minister. While ostensibly opening government to legislative examination, ministerial responsibility effectively prevents such examination'. Although the doctrine of ministerial responsibility began 'as an expression of the executive's accountability to parliament, it has become an excuse for avoiding such accountability. Originally, the trumpet call of parliament, it has become the incantation of the executive.' It was a conclusion that reflected widespread concern, cutting across parties, that the power of parliament, as measured by its ability to call the executive to acccount, was declining:[4] a concern which helps to explain in turn the spate of changes and innovation which marked the 1960s and 1970s. These were of two kinds. First, there were the changes in parliamentary procedures designed to strengthen the ability of MPs to make ministers more answerable (if not accountable in the strong sense) by strengthening the machinery for compelling explanations and justifications. Second, there were the institutional innovations designed to introduce new instruments of audit in the service of parliamentary accountability, as well as moves to strengthen the existing audit institutions.

The first line of development was to set up a series of select committees to give MPs an opportunity to scrutinize the policies and actions of individual ministers. The experiment began with the setting up of specialist committees, on an *ad hoc* basis, in 1969; since 1979, however, fourteen select committees mirroring White-hall's departmental structure have been appointed for the duration of parliament. It was a change long in the making. Among the first to consider the implications of growing complexity in government for accountability (among other things) had been the Haldane Committee on the Machinery of Government. Beatrice Webb, one of its members, recorded in her diary: 'We sit twice a week over tea and muffins in Haldane's comfortable dining room discussing the theory and practice of government. I try to make them face the newer problems of combining bureaucratic efficiency with democratic control; they are forever insisting that the working of parliament makes sensible, let alone scientific, admin-istration impracticable'.[5] In the outcome, the Haldane Report endorsed, if somewhat half-heartedly, the suggestion that a series of Standing Committees, 'each charged with consideration of the activities of the Departments which cover the main divisions of the business of Government' should be appointed.[6] Such 'Committees would require to be furnished with full information as to the course of administration pursued by the Departments with which they were concerned; and for this purpose, it would be requisite that Ministers, as well as the officers of Departments, should appear before them to explain and defend the acts for which they were responsible.' Which is, more or less, what was to happen almost fifty years later.

The new system of select committees is in effect an attempt to square the circle: to maintain the doctrine (or myth) of ministerial responsibility, while yet bringing departmental civil servants on to the public stage. The position, to quote Tim Nodder, a former Department of Health and Social Security (DHSS) civil servant is that:[7]

'The Minister is accountable to the House, and he is accountable in numerous ways – answering parliamentary questions, replying to correspondence from MPs and taking part in debates. We're concerned in our day to day business to assist him with all of these. I see the select committee procedure as an extension of that accountability, and therefore one in which the civil servant is assisting the minister in that process, which in this case involves assisting him to explain and justify himself and policies to a select committee.'

The same distinction between direct accountability to parliament, and assisting the minister to be accountable, has been drawn by Sir Patrick Nairne, a former DHSS Permanent Secretary:

'civil servants themselves have had to expound on policies and have had to be capable of explaining the reasons behind these policies to committees. The important point of principle is that civil servants, in doing that, have remained accountable to their ministers. They haven't become accountable to the committees themselves, but they have in a sense become answerable to the committees for that part of policy-making that falls to civil servants.'

Note the distinction made once again, between accountability and answerability, the line drawn between the master–servant, authority–subordinate, relationship implicit in accountability, as against a vaguer and less hierarchic relationship implied by answerability.

The second line of development was to set up a series of new institutions designed to extend accountability, seen as audit by disinterested experts, from the financial to the administrative sphere. In the financial field, the House of Commons had been able to draw on the expertise of the comptroller and auditor-general to call the government to account for its handling of money since 1866. In 1961 the Whyatt Report argued that the procedures for 'dealing with maladministration in the financial field' could and should be extended to other areas of public administration.[8] It concluded:

'It is clear, therefore, that there is a growing consciousness that a point has been reached in the development of public administration in this country when some machinery should be devised which will enable Parliament to exercise supervision and control over the general administration of Government Departments as effectively as the House of Commons does through the Public Accounts Committee and the Comptroller and Auditor-General in the financial field.'

From this flowed the recommendation, to be implemented in 1967, for the creation of a parliamentary commissioner to investigate complaints of maladministration against government departments. The parallel with the institutions of fiscal audit must not be pushed too far. Unlike the auditor-general, the parliamentary commissioner for administration does not have a general remit to audit the administrative practices of government: the role is limited to dealing with specific complaints channelled by members of parliament although the commissioner may, and does, draw general implications from individual cases. Like the auditor-general, the commissioner is the servant of parliament. The office can thus be seen as creating a new link in the *system* of accountability. By giving MPs an impartial expert who can directly examine the report on the actions of civil servants, this new institution helps to relieve the overload or blockage in the links that run from civil servants to parliament via ministers. But, crucially, the parliamentary commissioner is barred from examining or questioning policy decisions. His remit expressly prohibits him from questioning 'the merits of a decision taken' and authorizes him to deal only with maladministration, that is defects or failings in the administrative execution of policies or in the procedures followed by departments.[9] Essentially, therefore, his office is an instrument of managerial accountability. Implicit in its remit is the assumption that there are self-evident rules or standards of good administration which an impartial expert can apply in individual cases.

The parliamentary commissioner was only the first in a set of similar institutions. In 1973 the office of Health Service Commissioners was created; in 1974 the Commission for Local Administration was set up; in 1976 there followed the Police Complaints Board. None was explicitly designed to deal with the problem of accountability in the larger sense of making democracy more effective by compelling the rulers to justify themselves to the ruled; all, however, were designed to allow the individual citizen to seek answers and redress – in the sense of explanation if not compensation – for their grievances. In each case, one aspect of the new institution is worth noting as particularly relevant to an analysis of accountability. In the case of the Health Service Commissioner, the legislation explicitly barred any investigation of actions 'taken solely in the exercise of clinical judgments'.[10] In other words, the audit of administrative propriety does not extend to the professional service-deliverers: professional decisions are treated like political decisions – beyond the scope of investigation. In the case of the Commission for Local Administration the remit follows closely that of the parliamentary commissioner: that is the former's concern is with maladministration in local government services, just as the latter's is with maladministration in central government services.[11] What is remarkable, perhaps, is the perceived need to set up such an institution in the first place, given the ability (in theory) of the individual councillors to take up individual grievances in a way not open to MPs. Lastly it is worth noting that while the Police Complaints Board, unlike the Health Service Commissioner, is not explicitly barred from challenging the judgements of the service-deliverers, in practice it has found its investigatory role severely circumscribed. In part, this reflected its remit:[12] 'The independent element in the present system rests, in essence, on the Board's power to direct a chief officer to prefer a disciplinary charge against the officer who is the subject of a complaint'. In part, however, it also reflected a realization by the Board that only experts could call their fellow-experts to account: 'only trained officers are qualified to carry out the kind of detailed investigation necessary in these cases'. The machinery for dealing with police complaints is now in the process of being changed, but it is unlikely to dispose of this particular dilemma.

The notion of accountability shaping the development of the various kinds of ombudsmen reflected the traditional conception of financial audit, just as, ironically, the adequacy of the latter was being challenged and expanded. The idea of administrative audit, as reflected in the various ombudsmen institutions, mirrored the limited idea of financial audit as being about making sure that the appropriate rules had been followed and that there had been no impropriety in the use of public power. But in precisely the period that the ombudsmen were being set up, the pressures for widening the role of the comptroller and auditor-general were increasing; just as the Whyatt Report was evoking the advantages of an institution 'dealing with the maladministration in the financial field', so the inadequacies of the comptroller's office as an instrument in the service of parliamentary accountability were increasingly being criticized. In 1983 the Exchequer and Audit Department was transformed into the National Audit Office; the change of title was more than symbolic. It marked both an extension of the notion of financial accountability itself and the growing role of expertise in accountability.

Both points emerge clearly from the 1981 report of the Committee of Public Accounts which over the years had been pressing for change in company with a succession of other parliamentary committees.[13] In this, it commented on the government's Green Paper proposals for change.[14] The Green Paper marked a cautious climb up the ladder of accountability by the government from regularity to effectiveness. It accepted that the auditor's role should include both regularity and efficiency or value for money audit. But it was distinctly less enthusiastic about effectiveness audit, that is 'an examination to assess whether programmes or projects undertaken to meet established policy goals or objectives have met those aims'. The Committee of Public Accounts had no such inhibitions. It argued that the line between efficiency and effectiveness was in any case blurred, and that the comptroller and auditor-general should explicitly be empowered by legislation to pursue both kinds of audit; as, in the outcome, he was.

However, the arguments deployed by the government in urging caution about the development of effectiveness audit illustrate one of the difficulties of drawing clear lines between political and managerial accountability, between accountability seen as being about justification by argument and accountability seen as a neutral technical exercise. If the comptroller and auditor-general started to look at effectiveness, the Green Paper warned, there might be a danger of getting 'involved in debate about the merits of particular policy objectives'. If so, 'it would put at risk the traditional, non-partisan character' of the audit exercise. The reservation was brushed aside by the Public Accounts Committee: 'We consider that the C. & A. G. should draw Parliament's attention to aspects of particular policies where it is apparent from his investigations that there is reasonable doubt about their effectiveness.' Yet in a sense, the government's Green Paper was surely right. If it were to turn out that certain policy objectives are incapable of achievement through the policy instruments chosen (for example spending money on hiring more policemen to prevent crime), then it is difficult to see how such a neutral technical evaluation could be separated from political argument. The two forms of accountability inevitably blend and merge.

The 1981 report of the Committee of Public Accounts also reflects its faith in independent expertise. On the one hand, it argued that the status of auditors should be improved:

> 'until recently, most recruits to the Exchequer and Audit Department have not been graduates but have had qualifications approximating to university entrance level. This has now been changed, and all recruits are now honours graduates. . . . Nonetheless, audit staff on recruitment are almost all graded as executive officers. . . . We anticipate that it will be necessary to raise the status and grading of auditors to enable them to receive salaries more comparable with those paid in the private sector.'

Equally the committee stressed the importance of making both the comptroller and auditor-general and his staff directly appointed by, as well as reporting to, parliament – instead of being part of the civil service. In short, it wished to emphasize that the new National Audit Office was an instrument for strengthening parliament's ability to call the executive to account by reinforcing expertise in the service of a wider notion of accountability.

The search for ministerial control

But while parliament was seeking to strengthen its ability to call ministers to account, to find alternatives for the overloaded line of personal, direct accountability to the House of Commons, so

ministers were trying to strengthen their own capacity to control
their departments. For, if MPs were worried about their loss of
control, so were ministers. The Crossman Diaries, for example,
provided a text for those who believed that civil servants
consciously sought to manipulate their nominal masters.[15] And
how could ministers be expected to be accountable to anyone –
parliament, party, or public – if they themselves did not have an
effective managerial grip over their own departments? How could
the accountability of the machinery of government *to* ministers be
strengthened? The questions prompted a variety of responses, as
the reports of Royal Commissions and committees of inquiry,
Green and White Papers, academic and newspaper articles poured
off the presses. But two themes stand out.

The first theme is the assumption that efficiency and accountability are two sides of the same conceptual coin: indeed, many of
the changes, both proposed and introduced since the 1960s, were
prompted by the quest for greater efficiency in government – with
improved managerial accountability being seen as a necessary
condition for the promotion of efficiency. The second theme is the
assumption that accountability should be concerned less with
individual actions, of the kind subject to scrutiny by the parliamentary commissioner, than with overall performance. Both
themes emerge clearly from the 1969 Fulton Committee's report
on the Civil Service.[16] 'To function efficiently, large organisations
(including Government departments) need a structure in which
units and individual members have authority that is clearly
defined, and responsibilities for which they can be held accountable. There should be recognised methods of assessing their
success in achieving specified objectives', the report argued.
'Accountable management means holding individuals and units
responsible for performance measured as objectively as possible.'

Fifteen years later, almost precisely the same themes were to be
propounded in the Conservative government's White Paper on
Financial Management in Government Departments, if in a rather
different context.[17] This put forward two related arguments for
improving accountability by setting objectives against which
performance could then be assessed. On the one hand, specifying
objectives, and wherever possible, measuring the output, would

illuminate 'choices between competing claims on resources and provide a means of monitoring efficiency and effectiveness' for ministers and parliament. On the other hand, it would facilitate the devolution of responsibility:

> 'While the centre of the department receives regular information about the use of resources and the effectiveness of activities, individual managers can then be held accountable for their performance, and provided these conditions are met, can have more say in the composition of their budgets and greater freedom to manage them. This delegation of authority should help them to improve the efficiency and effectiveness of their units and to be more accountable for so doing.'

The 1983 initiative also illustrates two further aspects of the search for greater efficiency through improved managerial accountability in the public sector. There is, once again, the stress on greater expertise: improved accountability is seen as dependent on new techniques. New management and information systems had to be set up; adequate indicators and measures of performance had to be developed; the training of civil servants in 'specific skills and techniques' had to be stepped up. But there is also, providing a new note, an emphasis on information. There is a recognition that it is the flow of information which brings the machinery of accountability to life. Or, to vary the metaphor in the terms proposed at the end of the previous chapter, it is the quality of the information flowing through the pipes that determines the effectiveness of any system of accountability. 'Better information' was seen to be the key not only to strengthening ministerial control over their own departments but also as reinforcing parliament's ability to call ministers to account. Thus, the White Paper argued that the information generated about objectives and the indicators of progress would provide 'a ready starting point for examining the performance of a department in more detail' by the departmentally related select committee which, as we have seen, had evolved by the 1980s. Implicit in all this there appeared to be a clear, if simple, model of accountability. If ministers had to be explicit about their objectives, if there was information about progress towards them, parliament could then hold them accountable for `their performance. Effective political accountability was thus seen to be dependent on effective managerial accountability. The circle of accountability had been closed.

Moreover, the formula also seemed to offer a solution to the problem of modern accountability in so far as this reflects the growth in the sheer quantity and complexity of government activities. By delegating responsibility, by emancipating themselves from responsibility for individual actions by their nominal subordinates, ministers and parliament would be able to strengthen their effective control. The emphasis would switch from the control of activity to the control of performance: from regularity to output, from retrospective to prospective accountability – from calling for accounts not only about what was done in the past but also about 'processes, views, assumptions and reasons which *precede* policy decisions'.[18] The new institutions, the new techniques, and the new experts in the service of accountability would relieve overloaded linkages and provide an extra flow of information through the system.

It was a vision which, as we shall argue, was based on a number of over-optimistic assumptions. But it was also a vision which was followed with fervent and comprehensive enthusiasm. So far the discussion has centred on the national scene: the accountability of central government to parliament. However, many of the same themes re-emerge when we turn to the debate about local government which was rumbling alongside the developments in central government so far reviewed, if with significant variations. And indeed, one might well expect concern about accountability to be even greater outside the Whitehall–Westminster nexus than within it. For if, as argued in the previous chapter, the problems of accountability largely reflect the development of the service-delivery State – the problem of calling to account those actually responsible for the delivery of services to the public – then they might well be expected to be seen at their sharpest, the further away one travels from central government. The point is simply illustrated by one set of statistics. In the two decades of the debate here being analysed, from the 1960s to the 1980s, the number of civil servants directly employed by central government continued to hover around 700,000. Over the same period, the numbers employed in the National Health Service rose from 600,000 to

1,300,000 and those employed by local authorities (over half of them in education) from 1,900,000 to 2,900,000.[19]

The search for accountability in local government

The starting-point in the debate about local government was very different from that about central government, although, as we shall see, the conclusions reached were often remarkably similar. For, in one sense, local government appeared to be, almost by definition, more democratic than central government, in that those responsible for running local affairs were directly accountable to the public at the polls. Elected councillors were, after all, directly involved in government so that there could be no problem equivalent to that of ministerial responsibility.

However, it was precisely these assumptions that were challenged, in the year before the publication of the Fulton Committee, by the Maud Committee on the Management of Local Government:[20]

'We have found no evidence to support the common belief that our local government has some uniquely democratic content. Whether the test is public interest, as exemplified by the percentage poll at elections, or the extent to which members of the public, individually and in their associations, are drawn into its processes, our local government does not appear to be especially democratic.'

Further, the Committee argued:

'The idea that English local government is peculiarly democratic originates in the participation of the members in so much detail. For, unlike the members abroad, they believe, mistakenly in our opinion, that democratic government implies that to discharge their duties they must leave as little as possible to officers. As we explain later, we believe this misconception to be the root cause of local government's administrative troubles, and therefore the reason for our appointment.'

Whether or not democracy was a necessary condition for account-ability to the people, it certainly was not a sufficient one. In effect, to summarize the committee's complex arguments, the linkage between councillors and public had broken down. The social survey, carried out on behalf of the committee, showed wide-spread public alienation, thus confirming the evidence of apathy provided by the low turn-out at elections. While voters were largely ignorant about local government, councillors were seen widely as remote, inaccessible, and even irrelevant.

The reason for this state of affairs, the committee concluded, lay largely in an inefficient and ineffective organization which had undermined the *raison d'être* of local government, accountability to the people. The Maud Report argued:

'The system of local government administration has its roots in the nineteenth century respect for democratic forms, and in the old tradition of direct and detailed responsibility of local leaders for local affairs. The system was suited to a time when the range of activities of a local authority was limited, when government involvement in the affairs of society was minimal and when few professional staff were employed. Supervision by members was then not only possible; it was necessary.'

However, government by committees of councillors had become counter-productive:

'The work of departments grows more complex, partly as a result of scientific and technological development, and partly because the scope of the services is extended through public demand and national policies. It becomes increasingly difficult for committees to supervise the work of the departments because of the growth of business, lack of time and technical complexity of many of the problems. . . . We see the growth of business adding to the agenda of committees and squeezing out major issues which need time for consideration with the result that members are misled into a belief that they are controlling and directing the authority when often they are only deliberating on things which are unimportant and taking decisions on matters which do not merit their attention. . . . Leadership and

responsibility in the authority cannot easily be identified and
co-ordination of thought and work is made more difficult.'

In short, as in the case of central government, there could be no
effective accountability without effective control.

From this diagnosis flowed the cure: 'The organisation should
be based on the principle that members effectively and collectively
control officers, and are politically responsible and accountable to
the public.' But to be effective, members had to be selective. It
was for the members to 'take the key decisions on objectives of
the authority' and 'to review, periodically, progress and the
performance of the services'. However, it was for officers 'to be
responsible for the day-to-day administration of services, decisions
on case work, and routine inspection and control' and 'for
identifying and isolating the particular problem or case which *in
their view* and from *their understanding* [our italics] of the minds of
members, has such implications that members must consider
them'. In short, councillors should be more concerned with
outputs and less with inputs or process. There followed a series of
detailed recommendations for changing and rationalizing the
organizational structure of local councils, streamlining and limiting
the roles of the traditional committees.

It would be misleading, however, to suggest that the Maud
Committee was concerned exclusively with managerial accountability. Once again, it was the relationship between managerial
and political accountability which concerned it. If local government was seen as remote and unresponsive, the committee argued,
this was largely because it was a muddle: no one could understand
who was responsible for what. Once that muddle had been sorted
out, once responsibilities were more clearly defined, there had to
be more emphasis on accountability in the traditional Athenian
sense of face-to-face explanation. So, for example, the committee
recommended open meetings at which 'the public can meet leaders
of the authority', more emphasis on explaining their policies on
radio and television and the provision of more information.
Improved managerial accountability was thus to be complemented
by improved political accountability seen as transparency and
information.

The tension between efficiency and democracy, between

managerial and political accountability, also provides the theme for
the report of the Royal Commission on Local Government, which
represents yet a further attempt to reconcile the two by harnessing
the former to the latter.[21] The structure of local government, it
argued, had ceased to 'fit the pattern of life and work in modern
England'. Complexity and fragmentation were self-defeating.
Many local authorities were too small to be either effective or
efficient, while central government was reluctant to give them
'enough freedom to go their own way'. The result was that 'Local
Government is, at present, apt to be irrelevant to people's
problems, and often cannot solve them, even though it has
responsibility for so doing'. In turn, responsibility without power
helped to explain public indifference. From this, the committee
concluded that 'what is needed is a clarification of the local
government system'. Effective democracy required the ability to
act effectively: authorities large enough to bring together all the
main services, and to deploy 'the range and calibre of staff, and the
technical and financial resources' required for their 'effective
provision'. From this flowed the recommendation for the creation
of large, single-tier authorities, so strengthening accountability
(although the word was not used) by giving 'fresh encouragement
for citizens to take an active part in their own local government'.
Institutional change, by creating a more comprehensible, transparent, and effective structure, was thus seen as a way of remaking
the links between rulers and the ruled.

In the event, neither the recommendations of the Maud
Committee nor those of the Royal Commission were ever fully
implemented.[22] The logic of politics proved too strong for the logic
of institutional reform, seen as an essentially neutral managerial or
technical enterprise. However, the concerns of the 1960s did not
diminish, and were indeed exacerbated – and given a somewhat
different direction – by increasing financial stringency and the
growing anxiety of central government to control local authority
expenditure. The central dilemma of accountability came to be
seen, increasingly, as the conflict between accountability to the
local electorate and accountability to central government. Thus,
the Layfield Committee on Local Government Finance took as its
main theme the 'weakening of local accountability brought about
by the combination of two features of the present arrangements –

namely, the tendency for central government grants to grow as compared with the contribution from local taxation, and the natural concern of the government with the total of local government expenditure'.[23] The process of increasing central government control both over the total of spending, and over the level of provision for specific services, 'destroys local accountability'. From this flowed the Layfield recommendations (again ignored) for changing the system of local finance, and so aligning the locus of responsibility for revenue raising and of account-ability.

If the government resisted the arguments of the Layfield Committee for changing the system of local government finance, it had its own very different reasons for wishing to strengthen accountability, seen as making local decisions about money more visible to the public. If expenditure by local government was to be constrained, if the managerial imperative of getting better value for money was to be achieved, then there was an argument for strengthening accountability defined as providing more information in the hope that this could generate public pressure for greater efficiency and economy. That, at any rate, would seem to be the logic of the emphasis, mirroring what was happening in central government, on improving the flow of information about the performance of local government and introducing new audit institutions: again, expertise in the service of accountability.

In 1981, for example, the Department of the Environment issued a Code of Practice,[24] exhorting local authorities to include in their annual reports 'a short list of performance statistics relating to major services it provides'. Such indicators, the code of practice suggested, might include comparisons with other authorities, trends over time and between plans and achievements. The indicators might 'measure one or more of various aspects of performance, including the cost, scale and quality of service, the demand for the service, a degree of client satisfaction, relative efficiency and so on'. It was a development very much in line with the general direction of government policy already discussed, with its emphasis on moving towards the measurement of performance as the main instrument of managerial accountability. At the same time that local authorities were being urged to publish more information, the Department of Health and Social Security was developing a system of performance indicators for the National Health Service,[25] as part of a new system of 'accountability reviews':[26] a system discussed further in Chapter 4.

Lastly, the Local Government Finance Act, 1982 created an Audit Commission for Local Authorities. Previously each local authority had appointed its own auditor, drawn either from the District Audit Service or from a private firm. The 1982 Act added not only a new institution but also, in line with the change in the role of the comptroller and auditor-general, extended its function. In addition to the continuing responsibility for carrying out regularity audits, the new Audit Commission was charged with making sure that every local authority made appropriate 'overall arrangements for securing economy, efficiency and effectiveness in its use of resources'.[27]

In the discussions leading up to the creation of the Audit Commission, the local authority associations were sceptical about the need for the creation of a new institution. 'The best safeguards against waste, extravagance or inefficiency in local authorities' spending are the locally elected members who are the custodians of their authorities' objectives and oversee the execution of all their authorities' functions', the associations argued.[28] In contrast to the parliamentary demands for greater expertise in the service of accountability, local government remained faithful to a more traditional view of accountability: as something which was guaranteed, by definition, by the mere fact of local authorities being run by elected councillors. As the first controller of the Audit Commission was to write, echoing the Maud Committee fifteen years earlier, 'It is almost an article of faith within local government that the local council is accountable to and held accountable by the local electorate. Is this myth – or reality?'[29] In contrast to the national Audit Office, which was firmly linked into the system of accountability since its whole purpose was to provide parliament with information, the local Audit Commission therefore exists in a political vacuum: managerial accountability and political accountability are not linked. If accountability is seen exclusively and unproblematically as a function of elective status, then managerial accountability would seem to be largely redundant.

Puzzles and ambiguities

The view of accountability, seen as flowing from the fact of election, springs from traditional democratic theory uncontaminated by considerations about the complexities of large modern organizations or about the problems of large, uninterested electorates. It is a view which takes the linkages in the system of accountability for granted, since it assumes that councillors are automatically answerable to their voters and unquestioningly in control of the organizations for which they are accountable. As we have seen, the debate and developments of the past two decades reflect precisely the realization that neither of these two assumptions stands up.

However, these developments carry their own set of assumptions which require to be challenged. This is that impartial experts, using neutral techniques, can provide the information required to make political accountability effective. If objectives are defined, if performance is measured, if the relationship between inputs and outputs is examined, then accountability ceases to be problematic. The actions of the governors will be transparent to the governed: the problem of having an agreed, legitimate set of criteria, a common and accepted language of justification, will have been disposed of.

But of course, these are all highly questionable assumptions. To start with, who defines objectives?[30] What are the political processes which generate them? If it is ministers (for example) then is it they who are determining the criteria against which their own performance is to be judged? Yet it may well be that others (parliament or the public) might wish to challenge their performance precisely because it fails to meet a different set of criteria. Again, measuring performance is far from being a neutral, technical exercise. Not for nothing has accounting in the strictest technical sense been called the creation of the socially significant: 'Those with the power to determine what enters into organisational accounts have the means to articulate and diffuse their values and concerns, and subsequently to monitor, observe and regulate the actions of those that are now accounted for'.[31] If the concept of performance is often elusive, many-dimensional, and ambiguous –

and subsequent chapters address themselves to documenting precisely this – then the relationship between the customers of technical audit information (whether MPs, councillors, or the public) and the expert providers of accountability analysis may be problematic: a common and accepted language of justification may not exist.

Lastly, the debate and developments of the past two decades are, in retrospect, curiously lopsided. They revolve around the role of experts in accountability. They involve the creation of new institutions for improving the techniques of accountability. But they neglect the accountability *of* experts. For one of the characteristics of Welfare State service providers, as the previous chapter suggested, is precisely that they tend to regard themselves as accountable to their peers and are thus not linked into the institutionalized system through which political and managerial accountability flow. The following chapter seeks to justify and elaborate this assertion, as the first step in explaining our own approach to breaking down and disaggregating the notion of accountability in order to be able to explore its different dimensions in different contexts. For, if accountability cannot ever be reduced to a technical exercise, if it is inevitably and inescapably shot through with values and assumptions about the nature of the world, then its exercise is also bound to vary with its context.

REFERENCES

1 The classic discussion, pulling together the literature, of the dilemmas of ministerial responsibility is to be found in G. Marshall and G. C. Moodie (1959) *Some Problems of the Constitution*. London: Hutchinson, fifth (revised) edn. 1971. More recently the theme has again been explored by G. Marshall (1984) *Constitutional Conventions: The Rules and Forms of Political Accountability*. Oxford: Clarendon Press. Both these have been drawn upon in the discussion that follows.
2 The phrase is that of H. Elcock and S. Haywood (1980) *The Buck Stops Where? Accountability and Control in the National Health Service*. Hull: Institute for Health Studies, University of Hull.
3 I. Gilmour (1969) *The Body Politic*. London: Hutchinson: 166–67.
4 See, for example, B. Crick (1964) *The Reform of Parliament*. London: Weidenfeld & Nicolson.

5 Quoted in I. Gilmour (1969) *The Body Politic*. London: Hutchinson: 238.

6 Lord Haldane (Chairman) (1918) *Report of the Machinery of Government Committee*. London: HMSO Cd 9230: para. 53.

7 H. Young and A. Sloman (1982) *No Minister*. London: BBC Publications: 66. This is also the source for the followng quotation.

8 *The Citizen and the Administration: A Report by Justice* (1961) (Director of Research: Sir John Whyatt). London: Stevens & Sons.

9 Parliamentary Commission for Administration (1968) *First Report, Session, 1967–68*. London: HMSO HC 6.

10 Health Service Commissioner (1975) *Annual Report for 1974–75, First Report, Session 1974–75*. London: HMSO HC 407.

11 The Commission for Local Administration in England (1974) *Your Local Ombudsman*. London: The Commission.

12 Police Complaints Board (1980) *Triennial Review Report* London: HMSO Cmnd 7966: para. 13.

13 Committee of Public Accounts (1981) *The Role of the Comptroller and Auditor-General – Vol. 1. Report. First Special Report, Session 1980–81*. London: HMSO HC 115–1.

14 Chancellor of the Exchequer (1980) *The Role of the Comptroller and Auditor-General*. London: HMSO Cmnd 7845.

15 R. Crossman (1975, 1977) *The Diaries of a Cabinet Minister*. See especially vols 1 and 3. London: Hamish Hamilton and Jonathan Cape.

16 Lord Fulton (Chairman) (1968) *Report of the Committee on the Civil Service* vol. 1. London: HMSO Cmnd 3638.

17 Prime Minister and Chancellor of the Exchequer (1983) *Financial Management in Government Departments*. London: HMSO Cmnd 9058.

18 D. Howell (1970) *A New Style of Government*. London: Conservative Political Centre. This anticipates much of the later discussion and development.

19 Central Statistical Office (1984) *Social Trends no. 14*. London: HMSO Table 4.9.

20 Sir John Maud (Chairman) (1967) *Report of the Committee on the Management of Local Government* vol. 1. London: HMSO.

21 Lord Redcliffe-Maud (Chairman) (1969) *Report of the Royal Commission on Local Government in England* vol. 1. London: HMSO Cmnd 4040.

22 J. Dearlove (1979) *The Reorganisation of British Local Government*. Cambridge: Cambridge University Press: 352.

23 Frank Layfield QC (Chairman) *Report of the Committee of Enquiry on Local Government Finance*. London: HMSO Cmnd 6453.

24 Department of the Environment (1981) *Local Authority Annual Reports*. London: HMSO.
25 R. Klein (1982) Performance Evaluation and the N.H.S. *Public Administration* 60, 4, Winter: 385–409.
26 P. Day and R. Klein (1985) Central Accountability and Local Decision-Making: Towards a New N.H.S. *British Medical Journal* 290, 1 June: 1,676–678.
27 J. Banham (1984) Are We Being Served by Local Government – Some Initial Reflections. *Political Quarterly* 55, 3, July/September: 273–87.
28 Quoted in Committee of Public Accounts (1981) *First Special Report, Session 1980–81, The Role of the Comptroller and Auditor-General*. London: HMSO HC 115–1: xxxviii.
29 J. Banham (1984) Are We Being Served by Local Government – Some Initial Reflections. *Political Quarterly* 55, 3, July/September: 285.
30 R. Klein (1972) The Politics of PPB. *Political Quarterly* 43, 3, July/September.
31 A. Hopwood (1984) Accounting and the Pursuit of Efficiency: In A. Hopwood and C. Tompkins (eds) *Issues in Public Sector Accounting*. Oxford: Philip Allan: 178.

3

The accountability of expertise: complexity, heterogeneity, and uncertainty

So far we have traced the increasing interest in and development of institutionalized expertise in accountability over the past decades. Now we address the accountability of expertise. For it was this concern which shaped the strategy for the research on which we report in subsequent chapters. In this, our aim is to challenge the notion that accountability is a concept which can be analysed or discussed outside the context of specific services and to argue that the historical, cultural, and organizational characteristics of specific services and their delivery may be at least as important as their formal political institutions and managerial structures.

This contention rests, in turn, on a further set of assumptions. The first is that services are devised and delivered by people who may differ in their ability to define what the objectives, or outputs, are supposed to be. The second is that the ability to determine who is competent to assess progress towards the achievement of those aims may also vary: that is what is meant by performance and who is qualified to assess it according to what criteria. The third is that the ability of service deliverers to impose their own definitions may in turn reflect either the nature of the 'expertise' involved, such as the extent to which it claims to be based on arcane knowledge inaccessible to the non-expert, or the organizational power of the service deliverers (and quite possibly a combination of the two factors). The fourth is that the ability of the service deliverers to appropriate the currency of accountability may also reflect such characteristics of the services as the division of labour and interdependence between different groups of providers, and the consequent ease or difficulty of relating overall service performance to the actions of particular groups of providers.

All these points will be elaborated upon in the rest of this chapter, in which we outline our approach. At this stage of the exposition, a minimal justification of our strategy would seem to suffice. If accountability is all about the social and political processes involved in developing an agreed language of discourse about how to judge conduct, then it seems reasonable to assume that such processes will vary with the nature of the political arena in which they take place and the characteristics of the organizational actors. Furthermore, if accountability in complex organizations revolves around the ability to exercise control, then this may also be specific to particular settings.

Service deliverers, experts, and professionals

So far in this discussion we have deliberately and neutrally referred to 'service deliverers'. We will now break down this all-embracing phrase into experts, professionals, and others, looking mainly at the role of the first two groups. The Oxford English Dictionary gives two definitions of 'expert'. In the wider definition, an expert is someone 'trained by practice, skill'. In the narrow definition, an expert is someone 'whose special skill causes him to be an authority'. The former, therefore, applies to almost everyone delivering a service in the public sector, from dinner ladies to doctors, from the police to teachers, from school caretakers to social workers. All are trained by practice or skill, if to varying degrees. Whether or not they are also regarded as experts in the second and stronger sense, as authorities, is a matter for empirical investigation. One of our aims in this book is precisely to investigate which service deliverers are considered to be experts and which experts are considered to be authorities, since ascribed authority may be one of the factors determining the ability of service deliverers to determine the currency of accountability.

Professions, from this perspective, are organized groups of service deliverers who have been granted a monopoly of expertise by the State,[1] the right to control entry, and the qualifications required to practise. In effect, professionals are given the legal status of 'authorities', and their existence reflects an implicit social contract as argued in Chapter 1.[2] In exchange for the grant of a monopoly, the profession undertakes to ensure that its members are competent to practise. In turn, however, this means that it is the profession which defines what is meant by legitimate activity and adequate performance. In other words, professionalization is the occupational monopolization of the power to determine the language of discourse about how to judge conduct. The currency of accountability is, in effect, determined by the profession. This in turn is mirrored in the machinery of accountability. The individual professional is answerable only to his or her professional peers.

So in the case of doctors, the paradigm example of professionalism in the classical sense among the Welfare State's service deliverers, it is the General Medical Council which determines not only the qualifications required but also what constitutes proper conduct.[3] In the instance of the medical profession, furthermore, the principle of exclusive peer accountability is reflected in, and reinforced by, the absence of any hierarchical organizational accountability. Doctors in Britain are not accountable for their performance to their employers, the National Health Service, in that they cannot be made to answer for how they use the public resources put at their disposal. If an employing health authority wishes to rid itself of an incompetent or inadequate consultant, it usually has to invoke the 'Three Wise Men' procedure: that is a review by professional peers.[4]

The case of doctors provides a neat and clear-cut example of professionalism in the strict, traditional sense of a State-licensed monopoly of expertise and the privatization of accountability. But it raises a number of questions about just how 'professionalism' should be defined.[5] Does the ability to impose criteria of performance, and successfully to establish a system of internal accountability, reflect the level of expertise (in the strong sense of ascribed authority) or the power of a given occupational group to carve out a legal monopoly for itself? And what is the relationship between the level of expertise and power? Does power flow from expertise? Or does it reflect other factors, such as high social status? What is the relationship between expertise and status? Looking only at the case of doctors does not allow these questions to be answered, since the medical profession ranks high not only on acknowledged expertise but also on social status, whatever criteria – the Registrar-General's classification of occupations, income, or class background – are used to define this. Deriving general conclusions about the 'power of the professions' from the single case of doctors therefore risks tautology.

In any case, it is now generally accepted that to define professionalism exclusively in terms of the legal status of occupations is inadequate.[6] Not only doctors but also plumbers 'practise esoteric techniques for the benefit of people in distress'.[7] Not only doctors but also jazz musicians claim the right to define whether or not one of their colleagues has given an adequate performance: thus jazz musicians will resist letting 'any layman, even the one who is paying their wages, say that a musician is playing badly or even that he has struck the wrong note'.[8] The notion of professionalism in the loose and wide sense of occupational expertise has become all-pervasive: hence the phenomenon of what has been called the 'professionalization of everyone'.[9] Thus, it is possible to talk about footballers committing 'professional fouls' or to write about a cricket match: 'this was the type of professional survival operation the present England team is equipped to perform; though only extremely unprofessional play in the earlier stages had put them in the position of playing to survive'.[10] So professionalism may sometimes be equated with command over expertise, as these examples show, although it does not follow that all professionals are regarded as experts.

But to what extent and in what circumstances can command over expertise also be translated into the privatization of accountability? If professionalization in the demotic sense is becoming generalized, does this also mean that service deliverers of the Welfare State are successfully establishing a claim to defining performance and judging conduct in the same way as professionals in the strict, legal sense? And, if such claims are being pursued, is success in achieving them related either to the level of expertise (as judged, for example, by the educational qualifications required to pursue a particular occupation) or to the social status of those involved? These questions cannot be answered by looking at single occupations: here the debate about the role of the medical profession is a warning example since assertions that its power rests on either its level of expertise or high social status cannot be proved or disproved without looking at other occupations where these characteristics do not go hand-in-hand. A comparative approach is essential. The first aim of our research design (see pp. 71–3) was therefore to examine the problem of holding to account service deliverers of different kinds. If we looked at service deliverers varying both in their expertise and in their social status, we argued, we would be able to explore whether these *are* the decisive factors – or whether possibly the problems of accountability reflect other influences.

Service complexity, heterogeneity, and uncertainty

If the characteristics of service-providers are one factor in the exercise of accountability, the characteristics of the services themselves are another. To illustrate this point, let us return to ancient Athens. Let us imagine that the messenger sent to Marathon had been called to account by the citizens. There are a number of characteristics about the action he was performing, relevant for any discussion of accountability. First, it was a simple action, and the messenger was delivering only a single service: his duty was to run as fast as he could to deliver his message. Second, it was a solo action, and the messenger did not need the help of someone with a different skill (for example a driver) in order to be able to carry out his responsibility. Third, it was an action which spoke for itself, with no uncertainty about the objective and the relationship between means and ends: if his message was success-fully delivered, the achievement of his objective could not be in doubt. So provided he did not stray off his route to visit his wife or engage in some similarly flagrant dereliction of his duty, the messenger would have no problem in giving an account of himself. Nor for that matter would the citizens of Athens have any problem in devising appropriate criteria for judging his conduct.

This example suggests that there are three dimensions of

service characteristics relevant when it comes to considering problems of accountability. First, services may vary in their degree of *heterogeneity*, that is the extent to which a particular service-delivery agency, such as the National Health Service or the police, is delivering a single, simple product – or a variety of different products which happen to fall under the same administrative label. Second, services may vary in their degree of *complexity*, that is the extent to which the service needs to harness different skills for its delivery. Third, services may vary in the degree of *uncertainty* about the relationship between means and ends, that is the causal relationship between the input of resources, the processes involved, and the objective expressed as the achievement of a given impact. The three dimensions may be related. So it is likely in practice that both complexity and uncertainty increase with the degree of heterogeneity. But analytically it is useful to distinguish between them, and to discuss each of them separately. Let us take each of them in turn, in order to explore their implications for the exercise of accountability.

The simpler a service is, that is the less heterogeneous it is in terms of the variety of its products, the simpler also ought to be the exercise of accountability. If a service exists to turn out one product, there can be no argument about what the currency of accountability should be. The product defines the justification for the organization's activities. There is no scope for controversy about the justification for turning out one product rather than another, and the trade-offs between them. There may, of course, still be ambiguity about accountability for the efficient use of resources or for the achievement of desired impacts. There may, in the public sector at any rate, also be problems about accountability seen as being as much about the style in which services are produced as about the production of the services themselves. So, for example, it might be argued that Social Security has only one product: money. If the money is handed out promptly, accurately, and cheaply (in terms of administrative costs), that might well count as an adequate performance[11] – yet it might be argued that Social Security officers should also be accountable for courtesy and respect towards clients. So, even in simple services, accountability may be quite complex. But difficulties multiply when there has to be accountability for a mix of perhaps competing products, and when the assessment of performance involves making judgements about the relative desirability, efficiency, and impact of different mixes.

The complexity of a given service, that is the number of different skills involved in the processes of production is of course likely to be related to the variety of its products. But even given single-product services, there may still be large variations in the extent to which the co-operation of different skills is required for their production: contrast, for example, the limited number of skills required to produce a legal service as against the many involved in running a surgical unit. Complexity has implications therefore for accountability which are independent of heterogeneity. To return to the messenger to Marathon, his accountability was unproblematic largely because no other person was involved in the action he was performing. He did not depend on the co-operation of a map-reader or a driver. He was answerable only for what he did himself. He could not be blamed for the action of another, nor could he absolve himself by blaming someone else. But if accountability revolves around being able to assign responsibility – to define with precision what can be expected from whom – then the difficulty of so doing is likely to increase with the complexity of any given service, to the extent that the performance of any individual action is dependent on the actions of others. The division of labour within a service may also lead to a blurring of accountability. The point can be illustrated by taking the kind of case which the Health Service Commissioner is often called to investigate:[12] the dumping of a discharged patient at home without adequate support. This may involve questioning the performance not only of the ambulance service but also of doctors and nurses, and possibly social workers and home-helps. Where the success of a performance depends on the degree of co-operation between different skills, who is accountable for what?

To ask this question is also to underline another aspect of complexity. It is not just the number of different skills involved in delivering a particular product which may pose problems of accountability; so may the organizational relationship between the different skill groups. If there is a clear-cut hierarchy of command between different skill groups, if the doctor can command the nurse, if the nurse can command the ambulancemen and so on, then there is also a chain of accountability (although it remains an open question whether the formal ability to command can also be translated into an effective ability to control; conversely there may be an effective ability to command based on custom or convention, even where there is no formal hierarchy). Responsibility is defined by the hierarchy itself. If, however, there is no such hierarchy – if dependence on the skills of others is not matched by the ability to command – then indeed, accountability becomes problematic, all the more so if there is no hierarchy of command within skill groups. To hold someone accountable for the actions of others who are not accountable to him or her is to make nonsense of the concept: it is to suggest that someone can be made answerable for a performance which he or she does not 'own' – rather as if a conductor were to be held responsible for the performance of an orchestra where each player can choose what score to play from (and was answerable only to his or her fellow flautists or violinists for the competence with which he or she played his chosen part).

The notion of uncertainty introduces yet a further and different set of considerations. Accountability seen as being answerable for the achievement of stated objectives not only raises the question, as we have already suggested, of what social and political processes are involved in setting the objectives in the first place. Objectives are not necessarily self-evident. Nor are they necessarily or invariably clear and precise. Services may vary in the clarity and precision with which objectives can be defined: the degree of ambiguity or certainty about what they are all about. Moreover, to add to the difficulties involved, the social theories underlying objectives may vary in their adequacy. To set an objective means having a theory of the causal relationship between performing certain actions and producing intended results: if the messenger to Marathon ran as fast as he could, he would achieve his objective – by delivering his message. If the theory of social action implicit in the objective is faulty or inadequate, then by definition the objective is unattainable – and those charged with achieving it can hardly be made answerable or blamed for their failure in meeting it. The point is reinforced if objectives are to be defined in terms not merely of organizational activities but of social impact: that is if performance is to be judged not just by outputs but by outcomes. So, for example, it might be possible to define the objectives of the NHS in terms of activities or outputs (for example the number of patients treated every year), or in terms of impact or outcome (for example the improvement or deterioration in the health status of the country's population). In the latter case, the problem of uncertainty comes to the forefront. The relationship between the production of health services and the state of the nation's health is extremely uncertain (see Chapter 4): a great many factors, ranging from nutrition to housing, influence the population's health, and the contribution of the NHS is extraordinarily difficult to disentangle. So to the extent that services vary in the conceptual puzzles involved in assessing the relationship between their activities and their ability to have a desired (and feasible) impact, so the problems of accountability grow.

The framework for research and analysis

The conventional view of the problems of accountability, to sum up the argument so far, is that these stem from the nature of government in complex, modern societies. It is the view that has shaped the attempts reviewed in the previous chapter to find institutional solutions, whether by inventing new machinery or by changing the existing structure of government. New linkages have been created; existing ones have been reinforced. It is an approach influenced by the traditional preoccupation with parliamentary accountability which, by definition, reflects a general across-the-board concern with the relationship between rulers and the ruled. Such a general across-the-board approach ignores, however, the possibility that the problems of accountability may also reflect the characteristics of specific services, and the actors involved in them. Yet as we have tried to show, there are good reasons for assuming that service specific factors may be as important as institution specific factors.

To test our own assumption, as well as those of the traditional view, necessarily involves adopting a comparative approach and asking questions about the practice of accountability in different service settings. Accordingly our research strategy had to be designed to allow us to explore the relationship between the three sets of factors which, as our analysis has so far suggested, might be expected to influence the practice of accountability.

Institutional factors

One of the themes in the contemporary debate is, as we have seen, that if services are run directly by elected representatives of the people, then the notion of accountability becomes largely unproblematic. Local government equates with local democracy seen as accountability. The service providers are directly answerable to the elected representatives, so runs the theory underlying this view, while the latter are directly answerable to the people. To test this view we had accordingly to compare local government services with those operating in different institutional frameworks.

Service deliverer characteristics

If accountability involves the generation of a social consensus about what counts as good conduct and acceptable performance, then as we have also argued, the power of the organizational actors may be crucial. In turn, however, the power of the actors may be derived from their status as authoritative professionals, from their social status, from their imputed expertise, from their organizational strength (or quite conceivably, from a mixture of these factors). Furthermore, if accountability also involves the ability to make individual service providers answerable for what they do, this may vary from service to service depending on the ability of different groups of providers to make themselves invisible to scrutiny. To explore such questions we compared services which varied in these characteristics of the organizational actors.

Service characteristics

Services vary (see pp. 59–63) in terms of three dimensions relevant for the practice of accountability: complexity, heterogeneity, and uncertainty. To probe the implications of these factors, we again compared services which differed on these dimensions.

To accommodate these three sets of factors, we chose five services for our inquiry: education, social services, the police, health, and water. All five involve the delivery of services to the public: they therefore fit into our concern with the problem of accountability in the modern service delivery State. However, they offer scope for exploring the influence of institutional, service deliverer, and service characteristics. The differences between them in these respects are set out schematically in *Table 1* and are elaborated in the subsequent chapters dealing with each specific service in turn. In what follows we briefly set out the justification for choosing these services as laboratories for exploring the factors identified as relevant to the practice of accountability.

Taking first the institutional setting of the five services, education and social services are both the direct responsibility of local government committees made up of elected members (though these also co-opt other, non-elected members). They therefore provide examples of 'democratically run' services, if local government can be equated with democracy. The police provide an example of a mixed system, in that police authorities are composed both of elected members representing local authorities and of others representing the magistracy; in addition, a direct line of accountability runs between the police and central government (see Chapter 5). The NHS is different yet again in that it is a centrally financed service for which the Secretary of State for Social Services is directly accountable to parliament but is administered locally by direct authorities composed of nominated members. Similarly water is a national service run by nominated authorities accountable to the Secretary for the Environment, but differs from the NHS in that (uniquely among the five services) it sells its products and is self-financing.

Turning next to the degree of professionalization, classification is more difficult for a number of reasons. The services themselves are more complex, if to varying degrees, in that they may employ a range of different skill groups (see pp. 68–9). Furthermore, as already noted, the notion of professionalism is a protean one. The classification set out in *Table 1* is therefore both rough and ready and provisional. One of the intentions of our study was precisely to explore the extent to which different service deliverers are perceived as professionals: that is the degree of 'authority'

Table 1 A classification of the five services in the study

	'direct democratic control'			'professionalization'			heterogeneity			complexity			uncertainty		
	high	med.	low	high	med.	low	high	med.	low	high	med.	low	high	med.	low
education	X				X			X				X	X		
health service			X	X			X			X			X		
police		X				X	X					X	X		
social services	X				X				X	X			X		
water			X		X				X		X				X

imputed to them. We have ranked the National Health Service high on professionalization because it is dominated by doctors who represent the archetypal profession on every possible criterion – a legal monopoly over the exercise of certain skills, restrictions on entry, peer accountability, and so on. Education and social services have been assigned to a middle category on the grounds that both teachers and social workers represent aspiring would-be professions which, however, have yet to achieve the legal status of doctors. Water has also been put into this category, if with some hestitation, because the Institute of Water Engineers and Scientists is not a registration or licensing authority and does not therefore conform to the full professional model.[13] The police have been ranked low on professionalization since, on a strict construction of the term, they lack any of the distinguishing characteristics of a profession. To what extent professionalization is equated with imputed expertise (and the relationship between the two) is, of course, a matter for investigation in subsequent chapters.

If rough and ready, our classification is at least consistent with the social status of the occupations concerned as conventionally defined. In the categorization adopted by the Office of Population Censuses and Surveys (OPCS),[14] doctors appear in social class 1, teachers and social workers appear in social class 2, and policemen appear in social class 3. The three occupations tend to appear in the same order of prestige in various scales constructed by social scientists on the basis of popular perceptions, although it is worth noting that on one such scale (that constructed by Hope and Goldthorpe) police constables rank higher than teachers and social workers if still well below doctors.[15] Reinforcing our perplexity about the categorization of the water service, engineers are assigned to social class 1 by the OPCS but appear well below doctors on one scale of occupational prestige and above them in another.

Classifying services by heterogeneity turns out to be a perplexing task. For this categorization begs the question of what is meant by service 'products'. At the highest level of generalization, all our five services could be said to be delivering only one product – health care, social care, schooling, policing, and water. At the coal-face level of activity, all our five services turn out to involve a great many different, discrete kinds of products, so there is an element of arbitrariness in assigning them to different categories of heterogeneity.

The NHS delivers a bewildering variety of products designed for different client groups, ranging from intensive care treatment of patients with heart attacks to custodial care for mentally ill or handicapped people. It presents all the problems of a mixed-product service, in the sense that there is continuing controversy about what the mix should be and what the trade-offs are between products. Similarly social services deliver a wide range of products to a number of client groups, from residential care for the elderly to case work with the young. They share with the NHS all the characteristics and complications, if perhaps to a less extreme degree, of a mixed-product service and we therefore have no hesitation in ranking them 'high' on heterogeneity. Education and the police are more difficult to classify. Education has a smaller range of products and more limited client groups than the NHS or social services. While health and social services can be compared to department stores, education is more like a specialist shop. And although the police has some of the characteristics of the heterogeneous department store services – in particular the variety of client groups served – it does not have so many discrete products in terms of the variety of activities pursued by officers (although here heterogeneity is difficult to disentangle from complexity, and the difference between services in the mix of skills involved). We have therefore assigned both education and the police to the middle category of heterogeneity although arguably they might just scrape into the high category. Finally, water would seem to be an example of a more or less single-product service: water coming out of taps and flushing away household waste. The picture is complicated by the fact that water authorities also have responsibility for pollution and flood control, for dealing with sewerage, and even for providing recreational facilities. But given that the service's dominant function is to provide water, it would appear reasonable to put it into the 'low' category on heterogeneity.

Predictably the NHS once again emerges as being high on complexity. The heterogeneity of its products is mirrored in the number of different skills involved in delivering the service. Of the 835,000 people directly employed in the NHS in England, only 38,000 were doctors in 1980.[16] The rest included 370,000 nurses,

172,000 ancillary workers, 105,000 administrative and clerical staff, plus a host of assorted 'experts' ranging from pharmacists to radiographers, occupational therapists to electronics technicians. Social services, too, demonstrate a high – if lesser – degree of complexity. Social workers account only for a tenth of the total staff of 280,000. The rest included 22,000 administrative and clerical staff, 93,000 home-helps, 71,000 residential home staff and a mixed bag of nursery officers and child-care specialists. It is a service which clearly depends on the co-operation of a considerable range of different skills – at different levels of expertise – for its delivery. This is true to a lesser degree of water, which has been placed in the medium category of complexity. Alone among the five services it is capital rather than labour intensive, and its total workforce is only 60,000.[17] Of these, 12 per cent are graded as managerial and professional staff, 16 per cent as technicians, 24 per cent as support staff and supervisors, 7 per cent as craftsmen, and 38 per cent as manual operators. By contrast the police offers an example of a service which overwhelmingly relies on a single-skill labour force. In 1984 its total workforce, excluding special constables, was 168,000. Of these, 120,000 were policemen and women, and 5,000 were traffic wardens, supported by 20,000 clerical civilian workers, 10,000 technicians, and a variety of domestic workers.[18] Similarly a single occupation, teaching, dominates in the education service. Of the 1,100,000-plus people employed by LEAs in 1982, almost 700,000 were teachers. The rest were support staff of various kinds, of whom over half were part-timers like school dinner ladies.[19]

Uncertainty, unlike complexity, cannot be quantified, even crudely. Four out of the five services in our study seem, however, to rank high on uncertainty – whether this is defined as uncertainty about the objectives themselves or about the relationship between means and ends. In the case of the NHS, for example, outcome or impact objectives tend to be defined in extremely general terms, such as improving the state of the population's health. Although many specific products can be identified, the overall contribution of the health service is difficult to calculate. When objectives are defined more specifically, they tend to be limited in their scope to input or process aims, such as the provision of a specified number of beds or equity in access to any given level of provision.[20] Social services, again, lack clear-cut outcome or impact objectives, and where there are such objectives (for example the prevention of delinquency or enabling elderly people to continue living in their own homes) it is difficult to isolate the contribution of the social services from environmental factors or other public policy streams. Education might, at first sight, appear to be a somewhat different case, in that its objective would hardly seem to be in doubt: to produce an educated population. But not only is there disagreement about what is meant by an 'educated population': witness the debate about the desirable balance between training in basic skills, such as literacy and numeracy, and education in social skills and critical thinking.[21] But equally there is uncertainty about the contribution of schools, as distinct from the home environment towards the achievement of any of the objectives set. In all these respects, however, water is very different. If water does not run, if the lavatory does not flush, then the water authorities have failed in the achievement of their objectives. Moreover, their objectives can be quantified and expressed in terms not only of providing a specified level of service to consumers but also in terms of achieving a specific return on the capital invested. There is no doubt about the relationship between the input of resources and the outcome, or about the exclusive role of the water authorities.

All these are issues to be explored and developed further in the chapters that follow, each of which deals with one of the five services in our study. The classifications in *Table 1* are designed to provide a framework for our study, no more, and the analytic threads for our journey through the labyrinth of accountability. Like the scaffolding of a building, the framework can be dismantled once the work is complete. Even if our categorization is crude, it does serve to demonstrate the diversity of the five services on those criteria which, we have argued, are critical for the practice of accountability. The services are also diverse enough to permit an exploration of other, possibly relevant issues, such as the role of central government inspectorates (notably but not exclusively in the case of education and the police) in generating information about performance. If effective political accountability does indeed depend on the availability of an independent source of expertise or audit in assessing the performance of service deliverers, then this should emerge from the experience of the five services in our study.

The design of the research study

To examine the practice of accountability, we decided to focus on the role of the members of the authorities and committees responsible for delivering the service.[22] For these are in theory the critical links in the system of accountability. They are answerable either to the people (in the case of directly elected authorities, such as education and social services) or to the relevant secretary of state (in the case of health and water), with members of police authorities being perhaps examples of divided accountability. In turn, it is they who, if they are to be answerable to a third party, must be able to call the service deliverers to account. They represent, as it were, the two faces of accountability: answerability and control. If they do not function as theory demands, then our ideas about the system of accountability may need to be changed. By looking at their role, we can therefore examine whether and to what extent political and managerial accountability mesh, and what currency of accountability is used: that is what the criteria for judging right conduct and performance actually are.

Accordingly members of the authorities responsible for delivering the five services in one geographical area were interviewed. The aim was to explore the members' own perceptions of their accountability – to whom and for what; and how they themselves assessed the performance of the services for which they were responsible. (See Appendix 1 for survey details.) In designing the check-list of questions for interviews, we used the concepts and issues – such as the definition of objectives, the degree of imputed authority to professionals and experts, the currency of evaluation, the use of independent experts in accountability – which provide our analytic framework. But we quickly learned that while such concepts were useful for organizing our own approach, they largely represented an alien language for many members who had to be left to define their role in their own words (even the key word, accountability, often did not appear in their vocabulary without prompting). The findings reported in subsequent chapters therefore represent in a sense a report on a visit to a strange tribe, whose existence is taken for granted in the theoretical literature on accountability, and who are indeed crucial to it but whose views on accountability remain largely unexplored.

The interviews with members were supplemented by interviews with officers of the services concerned, attendance at committee meetings, and the analysis of minutes and reports. However, by concentrating on how the members themselves interpreted and performed their role – as distinct from how they are supposed to be carrying out that role, according to constitutional doctrine and the academic literature – inevitably we cannot present a complete picture. Indeed, it is difficult to see how this would be possible, short of a vast and unaffordable research enterprise which also embraced interviewing a representative sample of the public (to investigate how far they saw the members of authorities as being answerable to them) and of the service deliverers (to see how far these see themselves answerable to the members). In short, as always with research, the strengths of our approach are also the source of its main weakness: by comparing five services, we are able to investigate the influence of service context on accountability but must rely on inferences drawn from examining in detail only one, albeit crucial, link in the system of accountability.

Since the whole justification for our research strategy was to compare services, this also meant that we had to avoid other, confusing factors as far as possible, such as differences in the socio-economic environment and in political control. This is why we decided to choose five authorities in the same geographical area. This meant that we could concentrate on the differences between services, without worrying whether these were caused by environmental or political differences, since these were the same for all five. But again, there was a price to be paid for this. We cannot say, on the basis of our findings, whether or not a different socio-economic or political environment would produce different perceptions of accountability among the members of authorities – although we can and do examine whether party identification makes a difference in our study area.

So this is a report on perceptions of accountability in one geographical area, at one point in time (the interviews were carried out from mid-1983 to mid-1984). The study area, which cannot be identified in order to protect the anonymity of the members interviewed, consisted of a large, predominantly urban county where the education and social services committees, like the council as a whole, were controlled by the Labour Party. The three health authorities covered by our study were all within this county. However, the police and water authorities spilled over into neighbouring, Conservative-controlled counties.

In the chapters that follow, we put our findings for each of the services in the context of its national institutional setting and the assumptions made, by central government and others, about what the practice of accountability should be. The gap between practice and assumptions is, as we shall see, wide. But we do not, and indeed cannot on the basis of our research approach, claim to have given a definitive picture of the practice of accountability valid for all authorities for all time. All that our approach allows us to do is to generate insights about the problems encountered in trying to give meaning to the concept of accountability, and what these problems imply for future debate and policy-making.

REFERENCES

1 G. Millerson (1964) *The Qualifying Associations*. London: Routledge & Kegan Paul.
2 A. W. Merrison (Chairman) (1975) *Report of the Committee of Inquiry into the Regulation of the Medical Profession*. London: HMSO Cmnd 6018:3.
3 General Medical Council (1985) *Professional Conduct and Discipline: Fitness to Practise*. London: GMC, April.
4 For an illustration of the problems of calling a consultant to account, and the ineffective use of the 'Three Wise Men' procedure, see M. D. Sherrard (Chairman) (1978) *Report of the Committee of Inquiry into Normansfield Hospital*. Cmnd. 7357. London: HMSO.
5 The literature on professionalism is vast. See especially T. J. Johnson (1972) *Professions and Power*. London: Macmillan. R. Dingwall and P. Lewis (eds) (1983) *The Sociology of the Professions*. London: Macmillan. D. Portwood and A. Field (1981) Privilege and the Profession. *Sociological Review* 29, 4, November: 749–73.
6 *ibid.*

7 E. Hughes (1958) *Men and their Work*. London: Collier-Macmillan: 88.

8 H. S. Becker's study, quoted in E. Hughes (1958) *Men and their Work*. London: Collier-Macmillan: 93.

9 H. L. Wilensky (1964) The Professionalization of Everyone? *American Journal of Sociology* LXX, 2, September.

10 J. Arlott (1972) England Lives to Fight Again. *Guardian* 19 July. Quoted in R. Klein (1973) *Complaints Against Doctors*. London: Charles Knight.

11 See the performance indicators used by the Department of Health and Social Security, as set out in Chancellor of the Exchequer (1985) *The Government's Expenditure Plans 1985–86 to 1987–88*, vol. 2, Table 3.12.11. London: HMSO Cmnd 9428–II.

12 The instance given is an invented composite, but see for example Health Service Commissioner (1980) *First Report for Session 1980–81* Selected Investigations Completed April–September 1980, case no. W398/78–79. London: HMSO.

13 Institution of Water Engineers and Scientists (1978) *Evidence for the Committee of Inquiry into the Engineering Profession*. London: Council of the Institution.

14 Office of Population Censuses and Surveys (1980) *Classification of Occupations*. London: HMSO.

15 A. Stewart, K. Prandy, and R. M. Blackburn (1980) *Social Stratification and Occupations*. London: Macmillan. See also A. P. M. Coxon and C. L. Jones (1978) *The Images of Occupational Prestige*. London: Macmillan. A. P. M. Coxon and C. L. Jones (1979) *Class and Hierarchy*. London: Macmillan.

16 Department of Health and Social Security (1982) *Health and Personal Social Service Statistics for England 1982*. London: HMSO.

17 Water Industry Central Manpower Unit – personal communication.

18 Her Majesty's Chief Inspector of Constabulary (1985) *Report for the Year 1984*. London: HMSO.

19 Central Statistical Office (1985) *Social Trends no. 15*, Table 3.22. London: HMSO.

20 For the problems of defining the NHS's objectives, see Sir Alec Merrison (Chairman) (1979) *Report of the Royal Commission on the National Health Service*. London: HMSO Cmnd 7615.

21 Secretary of State for Education (1985) *Better Schools*. London: HMSO Cmnd 9469.

22 The literature on the roles and attitudes of councillors, and their relationship with officers, is of course vast. But little of it deals specifically with accountability as such. However, we have drawn upon: K. Newton (1976) *Second City Politics*. Oxford: Clarendon

Press. D. Walker (1983) *Municipal Empire*. London: Maurice Temple Smith. H. Heclo (1969) The Councillor's Job. *Public Administration* 47, Summer: 185–202. M. Laffin and K. Young (1985) The Changing Role of Local Authority Chief Officers. *Public Administration* 63, Spring: 41–59.

4

Accountability and the National Health Service

From its inception the National Health Service has embodied a particular, formal notion of accountability. Since the service is centrally financed, it is the minister responsible who must be accountable to parliament. Since the minister is accountable, all the subordinate health authorities must in turn be accountable to him. It was Aneurin Bevan who, in explaining his proposals to the Cabinet in 1945, set out what has remained the constitutional doctrine ever since. Describing the position of the bodies charged with the management of the NHS, both at the regional and local levels, he wrote: 'They will be the agents (though not, I hope, in any derogatory sense, the creatures) of my Department'.[1] Nor was it merely seen as financial accountability in the narrow audit sense. The minister was, and is, also answerable to the House of Commons for the activities carried out within the NHS. As Bevan remarked on another occasion, 'when a bedpan is dropped on a hospital floor, its noise should resound in the Palace of Westminster'.[2] Alone among the five services with which we are concerned in this book, the NHS has a hierarchy of accountability running from the coal-face of health service delivery to parliament.

But although the constitutional position is clear, the practice of accountability is less so. In particular, there has been a tension – evident from the start of the NHS – between seeing the members of health authorities as the *agents* of central government and as autonomous actors with responsibilities of their own. If members of health authorities were charged only with carrying out the directives of central government, there would be no problem: they would be answerable for the way in which they did so. This has never been the position in the NHS. Once again, Bevan made the position clear in a memorandum to the Cabinet written a few years after the launch of the NHS:[3]

'There would have been no theoretical difficulty – there is none now – in having from the outset a tightly centralised service with all that would mean in the way of rigid uniformity, bureaucratic machinery and "red tape". But that was not the policy we adopted when framing our legislation. . . . In framing the whole service, we did deliberately come down in favour of a maximum decentralisation to local bodies, a minimum of itemised central approval, and the exercise of financial control through global budgets, relying for economy not so much on a tight and detailed Department grip but on the education of the bodies concerned by the development of comparative costing, central supply and similar gradual methods of introducing efficiency and order among the heterogeneous mass of units we took over.'

So in theory, the NHS is an example of a service which is trying to combine the centralization of accountability with the decentralization of responsibility. On the one hand there is the stress of carrying out national policies. On the other hand there is also the emphasis on the large degree of discretion enjoyed by those responsible for carrying them out locally: the members of health authorities.

It is this tension which provides a constant theme running through the various reorganizations which the NHS has undergone since 1948.[4] The 1974 reorganization replaced regional hospital boards by regional health authorities, and hospital management committees by area health authorities. The aim was 'that there should be a maximum delegation downward, matched by accountability upwards. . . . The line of delegation downwards (with corresponding accountability upwards) will be from the Central Department to regional health authorities, and from the regional health authorities to area health authorities. The aim will be to set clear objectives and standards, and measure performance against them.'[5] But the health authorities were not to be mere agents responsible for implementing national 'objectives and standards'. The White Paper introducing the reorganization spoke with forked tongues:[6]

> 'A national service calls for a national strategy, with national objectives, standards and priorities. It is, however, equally important to encourage variety and flexibility in working the strategy over the country. Within the national framework, therefore, administration will be delegated to local bodies, *which will set their own objectives and be responsible for achieving them.*' [our emphasis]

If the 1974 reorganization stressed accountability to the centre first, and put delegation to health authorities second, the reverse is true of the 1982 reorganization. This abolished and replaced them by district health authorities (DHAs), leaving the regional health authorities (RHAs) untouched. The thrust of the proposals was made clear by Patrick Jenkin, then Secretary of State for Social Services:

> 'We are determined to see as many decisions as possible are taken at the local level – in the hospital and in the community. We are determined to have more local health authorities whose members will be encouraged to manage the Service, with the minimum of interference by any central authority, whether at the region or in central government departments. We ask that our proposals should be judged whether they achieve these aims.'[7]

The government's intention of giving more discretion to the new DHAs, and thereby attenuating the traditional 'bedpan' doctrine of parliamentary accountability, was subsequently spelled out in a dialogue with the Social Services Committee of the House of Commons. In response to pressure from that committee for more information about the performance of the NHS (echoing the demands of the Public Accounts Committee), the government stated:

'As the Government have stressed in the Consultative Paper "Patients First", it is at local level that patients' needs and the impact of policies are usually best assessed. The Government have accordingly made clear their determination to increase decentralisation and strengthen local autonomy within the constraints of national economic policy. . . . Ministers will certainly answer for the major political decisions of, for instance, a health authority, if questioned in the House or in correspondence. But they ought not to be expected to agree with and to defend each and every decision of that authority. That would inevitably imply a level of intervention by Whitehall in local decisions which would be unacceptable and bureaucratic.'[8]

In the event, the enthusiasm for increasing decentralization and strengthening local autonomy was to be short-lived.[9] The combined pressure of parliamentary committees and financial stringency persuaded the DHSS to adopt an increasingly directive role. Within two years of the 1982 reorganization, the DHSS had introduced a new managerial structure for the NHS following the Griffiths Report and a system of performance indicators and reviews which involved setting specific targets to individual regions and districts.[10] At the same time that the interviews for this study were carried out, these changes were still in the pipeline or had not yet begun to bite. However, even without taking these developments into account, it is evident that members of health authorities have to cope with ambiguous signals and expectations in their exercise of accountability.

The role of authority members

All members of the DHAs are nominated. Their broad composition is laid down by the National Health Services Act, 1977, as amended by the Health Services Act, 1980, which spelled out the changes consequent on the replacement of area health authorities by DHAs. The chairman is appointed directly by the secretary of state. Four members are appointed by local authorities. The remaining members are appointed by the regional health authority. There are five 'reserved' places for a hospital consultant, a general practitioner, a nurse, and a trade unionist, all to be chosen after 'appropriate consultation' as well as a nominee of the appropriate university with a medical school in the region. The rest are 'generalists', normally bringing the total membership to sixteen (although the districts in our study had eighteen members each). For making these nominations, regions are offered a number of criteria by guidance from the DHSS.[11] The members should 'be able to devote sufficient time to the DHA's business'; they should 'have the health and vigour to make an effective contribution throughout their term of office'. Finally, 'as well as providing for a suitable geographical balance among the membership, RHAs should bear in mind a reasonable balance of age and sex, together with such factors as experience of management and administration in business or the public service, experience in the mental health or handicap fields, and in appropriate cases, suitable representation of ethnic minorities'.

Nevertheless, the members are in no sense representatives of their district or of professional groups within the NHS in the same sense that it is possible to talk of councillors as being the representatives of the electorate. The DHSS's guidance is specific on this point: 'no member is appointed to represent a sectional or personal interest', while 'the underlying principle of medical and nursing representation is that such members should bring to bear their wide professional knowledge and experience of health services, rather than act as spokesmen of professional interests or staff representatives'. Indeed, such a representative role would be incompatible with the agency role of members as the 'creatures' ultimately, to use Bevan's terminology, of ministers. The agency role of members is further underlined by the fact that they can be dismissed, rather like the stewards of someone's estate, accountable to their master:

'If an appointing authority is of the opinion that it is not in the interest of the health service in the area or district of an authority, that a person whom it has appointed as the chairman or a member of that authority should continue to hold that office, that appointing authority may, subject, if it is a relevant regional authority, to the consent of the Secretary of State, forthwith terminate his tenure of office.'[12]

Once again, however, there are contradictory expectations. They emerge strongly from the following quotation – given at length to convey its full flavour – from evidence given in 1981 by Sir Patrick Nairne, the DHSS's Permanent Secretary, to the Committee of Public Accounts.[13] As Sir Patrick explained:

'The district health authorities are formally accountable for the exercise of their responsibilities through the RHAs to the Department and to the Secretary of State; in short, they are accountable upwards.'

But the Department was also investigating ways of

'enhancing efficiency and a sense of local accountability by requiring health authorities to publish information about their own performance, which is not published now, that could be made available, for example, to community health councils, perhaps published through the local Press, so that local opinion can be much better informed about the ways in which the authorities are using their resources. As Ministers see it, it all adds up to an approach which I would describe as analogous to the responsibility placed on local authorities by the Local Government and Land Act of 1980, to produce information for the purpose of local accountability. We entirely understand, I think I must add, the clear difference between our health authorities and the local authorities. I would sum up the position by saying that what we seek to have is the formal accountability upwards matched by a greater degree of informal accountability downwards.'

Whether and how members of district authorities also understand the 'clear difference' between the 'formal accountability upwards' and the 'informal accountability downwards' is, of course, another matter: one which we shall explore later in this chapter, when we set out the findings from our interviews with members.

Despite this element of ambiguity, there is little doubt that the members of health authorities are statutorily accountable to the secretary of state – on pain of dismissal in the last resort, as we have seen. But precisely what are they accountable *for*? Turning once again to the DHSS's guidelines and the definition of the role of district members, it is clear that they have wide, if somewhat vague, responsibilities. Their function is to 'determine policies and priorities for their Districts' within the framework of national and regional guidelines and priorities. They have to 'review, and where necessary, challenge proposals' put forward by their officers. They are further charged with monitoring the performance of their chief officers, and to concern themselves with the 'working conditions, general interests and welfare' of their staff. Finally, 'members should assess not only services to patients but should also keep the efficiency and effectiveness of their Authority's own management arrangements under review'.

Two points in all this require noting. First, the DHSS's circular contains no suggestion that district authorities collectively, or their members, are responsible for all decisions taken: indeed, how could they be since, as we shall see below, many of these decisions fall outside their control. There is no exact equivalent of the ministerial doctrine of responsibility. On the contrary, there is an explicit statement that 'it is not the member's role to intervene in day-to-day operational management'. Second, there is a conspicuous lack of specificity about the currency of accountability: the criteria that are to be used, and the information that is required, in assessing services. To assess the 'quality of services provided', members are exhorted to visit – though not too often and not too routinely (Polonius must have had a hand in drafting the guidelines). Members are also advised to use outside agencies such as the Health Advisory Service or the Development Team for the Mentally Handicapped. But while it is made clear that informed decisions require adequate knowledge and information, it was not made clear that this would be knowledge and information which, given the nature of the NHS, would always be ambiguous and open to challenge by the autonomous experts delivering the service: the theme to which we now turn.

Ambiguity and expertise in the NHS

The NHS, as noted in the previous chapter, ranks high not only on heterogeneity and complexity, that is the variety and diversity of its 'products', on the one hand, and the large number of interdependent skills that are required to deliver services, on the other. Equally it ranks high on uncertainty. What are the objectives of the NHS? How is it possible to assess the relationship between inputs and outputs, the effectiveness of the processes involved in the service delivery, and the activities of the NHS and the impact made on the population? None of these questions allows an easy answer. To explore the problems involved in addressing them is also to explore the difficulties involved in devising an appropriate currency of accountability, and the perplexities and frustrations of health authority members in carrying out their assigned tasks.

The problems of defining the objectives of the NHS are well caught in the Report of the Royal Commission on the NHS.[14] The Royal Commission believed that the NHS should 'encourage and assist individuals to remain healthy; provide equality of entitlement to health services; provide a broad range of services to a high standard; provide equality of access to these services; provide a service free at the time of use; satisfy the reasonable expectations of its users; remain a national service responsive to local needs'. It acknowledged that some of those objectives 'lack precision' while others are 'unattainable'. It conceded, further, that the aim enshrined in the 1946 Act, that the service should secure improvements 'in the physical and mental health of the people', was largely outside the control of the NHS. Indeed, there is a large literature devoted to demonstrating that the determinants of health are largely environmental and economic:[15] that health is the product of good social conditions (for example housing) and good nutrition, as well as the life-styles adopted by individuals. In short, looking at the health of the population served – using such conventional indicators as infant mortality or life expectancy – may help to identify the problems faced by the NHS. But they cannot, without many reservations, be used to assess the performance of the NHS since so many other factors, apart from the provision of medical care, are involved.

It is therefore not surprising that the currency of accountability and the criteria to be used for evaluating the performance of the NHS, are themselves contentious notions. Given uncertainty, there is inevitably argument. To quote the Royal Commission again:

'The absence of detailed and publicly declared principles and
objectives reflects to some degree the continuing political
debate about the service. Politicians and public alike are agreed
on the desirability of a national health service, but agreement
often stops there. Instead of principles, there are policies,
which change according to the priorities of the government of
the day and the particular interests of the ministers concerned.'

As far as the practice of accountability by members of health
authorities is concerned, this might, of course, not matter.
Indeed, it might simplify their task. Their accountability could be
defined not in cosmic terms of policy impacts, such as improving
the health of the population being served, but by the extent to
which they implement 'the priorities of the government of the day'
and heed the 'particular interests of the ministers concerned'. In
other words, they could be thought to be answerable merely for
carrying out the policies laid down by the DHSS, that is the policy
statements would themselves define the currency of accountability.

This is merely to redefine the problem, not to solve it. The
DHSS does, indeed, publish both broad policy statements and
detailed instructions. And while the detailed instructions – like
the circulars commanding districts to put out domestic services
such as laundry to competitive tender – are precise enough to
permit the DHSS to hold authority members accountable for their
implementation, the same is not true of the broad policy
statements. Since the mid-1970s the DHSS has published a series
of documents setting out the government's priorities for the
various services, which together form the NHS.[16] The theme of
these documents has, over the years, remained the same: to put
extra resources into the development of community services, and
provision for certain groups such as elderly, mentally ill, and
handicapped people. But the way in which these objectives have
been defined has changed over time.

The documents of the 1970s expressed priorities in terms of
service inputs, for example more nurses and beds for geriatric
patients. The implicit assumption was that if inputs increased, then
it would automatically follow that service outputs would improve.
The currency of accountability was, quite simply, money. If more
was spent on the favoured services and groups, the NHS was

running to Marathon. Come the 1980s and clarity gave way to ambiguity. Financial stringency among other factors led to disillusion with objectives defined in such a way that they could be achieved only by spending more money, that is in terms of inputs. The revised priorities document published by the government in 1981, *Care in Action*, did not abandon the general themes of its predecessors.[17] But it no longer expressed them in terms of achieving any particular pattern or level of inputs – or, come to that, service outputs.[18] It substituted general exhortations for specific targets. Instead of the specific injunction to run to Marathon, there was just the exhortation to go in the general direction of the Greek army. No specific criteria were offered against which the achievement of objectives could be assessed.

Although *Care in Action* was the first priority document to be specifically addressed to the chairmen and members of health authorities, it was designed more to 'educate' them (in Bevan's sense) than to provide a currency of accountability. Members were told to 'plan and develop services in the light of *local* needs and circumstances', but also to have 'a regard to *national* policies and priorities'. What if local needs conflicted with national policies? What if, to take by no means a fanciful example, the need perceived locally was to develop acute services rather than provision for mentally ill people? The questions are by no means rhetorical. For the problem of accountability in the NHS reflects not only uncertainty but also, to return to one of our organizing concepts, heterogeneity. Given that the NHS is essentially a conglomerate of different services, all competing for a fixed bundle of scarce resources, it is by no means self-evident whether the overall performance of an individual DHA should be evaluated in terms of the relative priorities given to the component services or in terms of the quality and scope of each of those services. Nor is it self-evident that these two sets of evaluative criteria need necessairly pull in the same direction: the growth of one service may mean deliberately starving, or at least undernourishing, another. The problem is further compounded by the fact that even seemingly homogenous, single-speciality services may cater for heterogeneous client groups: so, for instance, holding back spending in acute client services (in line with the government's priorities) like orthopaedic surgery, may damage the prospects of treatment of elderly people for hip replacements or similar procedures (contrary to the government's priorities). In short, authority members are accountable, if anything, for the way in which they resolve conflict about competing objectives, both as between different services and between local and national priorities and perceptions of need.

The conflict may, of course, be eased – though not resolved – if more money becomes available: if the conflict is about distributing extra resources rather than redistributing existing resources. But given that the NHS budget has grown only marginally in the 1980s,[19] and that within the global budget some DHAs have had their allocation cut back or frozen, this option has become steadily less available. Hence the increasing emphasis of government on assessing the performance of health authorities and their members, in terms of efficiency with which existing resources are being used: the theory being that if costs can be cut, more cash will be available. This is reflected in the use of the performance indicators which were being introduced by the DHSS at the time of our study.[20] These indicators use available NHS statistics (not so very different from the 'development of comparative costing' mentioned by Bevan in 1950) to provide a profile of both DHAs and the individual hospitals within them, of how resources are being used: cost per case, per bed, catering costs, staffing levels, and so on. Two features of the performance indicators, highly relevant for the exercise of accountability, require noting, however.

First, they are indicators not of efficiency in the strict sense but of relative costs only. That is, they do not measure the relationship between inputs and outputs (since the outputs of the DHS are too heterogeneous: even figures of cost per case for any given condition are difficult to interpret, since individual cases may vary in their severity). So, the indicators show only that the costs of any district hospital are out of line with those in other districts or hospitals. Second, the significance or meaning of the indicators depends on the local context. If costs are out of line, this may be (or so, at least, may be argued) because of the physical layout of the hospital concerned, the availability or otherwise of operating theatres, the peculiar case mix being handled or the clinical policies pursued by the responsible consultants. The paradox is that the service-providers whose performance is ostensibly measured by the indicators are the monopolists of the information required for their interpretation. Not surprisingly, the Permanent Secretary of the DHSS, Sir Kenneth Stowe, told the Public Accounts Committee in 1982:[21]

'We now have got a range of indicators which we think will be a relevant base for enabling the regions to ask the districts for us to ask the regions relevant questions about their performance. But the point that we want to stress is that they will not of themselves take you much beyond that stage of asking questions. They will be pointers rather than definitive judgements of performance.'

Moreover, Sir Kenneth also stressed the limitations of the kind of performance indicators being used.

'We are addressing a service, the end product of which is patients, better or cured, and that is the supreme performance indicator. The very real difficulty – it is both conceptually and technically difficult – is to bring into a direct relationship the outputs of the Health Service in that sense and the inputs of money and manpower.'

To evoke the concept of the end product of the NHS as being 'patients better or cured' is also to draw attention to the missing link, to use our earlier phraseology (Chapter 2), in the chain of accountability. It is doctors who, in the last resort, are responsible for ensuring that patients are better or cured, even though their ability to achieve this result will depend on the successful orchestration of a wide range of other skills – hence the importance, of course, of complexity in the NHS. Similarly, it is doctors who are responsible for the clinical policies which will determine whether or not resources are used 'efficiently': so, for example, they will largely determine lengths of stay and the intensity with which operating theatres are used. But doctors are not answerable to their employers for their clinical performance. They are accountable, as stressed earlier, only to their professional peers. So, symbolically, districts (unless they are authorities with a teaching hospital) do not even hold the contracts of consultants. In effect, then, their performance is largely determined by a set of

service providers over whom health authorities have very little
control.

What is true of doctors also applies, if to a lesser degree, to
other service providers with a claim to professional status, notably
nurses. Nursing labour force accounts for over a third of the total
NHS budget. There are wide variations in the level of staffing. Yet
there are no agreed criteria for determining what is an appropriate
level. To quote a report by the National Audit Office:[22] 'The
DHSS consider it is important to assess objectively the optimum
number of nursing staff for any given situation. The assessment
must be made locally, using an appropriate methodology supplemented by the judgement of experienced managers.' Once
again, therefore, it is professional judgements which are decisive.
It is the professionals who define what 'any given situation' is, and
draw the implications for the management of resources from it.
Not only do they determine, as in the case of doctors, what valid
information is, but also the inferences to be drawn from it. In
short, they largely determine what the currency of accountability
should be.

In challenging the judgements of the service-providers, districts
can draw on some alternative sources of expertise and information.
But these are restricted in scope. The limitations of performance
indicators have already been discussed. The Health Advisory
Service (HAS), cited in the DHSS's guidance to health authorities,
is an independent inspectorate which makes periodic reports on
services for elderly and mentally ill people.[23] But not only are its
reports on individual DHAs widely spaced over time, but also they
are based, once again, on professional judgements: in essence,
they are an example of professional peer review. The HAS teams
of inspectors consist of a cross-disciplinary group of doctors,
nurses, social workers, and others. Finally, there is the DHSS
Audit Directorate, which audits the accounts of all health
authorities.[24] But its main concern is 'with the review of systems of
financial control': that is audit seen in the strict technical sense of
ensuring financial regularity, with the focus on the process of
financial control. Only recently, and very tentatively, has the
Audit Directorate moved into value-for-money audit, looking at
the efficiency with which resources are being used.

The perplexities of health authority members

In the light of the above discussion of the conflicting expectations held of authority members, and the problems they face in terms of both access to information and exercising control, it is not surprising that previous studies of their role have tended to reveal a sense of frustration and lack of power. In the case of one study of policy-making for resource allocation, the role of members was found to be 'minimal . . . consistent with their account of themselves and their role, and their general feelings of remoteness and impotence.'[25] A study carried out for the Royal Commission on the NHS found that members 'found it difficult because of lack of time as much as of knowledge to come to grips with so complex a system', while 'their impact on the service was felt to be slim' by those working on it.[26] Nor does the picture, as revealed by research, appear to have been greatly affected by the replacement of areas by districts, at least in their early days. In a study carried out contemporaneously with our own, Haywood and Ranade found that in only two out of ten DHAs examined 'were members generally perceived by officers to have considerable influence on local policies'.[27] The conclusion drawn was that: 'our evidence suggests that members are influential only through the commitment and support of chairmen and/or chief officers who believed strongly in the legitimacy of member involvement and design mechanisms to ensure that it occurs. Without that support, it is difficult for members to have much impact unless they are unusually united and determined.' The same study also provides a categorization of members which is helpful for our own research. It distinguishes between three broad loyalties or orientations. Tribunes are chairmen or members whose prime loyalty is to the local community; prefects are those whose loyalty is upward to the government and/or to the region; patriarchs are those whose loyalty is to staff of the health authority. The categories accurately reflect the various strands and tensions – see pp. 81–2 – in the exhortations and guidelines produced by the DHSS about the role of authority members.

Our own approach to studying the role of members is more specific in its focus, concentrating as it does on their perceptions of accountability. Before plunging in to report our findings, however, it is important to put our research into its local context. The members of three health authorities were interviewed: in one case directly, in two cases by postal questionnaire (see Appendix 1). Without exception, members interviewed conformed to these central government expectations, having broad levels of skills and interests as well as wide-ranging but relevant experience in the overseeing of health and care services. Apart from the specialist medical and nursing members, the generalists' experience covered a wide range of occupations and interests, including university lecturers, trade union officials, and people running businesses. Although one member described herself occupationally as a mother, this title thinly disguised her extensive community work in both health and social services. Some of the members nominated by the district and county councils had community health council and trade union experience, and there were six past members of either regional or area health authorities. Many members, both specialist and generalist, were dovetailing their health authority involvement with other community work, many at committee level. Overall the impression of these members was one of appropriate appointment according to central government require-ments. Similarly the members conformed to the central govern-ment expectation that they should have the 'health and vigour' needed to make an effective contribution throughout their term of office – always assuming, of course, that vigour can be deduced from age. Their ages ranged from 34 to 65 years, with more than half the members aged between 40 and 50 years.

One authority was a teaching district under considerable financial pressure, threatened by the loss of revenue under the region's resource allocation formula, and faced with the task of coping with a body of prestigious consultants working in the teaching hospital. The other two did not face a financial crisis, although one of them had to cope with the special problem of how to divest itself of its historical responsibility for providing mentally handicapped services for a population stretching well beyond its own boundaries. In one case, the chairman was someone with a long history of similar responsibilities in the NHS; in another, it was someone with experience of the NHS, but not of chairmanship; in the third, it was someone with a previous career in business who was brought into the chairmanship at the time of the 1982 reorganization. So there was considerable variation in the context of the three authorities studied; a warning that the sheer diversity of the NHS not only makes the practice but also the study of accountability difficult. In our analysis, to which we now turn, we therefore concentrate on common themes, cutting across the three authorities studied rather than trying to make anything of the differences between them.

The experience and perception of members

In presenting the findings from our interviews, we have followed, in this chapter as in the subsequent ones, the logic of our line of questioning. This provides the themes around which this section is organized. We start from the assumption that accountability involves at least a sense of direction, and therefore report first on how members saw the objectives of the service, if indeed they had any objectives, and their own role in setting them. Next, we examine how members evaluated and monitored progress towards the achievement of such objectives as they had, and how they saw their relationship with officers and the division of labour both in the setting of objectives (policy) and the monitoring of progress. In all this, we put particular emphasis on exploring the way in which members perceived the available information, such as performance indicators or comparative statistics, about what the service was doing. Following on from this, we present the way in which members saw the problem of control, that is their ability to get a grip on the service in terms of their perception of expertise and professionalism. Lastly, we report how members themselves thought about accountability.

Not surprisingly, members found it difficult to define the objectives of their district: a difficulty which reflected not only their own relative inexperience in their role, but also more fundamentally, the problem of defining the objectives of the National Health Service – which, as noted in the previous section of this chapter, has fazed members of Royal Commissions, academics, and just about everyone who has tackled the issue. Overwhelmingly, the majority expressed great difficulty in defining

their objectives for the authority, that is what they saw themselves
accountable for. This sense of puzzlement was shared by all
members, both the specialist 'expert' members as well as the
generalist amateurs. Most of them chose to give the very broad
general aims of making the best use of resources, deciding on the
right priorities for the public/community and in a few cases,
finding out what the public/community want and providing it.
Those members whose aims were 'giving the public what they
want' were all university or specialist medical representatives and
did not, as might have been expected, include the local authority
nominees.

The only relatively precise aim put forward by some members
was, in line with prevailing fashion, that the emphasis on health
care in the district should move away from 'high technology
medicine' towards more resources for preventive medicine and the
'cinderella' services for mentally handicapped and elderly people:

> 'I think of my main objective as reorganizing priorities in the
> health service and moving away from high technology health
> care which sucks up most of the resources.'
>
> (local authority member)

If members had difficulties in expressing their health objectives
and translating them into specific district policies, then their ability
to find out what was happening in their district and to evaluate it
was even more problematic for them. As the interviews progressed,
it became apparent that, quite apart from not quite knowing what
the district was supposed to be doing, most did not know what the
district was actually doing anyway. A discussion of the DHSS's
own performance indicators as tools of evaluation (see previous
section) produced near-universal scepticism:

> 'We are still trying to find ways of measuring performance
> sensibly and intelligently. If you try to measure things,
> administrators will measure stupid things.'
>
> (university-appointed member)

> 'I don't know what performance aims are or how to measure
> them. I am a bit agnostic about this.'
>
> (generalist member)

In order to pursue the notions of performance and evaluation, the members were asked about their use of other statistical information. Most had as many reservations about the usefulness of home or independently produced statistics as they had about the DHSS's performance indicators in health care evaluation. While a majority thought that statistics were a good way of learning about the activities of a health district, particularly in the use of league tables to compare districts, they also saw statistics as limited in their use and lending themselves too easily to unscrupulous or unskilled application. Some were emphatic that present-day health statistics have focused on the wrong information, are incomplete, and are beside the point:

'We can do reasonable sums on predicting service needs and demand, but things can change very rapidly. Statistics and comparative data have an educative role rather than policy-making role.'

(local authority member)

In particular, some members stressed the ambiguity of statistics in the absence of an agreed framework which gives them meaning:

'I have listened to John Yates [an independent academic who produces regular statistical information about NHS services] on the collection and use of statistics, but have to say that I feel that some statistics are very unreliable. For example, length of stay – shorter or longer? A good or bad thing?'

(university-appointed member)

The counterpoint of scepticism about statistics among members was enthusiasm for hands-on experience of the service. Particularly at the start of their membership, most embarked on visits to hospitals and had spoken at length to staff. All who had done the rounds were full of praise for this as a method of getting to know the district and learning about being health authority members. They were enthusiastic about being able to talk to staff:

'Visits were very valuable and the only real opportunity for us as members to be lobbied. It is important to look at services but even more important to listen to what people are saying.'

(generalist member)

'Visits are to see roughly where hospitals are in the district, but
district members should talk to staff. Staff do have things to say.
I don't think it is necessary for DHA members to be lobbied by
patients – that is the role of community health councils.'

(generalist member)

'I do believe in visiting as often as possible.'

(local authority member)

But members were realistic about the limitations of visiting as a
way of generating information about the district's performance.
Only a few saw visiting as a way of monitoring district health
services. Most saw it as a partial but nevertheless tangibly
reasurring way of checking up on the reports submitted by the
district management team of officers (DMT). For, most strikingly,
members across all the authorities viewed information provided by
the DMT with deep suspicion:

'The information we do get in the district is largely determined
by the DMT and the person with information has power.'

(specialist nurse member)

'We need access to DMT minutes in order to be good authority
members. I would like to see how professions function. We, as
authority members, tend to end up at present with the finished,
polished product, which gives us few clues.'

(generalist member)

'We get bombarded with too much information – it could be
better in some areas.'

(trade union member)

'We do not get enough of the right kind of information.'

(local authority member)

'It is difficult to get information to keep yourself briefed.'

(generalist member)

Members of the teaching district authority suggested that its
state of permanent financial crisis, whether real, imagined, or
manufactured, was also a barrier to monitoring performance.
Some felt that even if the crisis was not manufactured, then it was
certainly being used with skilful opportunism by the district

management team to fend off members' pleas for relevant information, and to divert their attention. However, one saw financial stringency as an opportunity:

> 'Low resource situations can produce valuable insights and these financial cuts have made us look for cheaper, more efficient ways of doing things.'
>
> (university-appointed member)

But if the available information was regarded with suspicion, if statistics were seen as being of limited value, and if visiting was perceived to be more about learning than about monitoring, what did members see as their best means of evaluating the service? Most, while emphasizing the need for more open, complete, and soundly based information, said that in reality there was no way of judging the performance or effectiveness of health care in their districts at the present time and that this was not wholly due to their own inexperience or the manipulation of information by officers. In spite of their frustration at not being able to find out what was going on and to evaluate it, they saw the assessment of their district's health care performance as both necessary and urgent. But they also realized that their inability to assess and evaluate performance partly stemmed from the absence of clearly defined objectives in the service, that is the problem of having no currency of accountability:

> 'Performance indicators, a total bloody disaster so far. What are we looking for? First we don't know. What are we aiming for? . . . and when we know or if we ever know, how can we measure it?'
>
> (university-appointed member)

But who should set the aims or objectives? Members certainly saw it as their role to engage in the policy-making process – that is setting objectives – if in partnership with officers. However, they were not confident about their ability to carry out this role though some thought that they would become more effective once they had learnt the job and begun to work as a team. Generally members perceived their inexperience as less of an inhibition than the DMT's command over information:

'Basically, members make policy decisions but decisions are only as good as information provided by officers.'

(trade union member)

'The present set-up allows the DMT to set the policy. The authority ought to be involved in setting the policy, but members have a problem of information-gathering and synthesis.'

(university medical member)

'Authority members are cut off from the making of policy. That is, they don't formulate policy, rather they agree policy already determined by officers.'

(generalist member)

'Members are asked to do too little in the sense that we are not presented with policy options.'

(local authority member)

These quotations bring out the centrality of information in analysing accountability. On the one hand, information is needed to decide on aims or objectives; on the other hand, information is needed to assess the achievement of those aims or objectives. If there is no agreement about what represents appropriate information, about what meaning to attach to facts or figures, then members and officers may talk past each other rather than engaging in dialogue. This is what appears to have been happening in the case of our health authorities, where officers were criticized both for supplying inadequate information and for producing too much.

In turn, this point emphasizes the importance of trust between officers and members. If the meaning of facts and statistics is in dispute, much will depend on the way in which the 'source' or 'authority' for them is perceived. This came out clearly from the views of the members who thought that the production of 'good' information would follow only from an improved level of trust between them and officers. Indeed, the notion of trust and the word itself was mentioned frequently in the interviews as members sought to analyse their role and the tasks associated with it. Those members who expressed a preference for shared responsibility with officers in a joint decision-making process talked of the need for trust between themselves and the district management team and their attempts to forge a working relationship:

'A lot goes on trust between the DMT and the district authority, and this is what we are aiming to achieve.'

(university-appointed medical member)

'There has to be a great deal of trust between the information holders and those wanting to receive it, and we have yet to forge the right kind of relationship.'

(specialist nurse member)

In exploring the relationship between members and officers, we have also moved towards considering a crucial link in the chain of accountability. If accountability implies control by members over what is happening in the service, then the ability to do so in turn rests on the ability to control the top managerial echelon within the service: the DMT in the case of the health service. And the sense of powerlessness expressed by most members reflected their sense of dependence on the officers: maybe distrust was born of frustration. Some optimists among them thought that this would change over time. But most saw their dependence on the DMT as a function of the latter's access both to formal information and to tacit knowledge about the district. In short, the officers were seen as the monopolists of a particular kind of expertise, especially financial. And when members talked about the problems posed by professionalism in the NHS, they first and foremost were referring to the DMT officers who, they sometimes felt, saw themselves dealing with intellectual challenges rather than providing a service. The expertise of the DMT, particularly of the treasurers, was both admired and resented:

'Power has gone to the purveyors of bad news in the NHS. They [the DMT] hold the others in sway.'

(generalist member)

So preoccupied were members with the power of the DMT that they didn't, until prompted specifically by a question about the role of experts and professionals in the NHS, talk about the position of doctors. The problem of exercising control in an organization where there is no hierarchy of command over service-providers came second in their minds to the problem of exercising control over the officer team. However, once launched on this theme, members distinguished very clearly between professionals and experts: professionalism implying autonomy, status, and power, while expertise was considered to be more about specialist knowledge and techniques. In other words, while professionals were seen to have power, experts were seen to have authority. In the specific case of doctors, members largely took their *professional* power for granted, as a fact of life in the NHS, even while seeing them merely as one among many bodies of experts:

'We should distinguish between professionals and experts. Rather, there are other experts besides professionals and not all professionals are experts.'

(local authority member)

'Doctors are professionals but I don't regard them as the health service experts. They have no experience of running an organization the size of a district, nor do they know which health priorities people have.'

(generalist member)

Members were divided in how they saw the position of the medical profession. On the one hand, there were those who argued that the power of doctors was, if anything, increasing. Some attributed this to recent changes in the organization of the NHS which had strengthened vested interests, including the medical profession. Others perceived it to be the result of collusion between doctors and patients:

'The British Medical Association is increasingly powerful. Medical power is given by political means. The man in the bed and the taxpayer encourage and maintain the power of the doctors.'

(chairman)

'It is not entirely the fault of doctors and the service that the present system of emphasis on acute service continues. The surgeons can wield power but only because people want it that way. People want drama and they respond to this in the health service. They feel reassured by the mystique of doctors and medicine.'

(university-appointed member)

On the other hand, more optimistic members saw changes beginning to take place. In particular, the idea that the medical profession was beginning to lose its dominance:

> 'Times have changed. The younger generation of doctors has been dragged kicking and screaming into modern times.'
>
> (chairman)

Some members saw this as a change of heart within the profession itself, albeit because doctors are learning that what is technically possible in medicine may not be economically possible within the real life, present-day organization of the NHS:

> 'The district health authority has actually managed to organize a working party on consultant hours in the district. They may not get far but just forming a group to investigate represents a triumph.'
>
> (generalist member)

But it would be a mistake to see the problems of distrust and conflict as unique to the relationship between health authorities and officers or doctors. These, as one member argued, were the result of the domination of the NHS by a 'closed shop' mentality, common to all types of staff – professionals, experts, and others – which produced tension between groups of workers and meant that the patient had been left behind by the organization:

> 'Most medical knowledge is arbitrary, not much is absolute and definite. There is a lot of professional conflict in the NHS. The revolution in health services in the last three decades is from no administration to a new professional administration bringing about conflict between administration and medical factions. The NHS now equals experts against experts for experts.'
>
> (medical specialist member)

In this battle of experts, members saw themselves in a different role. Very few thought of themselves as experts but saw their job as bringing a sound good sense to the service, and acting as watchdogs. This denial of expertise was all the more surprising since many had considerable health and community experience and a few had jobs within the health service. Their feelings of being non-experts appeared to be based on their lack of overall knowledge of the district and its services, and their feelings of helplessness.

Given this sense of powerlessness in a complex organization where information was, at best, ambiguous, it is perhaps not surprising that the perception of members of their own account-ability differed sharply from the definition implicit in official pronouncements, that is direct accountability to the secretary of state. While a few said that they were ultimately accountable to the secretary of state, most saw themselves accountable to a variety of other bodies, including the authority itself. Not surprisingly, the three chairmen all gave the secretary of state as the focus of their accountability but so did one generalist member and one local authority county council member. But when members were asked whether in practice they could be held accountable, the majority (including one chairman) thought that it was not possible except in the narrowest financial terms. Rather they relied on the feelings of responsibility towards the community or their own conscience. One member who said that accountability in the strict sense was not possible went on to argue that this did not matter as everyone was 'highly motivated, highly intelligent and impressively concerned for the community' (university-appointed member).

Another generalist member showed equal unconcern for his admitted lack of 'real' accountability: the 'self-created' account-ability to his own intellectual integrity, he thought, was enough to sustain his role as a member of a health authority. Although the words accountability and responsibility were to a large extent freely exchanged by health members, there was a general impression that where a distinction was made, responsibility downwards to people in a somewhat paternalistic sense, was more important than accountability upwards to the secretary of state:

'Ultimately, we are accountable to the minister, but actually I don't think I feel accountable to anyone. I think I have a duty to worry about the delivery of health in the district, that is why we are here. I am accountable, we are all accountable to our own consciences.'

(specialist medical member)

'I, as an appointed member, am ultimately accountable to the secretary of state. I don't feel this personally. I feel a self-created accountability. I feel accountable to my own intellectual integrity.'

(generalist member)

'I feel responsible firstly to my own conscience.'

(local authority member)

'As a doctor I could say I have a responsibility first to the public.'

(university-appointed member)

In short, members tend to internalize accountability – to see it as a private dialogue between themselves and their consciences – rather than seeing it as part of a public, political, or institutional process.

Summary

According to central government's expectations of health authority members, they should, if they are responding appropriately, be aiming to combine accountability to the secretary of state with a responsibility towards their district. These expectations are shared by those who assume that appointed rather than elected members of public services will feel and indeed be more accountable to the government than to the people.

Our findings suggest strongly that health authority members do not accept this definition of their role and that even if they did, it is not possible to achieve it. Overwhelmingly, most members interviewed were, first and foremost, concerned to fulfil their responsibilities towards the district, whether it was called the community, the people, or the patients. Only a few members even mentioned their theoretical accountability upwards and then as a lower priority to their general feelings or responsibility downwards. Except as the source of funding, central government authority was seen as largely irrelevant and members did not consider themselves as in danger of reprimand or sacking, unless for some financial irregularity.

Since accountability to the centre was of such a low priority to members it could not be considered a serious area of tension for them. Rather the battleground was seen by them to be the local arena with conflict between themselves and the inflexible, inscrutable district organization. Somewhat surprisingly health members did not want to monopolize entirely the policy-making role, that is setting objectives for performance, allotted to them by central government. Most wanted to have a significant input but nevertheless to work with the district management team. As for the tension between national and local objectives and priorities implied by the more ambiguous reorganization documents, most members confessed to unclear aims and objectives and further suggested that they shared this confusion with administrators and health providers alike. Confusion was compounded by the perceived difficulty of relating inputs of resources to desired outcomes. Hence members were sceptical of most of the available information, particularly the DHSS's performance indicators, even while wanting to develop tools of evaluation.

Where health service objectives were contentious, difficult to define, or even observe, members saw this as a major barrier to their policy-making contribution as well as to the achievement of accountability. The inexperience of the authority and lack of co-ordinated teamwork, members thought, were exploited by officers. Although the power of the service providers was seen to have some significance, this power was seen as only partly responsible for the obscure and uncertain objectives which characterize the NHS at the present time and inhibit the exercise of accountability by members.

REFERENCES

1 National Health Service: Memorandum by the Minister of Health (1945) 16 October, CP (45) 231. PRO CAB 129.
2 Quoted in Sir Patrick Nairne (1984) Parliamentary Control and Accountability. In R. Maxwell and N. Weaver (eds) *Public Participation in Health*. London: King's Fund.
3 Committee on the National Health Service: Memorandum by the Minister of Health (1950) 15 July, NH (50) 17, PRO CAB 134.
4 For details see R. Klein (1983) *The Politics of the NHS*. London: Longman.

5 Secretary of State for Social Services (1971) *National Health Service Reorganisation: Consultative Document.* London: DHSS.

6 Secretary of State for Social Services (1972) *National Health Service Reorganisation: England.* London: HMSO Cmnd 5055.

7 Department of Health and Social Security (1979) *Patients First.* London: HMSO.

8 Department of Health and Social Security (1980) *Reply by the Government to the Third Report from the Social Services Committee, Session 1979–80.* London: HMSO Cmnd 8086.

9 R. Klein (1985) Health Policy, 1979–83: The Retreat from Ideology? In P. Jackson (ed.) *Implementing Policy Initiatives: The Thatcher Administration, 1979–83.* London: Royal Institute of Public Administration.

10 P. Day and R. Klein (1985) Central Accountability and Local Decision-Making. *British Medical Journal* 290, 1 June: 1,676–678.

11 Department of Health and Social Security (1981) *Health Circular: The Membership of District Health Authorities.* London: DHSS HC (81) 6.

12 Statutory Instruments 1981, no. 933 (1981) *The National Health Service (Health Authorities: Membership) Regulations 1981.* London: HMSO H81/904.

13 Committee of Public Accounts 1716 (1981) *Report Session 1980–81. Financial Control and Accountability in the National Health Service.* London: HMSO HC 255, Q. 1512.

14 Sir Alec Merrison (Chairman) (1979) *Report of the Royal Commission on the National Health Service.* London: HMSO Cmnd 7615: para. 2.6.

15 See, for example, T. McKeown (1979) *The Role of Medicine.* Oxford: Basil Blackwell. Also Sir Douglas Black (Chairman) (1980) *Report of the Working Group on Inequalities in Health.* London: DHSS.

16 Department of Health and Social Security (1976) *Priorities for Health and Personal Social Services in England.* London: HMSO. Department of Health and Social Security (1977) *The Way Forward.* London: HMSO.

17 Department of Health and Social Security (1981) *Care in Action.* London: HMSO.

18 Specific outputs targets were, however, set for individual health authorities by the performance review system. See P. Day and R. Klein (1985) Central Accountability and Local Decision-Making. *British Medical Journal* 290, 1 June: 1,676–678.

19 Social Services Committee (1985) *Sixth Report Session 1984–85. Public Expenditure on the Social Services.* London: HMSO HC 339.

20 R. Klein (1982) Performance, Evaluation and the NHS. *Public Administration* 60, Winter: 385–407.

21 Committee of Public Accounts (1983) *Seventeenth Report Session*

1981–82. Financial Control and Accountability in the National Health Service. London: HMSO HC 255.

22 National Audit Office (1985) *National Health Service: Control of Nursing Manpower.* London: HMSO HC 558.

23 Department of Health and Social Security (1976) *The Health Advisory Service.* London: DHSS HC (76) 21.

24 Department of Health and Social Security (1984) *Report of the Director of Audit, 1982/83.* London: DHSS.

25 D. Hunter (1980) *Coping with Uncertainty.* Chichester: Research Studies Press.

26 M. Kogan, N. Korman, M. Henkel, V. Heyes, H. Simons, and B. Goodwin (1978) *The Working of the National Health Service.* Royal Commission on the NHS Research Paper no. 1, London: HMSO.

27 S. Haywood and W. Ranade (1985) Health Authorities: Tribunes or Prefects? *Public Administration Bulletin* 35, April: 39–52. See also W. Ranade (1985) Motives and Behaviour in District Health Authorities. *Public Administration* 63, 2, Summer: 183–200.

5

Accountability and the police

If the National Health Service is an example of a service where the notion of accountability is simple in theory but turns out to be complex in practice, the police is an example of a service where the notion of accountability is not only complex in theory but also turns out to be even more complex in practice. The role of police authorities and their relationship with chief constables is constitutionally ambiguous,[1] and politically contentious,[2] never more so than in recent years. And if there is doubt or argument both about the scope of the chief constable's accountability to the police authority and its currency, it is clear that it is not an exclusive line of accountability. In short, in this chapter we are concerned with multiple accountability with contested criteria: a Babel of evaluative languages with little agreement about which should be used and by whom where. The point is well caught by the following quotation from a former police chief, Sir Robert Mark:[3]

'A police chief in Britain serves five masters. The first, the criminal law which he is sworn to uphold and enforce impartially. The second, his police authority. The third, the men and women he commands, whose interests may not always coincide with those of his police authority, in financial matters, for example. The fourth, the people of the police district under his command, who look to him for security and tranquillity. The fifth – and most important – his conscience. For in Britain, policemen are not merely allowed to have consciences, they are

required to have them. Their authority under the law is
personal, as is their accountability.'

Even this list is not exhaustive; curiously, it leaves out the chief
constable's accountability to central government. But it is sufficient
to put police authorities into context and explain why any analysis
of police accountability which limits itself to examining their role
would be inadequate: indeed, as we shall see, one of the reasons
why the role tends to be seen as restricted and marginal is precisely
because the police authority is only one of many 'masters'.
Whether multiple accountability also means effective accountability
is, of course, another matter: one about which there is intense
controversy and debate, which it is not the purpose of this chapter
to resolve.

Police authorities are hybrid creatures. Two-thirds of their
members are councillors drawn from the county councils which
make up the police area (two in the case of the police authority in
our study). The remaining third are magistrates, chosen by their
fellow magistrates in the area. They are neither nominated
authorities, in contrast to the NHS and water authorities in our
study; however, nor are they directly elected bodies, in contrast to
the education and social service committees in our study. Neither
the rhetoric of central accountability nor that of direct democratic
accountability sits easily upon them, therefore. Furthermore, the
police service is itself something of a constitutional hybrid. It is a
local service which draws 50 per cent of its finance direct from
central government and where the freedom of police authorities to
appoint their chief officers is more constrained than in the NHS.
Thus police authorities can neither appoint nor dismiss chief
constables without the approval of the home secretary. Interestingly
there is no similar statutory provision in the case of the NHS where
health authorities can, in theory, appoint their chief officers at will
(and where the DHSS's ability, in practice, to blackball unfavoured
candidates seems to rest on a legal bluff since there is no explicit
statutory basis for the exercise of such a veto).

The duty of a police authority, as defined by the Police Act,
1964, is 'to secure the maintenance of an adequate and efficient
police force for the area'. Further, it has responsibility for
appointing the chief constable, for determining the number of

persons of each rank in its force, and providing buildings. All these powers are, however, exercised 'subject to the approval of the Secretary of State'. The police force itself is 'under the direction and control of the Chief Constable' who may, once again with the approval of the secretary of state, be called upon 'to retire in the interests of efficiency' (not, in other words, because the police authority has lost confidence in the judgement or policies of its chief officer). The chief constable has a duty to submit to the police authority every year 'a general report', and to provide, if asked, a report on specific 'matters connected with the policing of the area'. However, the chief constable can appeal to the secretary of state if he thinks that such a report 'would contain information which in the public interest ought not to be disclosed, or it is not needed for the discharge of the functions of the police authority' (functions which, as already noted, are defined in only the most general terms in the 1964 Act).

The relationship between the police authority and the chief constable is therefore very different from that between the authorities and chief officers in the other services in our study. The point was made starkly in the 1962 Report of the Royal Commission on the Police, which helped to shape the 1964 Act. The Royal Commission stressed that:[4]

> 'The authority's role cannot, under the arrangements which we propose, extend beyond the giving of advice and it will not be entitled to give orders or instructions to a chief constable on matters connected with policing. Thus, the relationship between a police authority and its chief constable will in this field differ from that between other council committees and their chief officers. In the case of the police *these positions will be reversed* [our emphasis]. The role of the police authority will be to advise the chief constable on general matters connected with the policing of the area; but the decisions will be the responsibility of the chief constable.'

In making this point, which of course applies to the relationship between all the non-elected authorities in our study and with their chief officers, the Royal Commission drew an interesting but puzzling distinction between 'control' and 'accountability'. They

conceded that 'the problem of controlling the police can . . . be re-
stated as the problem of controlling the chief constable'. Further,
they recognized 'the lack of local control'. However, they
proposed to increase 'the chief constable's accountability for his
actions' by giving authorities the right to call for reports, a
recommendation which was implemented in the 1964 Act. In
short, implicit in the statutory position of the police, there would
seem to be a particular model of accountability: what Marshall has
called 'explanatory accountability'. That is there seems to be
implied a general obligation on chief constables to explain their
actions to police authorities. It is a model of accountability which
does not assume any sort of hierarchical relationship. It is an
instrumental view of accountability that is difficult to distinguish
from a strategy for the mobilization of support. It is about the chief
constable telling a story, or making a statement, in a situation
where there are no formal sanctions if he fails to convince. It is
about the creation of trust and confidence, not about a master–
servant relationship. The point comes out clearly from the
Scarman Report.[5] In this Lord Scarman approvingly quoted the
words of the then home secretary, William Whitelaw: 'it has
become increasingly desirable that police authorities should see
themselves not just as providers of resources but as a means
whereby the chief constable can give account of his policing policy
to the democratically elected representatives of the community,
and in turn, they can express to him the views of the community on
these matters.' And he himself concluded that 'A police force, the
chief officer of which does not discuss . . . matters of policing
policy openly and responsively with the community, is certain in
the long run to find its efficiency undermined by loss of community
support.' However, Lord Scarman also argued that 'The exercise
of police judgement has to be as independent as the exercise of
professional judgement by a doctor or a lawyer.'

To divorce the notion of accountability from the context of
hierarchy, to abandon the idea that accountability is about having
to answer for the exercise of delegated functions or powers which
can by definition be revoked if the explanation fails to satisfy,
leaves a lot of questions unanswered, Who defines the scope of
such accountability? Which 'matters of policing policy' should, or
should not, be discussed openly? Who, furthermore, defines the

currency of accountability – the criteria that are to be used in judging performance? It is precisely because there is no consensus about the answers to such questions that even the revised or weaker notion of accountability, as entailing no more than an obligation to explain, leaves scope for a great deal of friction, controversy, and uncertainty in the relationship between police authorities and their chief officers. In particular, the revised notion still skirts what is the critical issue in this relationship. This hinges on the historically successful assertion by the police, upheld in courts, that they are responsible only to the law for the enforcement of the law. In the words of Lord Denning, Master of the Rolls:[6]

> 'I hold it to be the duty of the Commissioner of Police, as it is of every chief constable, to enforce the law of the land. He must take steps so to post his men that crimes may be detected; and that honest citizens may go about their affairs in peace. He must decide whether or no suspected persons are to be prosecuted and, if need be, bring the prosecution or see that it is brought; but in all these things, he is not the servant of anyone, save of the law itself. No Minister of the Crown can tell him that he must or must not keep observation of this place or that; or that he must or must not prosecute this man or that one. Nor can any police authority tell him so. The responsibility for law enforcement lies on him. He is answerable to the law and to the law alone.'

It is this legal doctrine that has traditionally been used to justify the claim of chief constables that they are not answerable to police authorities for operational policies, even though they might voluntarily choose to explain them if asked nicely. The difficulty is that the legal definition implies an extremely restrictive – and indeed completely unrealistic – definition of the role of the police.[7] Enforcing the law of the land is only one of the duties of the police. As Robert Reiner has argued: 'The core mandate of policing, historically and in terms of concrete demands placed upon the police, is the more diffuse one of order maintenance.' Indeed, policing policy often involves, most controversially, decisions about when *not* to enforce the law of the land in the interests of maintaining order or gaining the confidence of a particular community. Moreover, the legal definition glosses over the fact that chief constables do not take unconstrained decisions about enforcing the law of the land. Like all chief officers in the public sector, they have to take decisions about the allocation of scarce resources between competing objectives. In short, the judicial doctrine ignores economic scarcity which compels choices about which laws to enforce, at what level of resource intensity. The courts themselves have shown no disposition to accept responsibility for ranking competing objectives even in the restricted field of law enforcement (let alone all the other duties of the police). The chief constable is therefore not accountable (in the strict sense) for his choice of priorities either to the law or to the police authority; the doctrine of accountability to the courts for individual acts or omissions has come to justify immunity from accountability for policy decisions to police authorities.

It is therefore not surprising that the Royal Commission argued that the chief constable enjoyed an extraordinary degree of 'unfettered discretion', and the following conclusion reached in its report has not been greatly affected by legislative changes and events since it was published in 1962:[8]

'Thus he is accountable to no one, and subject to no one's orders for the way in which, for example, he settles his general policies in regard to law enforcement over the area covered by his force, the disposition of his force, the concentration of his resources on any particular type of crime or area, the manner in which he handles political demonstrations or processions and allocates and instructs his men when preventing breaches of the peace arising from industrial disputes, the methods he employs in dealing with an outbreak of violence or of passive resistance to authority, his policy in enforcing the traffic laws and in dealing with parked vehicles, and so on.'

There remains, as already noted, the statutory responsibility of the police authority to 'secure the maintenance of an adequate and efficient police force'. But this suggests a paradox; adequacy and efficiency can be assessed only in terms of the policies being pursued. They are relative, not absolute, concepts. If the policies themselves are determined by the chief constable, then how can the police authority assess either adequacy or efficiency? The problem is compounded by the fact that the chief constable is also accountable to central government. It is the Home Office which authorizes the manpower establishment of the police force, that is in effect decides what is an 'adequate' police force for a given area. It is Her Majesty's Inspectors of Constabulary who report every year to the secretary of state on the 'efficiency of police forces', as laid down by Section 38 of the Police Act, 1964. Indeed, the Royal Commission recommended that 'police authorities be relieved of any legal responsibility they may have for the efficient policing of the area', arguing that it was anomalous that 'a police authority appears to have responsibility for the efficient policing of its area, yet has no technical competence in the matter and no adequate system of inspection'. Instead, it proposed that the central inspectorate should be strengthened, and that 'the inspector always meet the chairman and members of the authority during the course of an official inspection and discuss with them matters for which the authority is legally responsible'.

In the event, the logic of the Royal Commission's arguments was ignored in the subsequent legislation. The inspectorate was strengthened, but the legal responsibility of police authorities for efficient policing remained enshrined in the statutes. And the role of the inspectorate has become increasingly, as is evident from the chief inspector's annual reports, to make sure that local forces conform to national standards and priorities. So, for example, the 1982 report addressed to the home secretary described the role of the inspectorate in the following terms:[9]

'Decisions taken about policing at the national level must not only shape and support local initiatives, but reflect the variety of local circumstances. Her Majesty's Inspectors, who are in touch with policing locally through their day-to-day contacts with forces in their regions, and with national policy develop-ments as your professional advisers, are in a unique position from which to offer advice at both these levels.'

The report also recognized the shift from local to national policy-making:

'While the organisation and functioning of individual forces are matters which are determined locally, the effectiveness and efficiency of the police force as a whole are also of major concern to you (that is the secretary of state). The last few years have seen an increasingly national dimension to many problems facing the police, particularly in relation to terrorism, public order and highly organised crime, and a growing need for high national standards, for example, in training. Against this background, you asked my predecessor to concentrate his attention on the way in which policing priorities are set, how resources are managed and how good practices can be promoted.'

The above quotations are significant, not only for what they imply about accountability to the centre but also for their emphasis on the role of the inspectorate in giving *professional* advice. If one of the characteristics of a profession is, as argued in Chapter 2, that its members see themselves primarily accountable to their peers, then the police appear to be increasingly claiming the privilege of such a status. So, for example, a recent handbook published by the Metropolitan Police is entitled *The Principles of Policing and Guidance for Professional Behaviour.*[10] This includes a 'Code of Professional Duties'. It stresses, on the one hand, that 'no group of people in any other walk of life has quite the same, all pervasive obligations to their fellows' and, on the other, the need for 'group loyalty'. In turn, this means that 'we each have an obligation to work to increase our professional skills, and to widen our experience, so that we can better advise and support our colleagues as well as perform our duties more effectively' and carries a responsibility to 'speak out and ACT' if there is any evidence of malpractice by a fellow officer. In short, as in a profession, there is deemed to be a collective responsibility 'to guard the good reputation of the Force, to work constantly to maintain its high ideals, to encourage others to do so by good example and leadership, and to contribute to its excellence by showing resolution and honesty if faced with police malpractice'.

The emphasis on professionalism in policing brings together two very different arguments, one based on tradition and the other on evolving patterns of practice. The first argument rests on the traditional role of the constable as independent officers of the Crown carrying personal responsibility for the way in which they perform their office. To quote the Metropolitan Police document again:

> 'A constable, though he must obey lawful and reasonable orders from any senior rank, does not hold his office and exercise his powers at the behest of a more senior officer who, in any case, whatever his title is constitutionally a constable also. Nor is he answerable to any government official, or to the Home Office or to Parliament. He is answerable to the law and holds his office independently of anyone else; on taking his declaration of office, he has assumed obligations which accrue to him personally.'

The constable's role is thus marked by the discretion he or she enjoys in interpreting his or her responsibilities; again, a trait shared with the professions in the strict sense. At the same time, to turn to the second argument, changes in police practice have meant increasing use of sophisticated modern techniques. Thus the 1978 Committee on Police Pay remarked that 'a considerable proportion of the evidence we received drew our attention to the greatly increased demands made on the police service by modern society and to the professionalism required to meet them'.[11]

In all the rhetoric of police professionalism, there is a paradox. This is that, despite the emphasis on discretion and personal responsibility, the police service is a hierarchical organization. The actions of individual constables, and indeed their private lives, are liable to scrutiny and direction by their officers. There are elaborate internal disciplinary procedures which help to explain the long-drawn-out battle over the introduction of an independent machinery for the hearing of complaints.[12] The Police Regulations impose considerable restrictions on the private life of a police officer, and, for example, give chief constables the power to order a member of his force to occupy a particular police house. Once again, the 1962 Royal Commission made the point well:[13]

> 'There are many people such as surgeons in the National Health Service, masters of ships and captains of aircraft, to name but a

few, who enjoy wide discretion based on professional skill in the way in which they carry out their duties; but these people are all servants and enjoy no special legal status implying the degree of independence which, in practice, they exercise. Indeed, the degree of independence within such occupations as these is considerably greater than that exercised by the constable, since the latter is a member of a disciplined service, subject to lawful orders from his superior officer. Consequently, it appears odd that the constable enjoys a traditional status which implies a degree of independence belied by his subordinate rank in the force.'

But if much of the evocation of professionalism is only rhetoric, its role in helping to justify the relationship between police authorities and chief constables remains important. The ideology of professionalism, it has been pointed out: 'attempts to persuade us that the police are in the best position to make judgements about the nature of crime and its control . . . it explains crime and crime control as technical-apolitical matters that are best left in the hands of trustworthy experts.'[14] At the same time, although this aspect of police professionalism is less stressed in official rhetoric, it helps to justify the fact that chief constables in practice find it difficult to control the behaviour of their subordinate officers: control, as argued earlier, is the necessary (if not sufficient) condition for the exercise of accountability. If constables do indeed enjoy the professional attributes of discretion and autonomy, then it is not surprising that what happens on the beat or in police stations is often at odds with the rules laid down by the hierarchy of command. In these circumstances, activities may be 'invisible' to senior officers. There is inevitably a seepage of control, which may extend to those in command deliberately closing their eyes to what is happening at the bottom.[15] The ideology of professionalism ironically helps to explain the widespread extent of unprofessional practices.

Moreover, and crucially for any analysis of the role of police authorities, the problems of organizational control appear to be common across countries with very different constitutional arrangements for the accountability of the police. Thus a study of the New York police found a conflict between the 'management cop culture' and the 'street cop culture',[16] while a study of the Amsterdam police discovered 'a deep dichotomy between the values, styles and vulnerability of lower ranks and senior officers, which is characterised by social distance, mutual distrust and varying levels of manipulation, control and acquiescence in deviant practices'.[17] In other words, it would be dangerous to conclude that if members of police authorities find it difficult to get a grip on the service for which they are nominally responsible – and they do, as we shall see in the section of this chapter reporting on our interviews – then this is necessarily or exclusively attributable to the peculiar constitutional position in which they find themselves.

Nor does the problem become any easier if the focus changes from accountability, seen as being answerable for process or individual actions to accountability, seen as being answerable for outcomes or the collective performance of the service. Again, it is important to note the conceptual difficulties, independent of institutional arrangements. To put the matter simply, 'Most police forces in the world quite literally do not know what they are doing', as one survey of the international literature has concluded.[18] In other words, remarkably little is known about the relationship between inputs and outputs: between the input of resources – notably police numbers – and the output or outcome in terms of crime levels or public order maintenance. Establishing such a relationship means being able, in the first place, to specify the objectives of the police, and then to measure progress towards their achievement: only so, is it possible to assess the effectiveness and efficacy with which the police are using their resources.

However, a survey commissioned by the Home Office concluded that there are two main sets of problems about this aproach to trying to evaluate the performance of the police.[19] The first is 'the difficulty of defining what the police and patrolling police officers are trying to do and of determining how much of their time they devote to one purpose over another'. This problem is compounded by the phenomenon of multiple, not necessarily consistent, outputs: 'the policemen who in pursuit of a felon descend on a quiet country town may arrest a criminal but also create public resentment. They may, therefore, create problems for their colleagues pursuing goals related to crime prevention and community relations.' The second set stems from the difficulty of relating changes in police practice or numbers to changes in crime. And the problems that apply to measuring the overall performance of a police force apply equally to assessing the effectiveness or the impact of particular strategies of policing.[20] In turn, this means that the statistics conventionally presented in the annual reports of chief constables – such as the number of crimes recorded and the proportion cleared up – are ambiguous at best and meaningless at worst. Such statistics may reflect changes in the socio-economic environment, or in police practices and record-keeping. It is very doubtful, however, whether they have any direct relationship to either effectiveness or efficiency.

It is precisely this problem of giving meaning to the routinely collected police statistics which explains the Home Office's reaction to the government's Financial Management Initiative, disussed in Chapter 2. In contrast to the DHSS, the Home Office has decided against using such statistics as formal performance indicators. Instead, the emphasis is on relying on the 'professional judgement of the Inspectorate'.[21] Even professional judgements tend to be concerned with process rather than outcomes: that is the emphasis is on ensuring that police forces are answerable for using the appropriate managerial techniques – such as setting explicit objectives and priorities – rather than for achieving particular outcomes. Indeed, one of the ironies of the 1980s has been the anxiety of chief constables, as reflected in their annual reports, to repudiate responsibility for outcomes. The emphasis has been on the responsibility of society as a whole for crime: a trend which is not so very different from that evident in the health care field, where the emphasis has switched from proclaiming the role of the medical profession in promoting the health of the population to stressing the role of individual behaviour and the socio-economic environment. If the performance of the police cannot be judged in terms of crime rates – if this is attributable to unemployment or whatever other social factors may be judged relevant – then the police cannot be blamed if crime rates continue to rise even though the strength of the police force has increased greatly over the past decade. And if the performance of the police is not to be judged in terms of such outcomes, what then is the currency of accountability?

Given that the performance of the police is, in part at least, a function of the environment in which the force operates, it is not surprising that the increasingly turbulent social climate of the 1980s has also led to an interest in downward accountability: that is accountability seen as a duty to explain and justify police actions and policies to the community at large in order to enlist public support. Influenced by the Scarman Report's emphasis on the need for consultation and explanation, noted earlier in this chapter, the government decided to create a network of local police consultative committees (PLCs) composed of district, town, or parish councillors, and representatives of welfare agencies and community groups.[22] Thus, Section 106 of the Police and Criminal Evidence Act, 1984, requires that 'arrangements shall be made in each police area for obtaining the views of the people in that area about matters concerning the policing of the area, and for obtaining their co-operation with the police in preventing crime'. If the prime aim is, as this quotation would suggest, the mobilization of support *for* the police, the means chosen is a forum in which there is an obligation *by* the police to give an account of what they are doing to the people most directly concerned. Although it is not as yet clear just how effective PLCs are in this role, their creation can be seen as part of a more general move to give the activities of the police more visibility. This has included provision for lay visitors to police stations and stricter requirements for individual constables to record their activities, particularly when operating stop-and-search procedures. To what extent such developments should be seen as a substitute for accountability to police authorities, or as a means of reinforcing their control over the service for which they are responsible, is an open question.

Given the constitutional and conceptual problems of police accountability, it is therefore not surprising that police authorities here tended to play at most a recessive role. There is a large and growing literature,[23] which suggests a mixture of passive acceptance by police authorities of the dominant role of the chief constable and occasional angry confrontations, but provides little evidence of the kind of active dialogue using an agreed language of evaluation which the ideal model of accountability would suggest. While it is the angry confrontations which capture the headlines, it is the passive acceptance of the chief constable's authority which appears to be the norm. This emerges clearly from a survey carried out in 1984 by the Association of County Councils and the Association of Metropolitan Authorities.[24] So, for example, while fourteen police authorities frequently asked the chief constable for information, twenty-eight did so 'infrequently'. Again, while thirty-eight police authorities discussed expenditure on building equipment, only twenty-eight discussed the efficiency of the force. Even during the miners' strike, a majority of police authorities supported the decisions taken by their chief constables during the dispute, although they were not consulted before the decision was taken to ask for or send officers in mutual aid.[25]

Inactivity or the passive acceptance of the chief constable's decision is, however, an ambiguous indicator of the relationship between police authorities and their chief officers. It may reflect either trust or a sense of frustrated inability to ask the kinds of questions required to make accountability effective. Next, we therefore turn to exploring the way in which members of the police authority in our study perceived their role: how they perceived (if indeed they did) the kind of constitutional and conceptual problems reviewed so far.

The experience and perception of members

The meeting of the police authority opened with the entry of the chief constable. Followed by his entourage of senior officers, he took his place. The effect was that of a special guest arriving at a party, who may or may not stay to be sociable. 'The chief', as he was referred to throughout, and his officers, gave the impression of leading an altogether separate life from the members, whose role was not to participate in, but to observe the service. During the course of the meeting, members began to engage in a questioning dialogue. Gradually the meeting became more like those of the other authorities observed during the study. But, if only symbolically, the police authority meeting underlined the fact that the chief constable had a quasi-military status quite different from that of other chief officers, and the police authority members in our study were used to a very different style of committee management.

In part, this may reflect the fact that police authorities in the past have tended to be made up of the less assertive councillors and magistrates, given a prevailing sense of impotence. A process of low expectations may have become self-reinforcing, all the more so since political parties tended not to put up their most ambitious members on the police authority. Among the members interviewed, however, there were signs of change: our study was carried out just as the police was becoming an issue in party politics. But the change itself presented a problem, since it meant that many of the members were relative newcomers. A large proportion of both county councillors and magistrates interviewed had less than two years' experience of police authority membership. Further, many of the councillors were new to politics, having been elected for the first time only eighteen months previously. This 'inexperience' of county councillors was also considered to be traditional in police authorities which used to have a low status among county council committees. Very few of the members thought of themselves as experienced in the police service, even the magistrates; but those 'inexperienced' members declared themselves to be uncertain as to what constituted relevant know-how for police authority members. While some members thought the magistrates knew about the law and might therefore be called experienced, others wondered about the relevance of law to the police service. As in health authorities, members had a wide range of general backgrounds in politics, business, and community activities, and several of the councillors were also magistrates.

As in the case of health authorities, too, members of the police committee tended to take refuge in large generalities and to stress the wishes of the community when asked about their objectives for their service (although, unlike the health authority members, they tended to do so with confidence, rather than wringing their hands about the lack of precision). More than half the members defined their priority aim as the satisfaction of the community. Almost all the others had the preservation of law and order as a desired outcome of the service, while only a few saw crime prevention as a major objective, in its own right, unrelated to the pursuit of an orderly community. Even the preservation of law and order was seen as a prerequisite of a peaceful society, and in accordance with the wishes of the community at large. The general tone among both councillors and magistrates indicated a direct concern for the wishes of the people and their definition of a good police service. Even the member whose objective was 'peace and tranquillity in the community' placed himself in the 'satisfaction of the people' category:

'The end product of the police service is to obtain the confidence of the greater part of the area covered by the force.'

(Labour member)

'The objective of the police authority is that the community is satisfied with the policing it gets and that the police force is efficient.'

(Conservative member)

'Value for money must include fostering a better relationship between the police and the public.'

(magistrate member)

Some members saw getting value for money, that is looking at costs, as an urgent objective, and one Conservative member said that there was a pressing need for a cost-benefit analysis of the police. Value for money considerations were high on the list of priorities for most members who were looking for savings in the service; however, many of them said they could see limitations on money-saving activities, since 80 per cent of expenditure on the service was accounted for by wages, salaries, and related expenses, as in other public services. Not surprisingly, the articulated pressure for financial savings came more from elected council members but not from any one party. Indeed, it was the Conservative councillors who took the most forceful line in urging an inquiry into police spending. Although the Home Office had produced no formal performance indicators most members were familiar with the concept and thought that in principle they should eventually be applied to the police service:

'I do think it should be possible to apply performance aims to the police service . . . any service or product can be measured, monitored, costed, and evaluated.'

(Conservative member)

'The authority's role on police spending is supposed to be their priority role. They are actually supposed to be looking at value for money. I have pursued personally the section of the police budget containing rent allowances . . . this amounts to a very large extra on top of a very generous salary.'

(Labour member)

'As a councillor, I do look for a lower cost for public services. Shortage of money is the best thing that has ever happened to local government – it has enabled a great leap forward to be made by looking at why we are doing things and how we are doing things. We are refining as well as reducing services. On a general level, and across all types of political barriers, people assuage their consciences and purge their guilt by providing money. All types of political party councillors do this or have done in the past, when resources were more freely available. Councillors of all parties tend to identify themselves with the local government machine. Councillors feel strongly about their "property", that is buildings, services, and people.'

(Conservative member)

'We must ask ourselves what are our values when we talk about value for money. In other words, what are our objectives. In theory, value for money should be the responsibility of the police authority who have financial responsibility but given that 70–80 per cent of finance is staff, and staff is the sole concern of the Home Office, it immediately moves outside the authority responsibility.'

(magistrate member)

'I think that the police force and the authority waste more money than any other type of public service. First, the Home Office standards are so high for police facilities; the standard of maintenance of police houses is very high. If I kept my house to an equivalent standard, I would be bankrupt. The police are operating at a high level of cost, unrealistically high in these times of stringency and the Home Office has made no attempt to economise or lower standards. The present government has also contributed to the police having disproportionately high standards by raising wages to such a level when everyone else faces cuts and unemployment, and certainly not any wage rises.'

(Conservative member)

Given that a large proportion of members had defined the objectives of the police service as the satisfaction of the community, it was not surprising that they also felt that an appropriate way of measuring the achievement of this aim, as part of their own accountability role, was to look at and listen to the people in the community. Only a few members thought that visiting the 'police on the job' was either appropriate or useful in monitoring the service, as visits could not be made spontaneously and were usually carefully stage-managed by senior officers. Indeed, as in the health service, members found themselves to be strictly under the control of officers with their exclusive access to information. The usefulness of statistical information was seen as fairly limited. This was for a variety of reasons including the commonly held opinion that statistics can be used rather 'too flexibly' for accurate and meaningful assessment of a service and, more significantly, that some statistics on the incidence of crime show a dubious relationship with the input of police officer activity:

'I am certainly very chary of criminal statistics as indicators of police activity. I can't see any way of arriving at performance aims for the police forces at the present time. The police part in the prevention of crime is not as great as general social and economic conditions prevailing and their relationship with the solving of crime is equally dubious.'   (magistrate member)

A few members declared themselves to be more optimistic about statistics and performance assessment in the police service, providing the right kind of information was asked for, and it was used wisely:

'Statistics, if properly used, are a good way of assessing the commodity. One has to use statistics sensibly and ask the right questions of the chief constable's report. If members are perceptive, they can ask the right question of the chief constable.'   (Conservative member)

These members said that it would be wrong to interpret their views on statistics as an unwillingness or inability to come to terms with precise methods of evaluation but that their attitude rather reflected suspicion of available statistics, many of which are irrelevant to a proper service evaluation. Her Majesty's Inspectors of Police and their reports did not figure much in the lives of police authority members interviewed, and were not used in pursuit of their role as public service watchdogs. Members felt that the yearly HMI inspection was none of their business, in the sense that it was mostly about staff morale. According to some, senior police officers had suggested that the inspectors were not going to be able to tell them anything they did not already know. The pressure for value for money policies from county councils was clearly on the minds of members who were beginning to look in more detail at what was being done in the police service and how much it was costing. As with other public services, the search for financial efficiency was highlighting those areas where service objectives had not been clearly defined and where the relationship between inputs of resources was not clearly related either to outcomes or objectives.

The police authority members were carrying out their duties, however vague their objectives, within a service where the ambiguity of their role has been written into the statutes and where, traditionally, this has resulted in a high level of uncertainty for them and a correspondingly high level of confidence among senior police officers about the scope of their respective roles. This long-standing ambiguity has persisted, in spite of the recommendations of the final report of the Royal Commission on the police published in 1962, as noted in the previous section. Whereas this ambiguity has been said to have undermined the role of police authorities and consolidated the role of chief constables, members indicated a surprising lack of direct conflict between themselves and the chief constable. Three-quarters of members saw the scope of their role constrained more by the Home Office than by the chief constable and his police force. Blurred areas of responsibility and confusion about the division between policy and operations were blamed on statutory legislation and the power of the Home Office:

'Members don't get involved in policy making. I assume the overall outlines of policy are the work of the Home Office.'

(magistrate member)

Most members were, in fact, genuinely confused about the distinction between policy and operations and even where the majority said that their function was a finance, resource, or 'housekeeping' function, it was admitted that finances do have both policy and operations implications. Similarly, when asked about the role of the chief constable, members thought that although he was responsible for the day-to-day operations of the police force, his role could be seen equally as policy-making. Although also seen as constrained by the Home Office, the chief constable was said by some members to have the political advantage over them; the ambiguity of roles was perceived as serving the interests of police officers rather than authority members:

'The problem is that the distinction between policy and operations is blurred in the police service and it appears that the chief constable is left virtually in control of both.'

(Labour member)

However, some members said that they had been witnessing changes in police officer power in the recent past:

'I feel that the police are getting the message from authority members. They have taken on board a great deal in a very short time and Scarman is here to stay.'

(Liberal member)

'In the last five years or so the police are conscious of the authority, if not breathing down their necks, then having a jolly good look.'

(Conservative member)

'I am not sure about the chief constable's sum total of operational power. He is guided by the Home Office and a lot depends on the personality and ability of the individual chief constable and the skill and effectiveness with which he translates the Home Office guidelines into policy and action.'

(Liberal member)

Most members, however, did not see the concept of ultimate responsibility for policy-making as a crucial issue. They did not think that it mattered what the source of policy was in a police authority as long as members had an input and as long as they were able to question the chief constable: that is as long as the authority was able to extract from the chief constable an acceptable account of his activities.

On the question of resources and their allocation, even on internal housekeeping arrangements, the Home Office was seen to have the first and the last word. Because of this, the role of county councils as keepers of half the purse was thought to be largely ineffectual in police policy-making:

> 'Although the number of police officers in a force is a financial matter, to a large extent this is the decision of the Home Office, not the authority.'
>
> (Labour member)

One member did suggest that the role of the county council might be changing with an increased interest not only in the resourcing of the police force but also in the role of the chief constable. There was, in fact, a feeling among both councillors and magistrates that the real world was drawing the police service into areas of public scrutiny previously inhabited only by conventional public services:

> 'We have just started a new system as county councillors of reporting back to our county. This has never happened before. It does make sense, since the chief constable is the only chief officer who does not go to county council.'
>
> (Conservative member)

Most members did not think, however, that the police service ought to be controlled by politics in the sense of party politics. The level of political involvement was said to be about right and there was general disapproval of the idea of changing the authority to an all-elected body. But one county council member did not see any way of putting pressure on the police service unless the authority was 'party politicized'; he suggested that all the positive progress towards changing the powers of the chief constable had been made by his fellow politicians. In contrast, another councillor argued that the political activities of certain members had been largely counterproductive in extracting information:

'Some councillors ask questions of the chief constable while displaying their obvious self-conscious assumptions that it isn't really their business. This is reflected in their aggressiveness, use of jargon, and constant referral to statutory rights, etc., and the net result is a question that the chief constable is not going to answer as he would if he was asked in a more confident, non-political way. It seems in the circumstances to be the wrong way of tackling the chief constable.'

(Conservative member)

Just as 'expertise' is being called into question in the case of the health service, so it is in the case of the police. Police authority members considered carefully the type and extent of expertise in the police service, in tones of scepticism. Most differentiated clearly between professionals and experts. Both magistrates and councillors thought that no part of the police service constituted a profession although they conceded a level of expertise in limited areas. Searching for ways of describing police service activity, many members suggested 'specialist' and 'experienced' as more appropriate adjectives to apply to the police than professional or expert:

'The role of the officer in local government is clearer than that of the chief constable and his officers. It is not even clear where police professional expertise lies. Police officers are certainly not financial experts, nor do they decide on the laws of the land. They are not really experts in crime solving – 80 per cent of crime is solved through information received through the intimate relationship between the police and the criminal world. Professionalism and expertise should be concentrated in the police officers' role in surveillance of traffic and in the prevention of crime. There is scope in these areas to extend both their professionalism and their expertise.'

(Labour member)

'A member should ask about crimes solved by detection compared with those solved by received information. This reflects on the activity of the police in crime solving. Quite a lot of crime solving is automatic with no police effort in the sense that as soon as it is committed, information will be received in enough detail to make arrests and take someone to court.'

(Conservative member)

Members' discussion of professionals and experts definitely reflected their feelings that in the positive sense of the word, the police were less than qualified to call themselves professionals and that in the negative sense they had used professionalization for their own ends:

'Generally, the police have acquired a greatly enhanced economic position. This is at the risk of distancing themselves from the rest of the community. The "middle classing" of the police has done damage to the policing of small villages in particular, where the policeman was part of the community. I think that police houses are sold on too good terms to police officers.'

(Liberal member)

'The police are still in the process of arranging their "professionalism" and deciding on its constitutional parts. They are in the process of asserting their financial superiority and professional autonomy.'

(magistrate member)

'Police officers are professionals, not in terms of a body of knowledge, but as operating and bargaining professional hardnecks who know how to handle the present situation between central government, chief constables and police authorities.'

(Labour member)

There was also a sense that the police were trying to appropriate as 'professional' decisions matters where they had no special expertise, where they were actually wrong in their assessments, and where there were considerable financial implications. This reflected the further suspicion that the police (like doctors) are inclined to over-invest in technological toys, a point caught in the following quotation from a member of the water authority who also happened to be a member of a neighbouring police authority:

> 'On the financial agenda was the intended purchase of a police launch costing £250,000. The report to the committee gave a very sketchy outline of the cost. I persuaded the police committee to ask for a full report on the cost which included information on what the boat was to be used for. I was able to tell the chief constable and the committee that this particular boat was not suitable to the police's job of patrolling the harbour. And although it was suitable for use out at sea, the chief constable was not entitled to be patrolling the high seas – which are outside his terms of reference. So, a second set of proposals were then submitted by the chief constable for a less powerful boat costing £100,000 – which was the right boat for the job. And the committee accepted the proposal.'
>
> (Conservative member)

In sharp contrast to the uncertainty about objectives, information, and policy, members were very clear about the direction of their accountability. Almost all members said that their accountability or responsibility was downward to the community. Whether members defined this feeling as accountability or responsibility – and there was a high degree of confusion between the two words – it was definitely downwards to the community with the emphasis on retrospective accountability; that is keeping an ear to the ground and making sure that people's grievances with the police were quickly dealt with. Members stressed this aspect of their accountability role and many said it was more important than producing an overall policy for the service:

> 'Accountability is a shifting concept. I am directly accountable to an elected committee for my police authority membership. The police authority as a whole is directly responsible to the Home Office and elected members feel very responsible to the people – are they getting the police force they need and want? Accountability is brought to the foreground when there are local public queries or crisis situations resulting from police activity. Accountability is real only in a crisis in the police

service. It is accountability in the sense of answering and taking the blame rather than working the system back to find out where it went wrong and why, and possibly avoiding it in the future.'

(Conservative member)

'I am accountable to the general public – as a councillor my accountability comes every four years at election time. Responsibility goes hand in hand with this, although it is not the same concept. My responsibility is to the general public. I am not accountable to a particular group, certainly not my Conservative group. I have made it plain that I don't subscribe to this aspect of politics.'

(Conservative member)

'Authority members cannot be accountable – it is not possible. However, I feel responsible to the magistrates' courts committee and to the people in my county.'

(magistrate member)

'One tends to be accountable to the general public. One tries to think what the average person would think.'

(magistrate member)

Only a few members saw themselves to be accountable, not only to the community or the people, but also to their own consciences and selves – or the Queen:

'On responsibility, everyone makes up their own mind really. We aren't really accountable to other people except we *feel* responsible. I question that the idea of democracy is answering to the people.'

(Labour member)

Like their health authority counterparts, police members generally saw their responsibility as assuring the satisfaction of the community and, in some sense, keeping an ear to the ground. However, most had never been involved with any public or community queries or complaints. Nor had they been in public situations where the requests or needs of the community for a particular type of police service had been discussed. This applied equally to both elected councillors and magistrates and across all political shades. That county councillors were more visible and more available through their surgeries than magistrates did not result in any greater contact between members and the public on police issues.[26]

Only three members interviewed had involved themselves heavily with issues raised by the public. One councillor who was directly engaged in community policing in his constituency said that the bulk of complaints were about domestic disputes. Another county councillor had taken up the motorists' lobby for complaints against the police in his area and was pursuing 'excessive breathalysing'. A third councillor had been busy dealing with complaints about not enough policemen being visible in his area, and a one-off complaint about constables seen without hats. Overall, the dominating irony was that while members felt themselves to be accountable to the community, the links between them and the community appeared to be fitful and tenuous.

Summary

One significant paradox emerges strongly from the study of the police. Members in the *National* Health Service authorities saw the main constraint on their role as the power of the local district management team rather than that of the central government department. In contrast, members in the *local* police authority saw the main constraint on their role as the power of the Home Office rather than that of the chief constable. It was the Home Office, in the eyes of members, which had created a situation in which lines of accountability were fudged and the chief constable operated in a grey area of autonomy. To the extent that the chief constable was seen as the strong arm of the Home Office, and it was the Home Office which controlled finances and manpower, so members felt frustrated and impotent. For how could they themselves hold to account a service where policies – financial and operational – were largely determined by the centre?

The sense of frustration did not, however, reflect a particularly ambitious definition of accountability. If members wanted to get more of a grip over the police service, it was only in limited ways.

They were realistic enough not to want to set service objectives except in very general ways. They were aware that there seemed to be no way of relating inputs of resources and outcomes, but were fairly sceptical about the use of statistical information. They did not see the police as experts or professionals, but on the whole appeared to be content that (like doctors) officers should be left to engage in their mystery. But they did want the chief constable to give a satisfactory account, in the sense of telling a convincing story, of what had been done, and to explain his housekeeping: members were particularly concerned that the police sought to claim 'professional privilege' for routine financial decisions, such as the purchase of boats, cars, or uniforms, which were appropriate for scrutiny by lay members, some of whom were more expert than the police in the matters at issue.

Speculatively, it may be precisely this sense of frustration – the baffled attempt to get more control over the service – that explains the emphasis of members on their own downward accountability to the community. For there was an element of myth-making in this emphasis, in that it was not at all clear how this downward accountability was intended to be exercised. It was very much a notion in the heads of members. But their emphasis on this notion (as on the idea of reporting back to councils) makes sense if it is seen as part of a strategy for strengthening their own ability, by demonstrating their legitimacy, to call the chief constable to account.

REFERENCES

1 G. Marshall (1978) Police Accountability Revisited. In D. Butler and A. H. Halsey (eds) *Policy and Politics*. London: Macmillan. G. Marshall (1984) *Constitutional Conventions*, ch. VIII. Oxford: Clarendon Press.
2 For an analysis of some of the issues and conflicts thrown up by the miners' strike, see B. Loveday (1986) Central Co-ordination, Police Authorities and the Miners' Strike. *Political Quarterly* 57, 1, January/March: 60–74.
3 Quoted in T. Jefferson and R. Grimshaw (1984) *Controlling the Constable*. London: Frederick Muller: The Cobden Trust: 66.
4 Royal Commission on the Police (1962) *Final Report*. London: HMSO Cmnd 1728: para. 166.

5 Lord Scarman (Chairman) (1982) *The Scarman Report.* Harmondsworth: Penguin.
6 Quoted in T. Jefferson and R. Grimshaw (1984) *Controlling the
  Constable.* London: Frederick Muller: The Cobden Trust: 55.
7 R. Reiner (1985) *The Politics of the Police.* Brighton: Harvester Press.
  In what follows, we have drawn heavily on this analysis.
8 Royal Commission on the Police (1962) *Final Report.* London: HMSO
  Cmnd 1728: para. 89.
9 Her Majesty's Chief Inspector of Constabulary (1983) *Report for the
  Year 1982.* London: HMSO HC 15.
10 *The Principles of Policing and Guidance for Professional Behaviour*
  (1985) London: Metropolitan Police.
11 Committee of Inquiry into the Police (1978) *Reports on Negotiating
  Machinery and Pay.* London: HMSO.
12 The police complaints machinery, although it can be argued to be an
  instrument of accountability, is not directly related to the role of police
  authorities and is therefore not discussed in this chapter. But for a
  recent review of the state of play, see G. Marshall (1984) *Constitutional
  Conventions.* Oxford: Clarendon Press.
13 Royal Commission on the Police (1962) *Final Report.* London:
  HMSO: para. 89.
14 B. A. Meuke, M. F. White, and W. L. Carey (1982) Police Professionalization: Pursuit of Excellence or Political Power? In J. R.
  Greene (ed.) *Managing Police Work.* Beverly Hills, Calif: Sage.
15 See for example S. Holdaway (1983) *Inside the British Police.* Oxford:
  Basil Blackwell.
16 E. Reuss-Ianni and F. A. D. Ianni (1983) Street Cops and Management Cops. In M. Punch (ed.) *Control in Police Organizations.*
  Cambridge, Mass: MIT Press.
17 M. Punch (1983) Officers and Men. In M. Punch (ed.) *Control in
  Police Organizations.* Cambridge, Mass: MIT Press.
18 D. H. Bayley (1983) Knowledge of the Police. In M. Punch (ed.)
  Control in Police Organizations. Cambridge, Mass: MIT Press.
19 I. Sinclair and C. Miller (1984) *Measures of Police Effectiveness and
  Efficiency.* London: Home Office, Research and Planning Unit, Paper
  25.
20 R. V. Clarke and M. Hough (1984) *Crime and Police Effectiveness.*
  London: HMSO, Home Office Research Study no. 79.
21 I. Sinclair and C. Miller, (1984) *Measures of Police Effectiveness and
  Efficiency.* London: Home Office, Research and Planning Unit, Paper
  25.
22 R. Morgan and C. Maggs (1985) *Setting the PACE.* Bath Social Policy
  Paper no. 4, Bath: Centre for the Analysis of Social Policy. See also S.

Savage (1984) The Police: Political Control or Community Liaison. *Political Quarterly* 55, 1, January/March: 48–59. R. Morgan (1986) Police Consultative Groups. *Political Quarterly* 57, 1, January/March: 83–8.

23 See for example Controlling the Police? *State Research Bulletin* 4, 3, April/May: 110–23. B. Loveday (1983) The Role of the Police Committee. *Local Government Studies* 9, 1, January/February: 39–53. P. A. J. Waddington (1984) The Role of the Police Committee: Constitutional Arrangements and Social Realities. *Local Government Studies* 10, 5, September/October: 27–49. M. Simey (1984) Partnership Policing. In J. Benyon (ed.) *Scarman and After*. Oxford: Pergamon Press.

24 This unpublished survey is quoted by permission of the Association of Metropolitan Authorities.

25 S. Spencer (1985) The Weakness of Police Authorities and the Case for Reform. *Local Government Studies* II, 6, November/December: 31–4.

26 The interviews were carried out before the new Police Liaison Committee had become fully operational; their activities may subsequently have promoted more contact between members and the community.

6

Accountability and the water authority

Alone among the five services studied in this book, water authorities are monopoly suppliers of essential services for which the users have to pay. They are, in effect, publicly owned commercial undertakings which have to make their books balance.[1] They also have, as we shall see, a range of other responsibilities: in particular a range of regulatory functions which affect the physical environment in which we all live. But dominating their activities, and their budgets, are two functions: making sure that water is on tap to, and that waste is carried away from, homes, factories, shops, offices, and farms throughout the country. To finance these activities, water authorities are empowered to charge customers either directly or through the water rates. They are unlike the other national service being studied, the NHS, in that they are self-financing. But they are similar to the NHS in that water authorities, like health authorities, are directly accountable to central government, that is the secretary of state for the environment. Equally like health authorities, they are responsible for delivering a national service in widely varying local environments. In examining the role of authority members in the accountability process, we are dealing with a service which allows us to look at how that role is defined in a very different setting from those considered in previous or succeeding chapters. In other words, we are able to explore how perceptions of the notion itself are affected both by its institutionalized context and by the nature of the activities being carried out.

Water authorities are the product of the search for national efficiency through institutional reform that marked the decade from 1965 to 1975. They are a monument, as it were, to technocratic rationality. The Water Act, 1973, swept away the 1,600 bodies – chiefly local authorities, but also including 30 water companies – which had previously been responsible for water management in its various aspects. Instead, it created nine regional water authorities in England and one in Wales. Only by combining the various aspcts of water management on a sufficiently large geographical scale, the government argued, would it be possible to plan the massive investment programme needed and to make the appropriate strategic choices.[2] The emphasis in presenting the plans for the new authorities was on integrating a fragmented system, on improving the techniques of investment appraisal, and on rationalizing the system of charging in order to encourage an efficient use of water resources. No doubt unconsciously, many of the arguments put forward for creating water authorities echoed those advanced in support of the creation of the NHS almost thirty years previously. In both instances, nationalization and regionalization were designed to enhance performance through the elimination of the historic jumble of multiple providers.[3]

The government's intentions in carrying through the 1973 reorganization of the water industry were clearly spelled out.[4] The objectives of the new machinery were set out explicitly and they are worth quoting in full since they cover, now as then, the main functions of water authorities:

'To secure an ample supply of water of appropriate quality to meet the growing demands of the people, industry, and agriculture – while at the same time ensuring that it is not wasted.

To provide adequate sewerage and sewage disposal facilities to cope with the natural increase in water use and with new housing, industrial and agricultural developments.

To ensure that the vital contribution of land drainage and flood protection to both urban and agricultural areas alike is maintained and, where appropriate, expanded.

To achieve a massive clean up of the country's rivers and estuaries by the early 1980s.

To make the widest use of water space for other purposes, including recreation and amenity and, where appropriate, the protection and development of salmon and fresh water fisheries and the provision of water needed for navigation.

To protect the interests of those who may be affected by proposals for the development of water resources in any one of these respects.'

Although the list of objectives is long, the activities of water authorities are concentrated on the first two: water provision and waste disposal and control. Thus in 1983/84, out of a total capital expenditure budget of £824 million (greater than that of the NHS or any of the other services in our study), 37 per cent was devoted to investment in water resources and supply, and 47 per cent was spent on sewerage, sewage disposal, and pollution control. The distribution of the capital budget is a better indicator of the distribution of activities than the composition of the current budget since water (in sharp contrast to other services) is a capital-intensive industry. Again, the point is made by a simple set of figures. In 1983/84 revenue expenditure was split as follows: 27 per cent to manpower, 35 per cent to other operating costs, and 38 per cent to capital charges.[5] This once more distinguishes water from our other services which spend 70 to 80 per cent of their total budget on the labour force.

If the intention in setting up water authorities was primarily to create a system for the more efficient management of resources, their membership reflected a different set of considerations. The establishment of water authorities meant that, as already noted, local authorities lost one of their functions. Not only did this create a problem of political acceptability for the change, but also it meant the elimination of directly elected local representation. Accordingly the 1973 legislation provided for a mixed membership with the government yielding to pressure from the local authority lobby.[6] Some members, including the chairman, were to be nominated by the secretary of state for their special knowledge and experience; others, the majority, were to be nominated by the local authorities in the area of the water authority. One result was a wide range in the size of the water authorities, since this depended on the number of local authorities in the area. Thus, at one extreme, one water authority had fifty-eight members; two others, at the other end of the distribution, had only fifteen. The average membership was twenty-nine.[7]

The result was a potential tension, not to be resolved until the Water Act, 1983 removed local authority representation (see pp. 146–7), between the constitutional position of water authorities as bodies accountable to central government and the traditions of local accountability by elected members: a tension similar in some respects to that noted in Chapter 4 in the case of health authorities. The difficulty was addressed by the Ogden Committee set up in advance of the creation of the new water authorities:[8] a committee composed exclusively of managers and civil servants. This noted that 'The tradition of representative local government will make it difficult for the local authority members to repress their instinctive response to geographical constituency consider-ations', and that there might be a danger of 'conflicts developing' between the local authority members and the expert members nominated by the secretary of state. Accordingly, the committee argued:

'We hope that the members of the authorities themselves will develop a corporate approach, and will view the problems of the region as a whole, and not from a "local constituency" or "special interest" position. Whilst there may be many diverse views on the means, they can surely be only one major aim, the optimum use of water for all the varied purposes to which it might be put. It would be tragic if different lobbies developed to a degree which vitiated this corporate approach.'

In short, the emphasis was on the authority as an *essentially* managerial body, dealing with *essentially* technical rather than political problems, with members and officers as partners: a somewhat different emphasis from that evident in the other services. Not only did this imply, the committee argued, that 'it is axiomatic that all information . . . must be freely available to every member of the authority'. But perhaps more radically still, the committee concluded:

'In this process there can be no clear dividing line between the preserves of members and those of officers. Traditional simplifications present the officers as assembling the case and members deciding it; or as members being responsible for policy and officers for implementation. Neither of these simple pictures is true and informed opinion is increasingly turning to a view of the relationship as a shared one, not with different functions but with different emphases. . . . In practice, policies and plans are forged in partnership; likewise their implementation.'

If the new water authorities were given what was seen to be primarily a managerial task, the role of efficiently planning water resources, there remained the question of just what their currency of accountability should be. If they were to be answerable to the secretary of state, how would he assess the performance of the service for which they were responsible? And what criteria would be used by the members of water authorities in determining whether their own service was achieving the performance required by the secretary of state? In the case of water authorities the answers to these questions are far more specific than in any of the other services in this study. In part, this reflects the nature of the service itself: the fact that, as we have seen, it is possible to define the functions of water authorities with some degree of specificity – and to derive measurable objectives from these. In part, too, it reflects the financing of water authorities: the fact that they generate their own income by selling their service, instead of being dependent on taxes or rates. In what follows, we shall deal with each of these aspects in turn, starting with the financial dimension of accountability.

Section 29 of the Water Act, 1973, imposed on water authorities a duty 'so to discharge their functions as to secure that, taking one year with another, their revenue is not less than sufficient to meet their total outgoings properly chargeable to revenue account'. In short, they are accountable for balancing their books. However, this defines the problem rather than solving it. For water authorities are, as noted at the start of this chapter, monopoly suppliers of essential services which are indispensable to most consumers. It is in this respect that they are different from other nationalized industries, which in other ways they resemble. In theory, therefore, they could balance their books by making ever-higher charges to compensate for what might well be an inefficient or incompetent performance. For example they might embark on extravagant investment programmes, or conversely let their capital plant run down, while still balancing their books. So while the requirement to balance the books may be a necessary condition of accountability, it is certainly not a sufficient one. And it is precisely this dilemma which helps to explain government policy since 1973. First, it has imposed ever tighter criteria on the use of investment funds: second, it has complemented this by introducing a set of performance 'aims' or 'ratios' designed to assess the efficiency with which the capital plant is used.

Like other nationalized industries, water authorities require government approval of their capital investment plans. The process has become increasingly rigorous since 1973, particularly so in the 1980s as part of the government's overall strategy for controlling public expenditure. Not only does the Department of the Environment (DoE) set an overall target of the expected return on the total capital assets of each water authority, that is including the historic legacy of inherited capital plant. In 1983/84 this was 1.25 per cent and the government's policy was gradually to increase it to 1.9 per cent over time. But new capital investment schemes have, in addition, to be justified to the Department of the Environment. It is a process which combines quantitative analysis and qualitative judgements, as the Second Permanent Secretary of State of the DoE, Sir Peter Harrop, made clear in giving evidence to the Public Accounts Committee in 1985:[9]

'We are, generally speaking, attempting to systematise the way in which water authorities set about not only their programming of investment but also the way in which they arrive at projects they want to include in their programme. It is in fact a difficult matter because financial appraisal, for the most part, is not available. If the investment is cost saving, they can do a financial appraisal and see whether it is worthwhile. For the others, you are in the field of judgement about what benefit you secure from the investment. Where we have reached at the

present time is to get water authorities to systematise their
approach to investment planning, to see that the projects that
they select are those which are needed to improve levels of
service, which meet the objectives which the authorities
themselves have set themselves.'

The process of determining the investment programme is part of
a continuing dialogue between water authorities and the department, in which the corporate plan produced by each authority is an.
essential part. It is a dialogue chiefly between officers and civil
servants, in which the latter (in the words of one of them) see their
role as being 'not to second guess water authorities, but to probe
and challenge'. There are also formal meetings (as in the case of
the NHS's performance review system) between ministers and
water authority chairmen and -women. For ministers, again as in
the case of the NHS, are accountable to parliament for the
performance of the water industry – with one all-important
difference, however. The model of accountability for the water
industry is the same as that for nationalized industries: that is
ministers are answerable for the overall performance of the
industry, not for individual cases or acts. There is, in other words,
no equivalent of the 'bedpan doctrine': MPs may not ask questions
about individual cases. So the purpose of the annual meetings
between ministers and chairmen is mainly to discuss the plans of
the authorities, and the efficiency with which authorities are
carrying out their operations.

For efficiency is a key word and concept in the system of
accountability, running from water authorities to central government, that has been built up. This stems, as already argued, from
the monopoly position of the water industry which means that
meeting financial targets could be compatible with incompetence.
To quote the report of the Public Accounts Committee:[10] 'the
Department had confirmed that in a monopoly situation, the
target of securing a financial return on assets could not be
expected to provide much of a stimulus to efficiency. They had
therefore set performance aims which required the industries to
reduce operating costs'. But measuring efficiency is not without its
problems, even in the water industry. The point emerges clearly
from the report of the Monopolies and Mergers Commission

which in 1981 investigated the affairs of one of the water authorities.[11] This explained the background to the government's policies:

> 'Originally, the government envisaged that performance aims would be expressed in terms of real costs per unit of output. . . . However, there was disagreement between the industry and government on setting aims in terms of unit costs. The industry argued that output could not be measured and that even if it could be measured, its costs were related much more to the size of the system than to the throughput. As a compromise, therefore, it was agreed that performance aims would be expressed in terms of total expenditure, with background information on movements in real unit costs measured by expenditure per head of effective population.'

In effect, then, the government has abandoned the attempt to assess the efficiency of any one water authority by comparing its costs to those of others. Instead, the emphasis is on looking at efficiency over time – as measured by the decline of unit costs – within each authority. To quote Sir Peter Harrop again:[12]

> 'We do have performance indicators in the form of performance ratios which show unit costs or the cost of service per head of population, that sort of thing . . . but the fact is that there are very considerable difficulties in using these indicators to compare performance. For a start, the physical characteristics of the water authorities differ a good deal, maybe in rainfall, maybe in their topography. There are many reasons why the costs of performing the service in one authority should differ from another authority. We can only regard these ratios at the present time as useful pointers, challenges if you like; where an authority has a high ratio to ask why it is like that.'

So even in the water industry, despite the fact that it appears to be producing a measurable product at a measurable price, the currency of accountability is problematic. As in the case of the other services being studied, where again there are statistics of comparative costs, accountability involves argument about the interpretation of what at first sight appears to be 'hard' data. Accountability is all about dialogue, the interpretation of 'facts' and the use of judgement.

However, in one crucial respect the water industry *is* different from the other services discussed in this book. So far our analysis has been devoted to the financial aspects of the industry's management. Turning to the other aspect of accountability distinguished earlier in this chapter, accountability for the achievement of measurable objectives or outputs, the water industry turns out to be very much the exception. It is not only possible to set objectives but to measure their achievement, both quantitatively and qualitatively. While defining the objectives of the NHS or the police is, as we have seen, extremely problematic – given the often ill-understood relationship between inputs and outputs, their vagueness, and the possibility of conflict between competing aims – the difficulties appear to be much less in the case of the water industry. There actually is an accepted currency of accountability, or criteria for measuring performance linked to objectives, when it comes to looking at the industry's outputs. Members of water authorities, uniquely perhaps among the five services, have relatively unambiguous, clear-cut, and measurable criteria against which they can assess the outputs of the organization for which they are responsible.

These are the 'level of service indicators' produced by the Department of the Environment, which set out in considerable and precise detail the way in which each water authority should analyse its performance in its corporate plan.[13] Those 'level of service indicators' differ from the performance indicators produced by the DHSS for the NHS, and from the routine statistical returns produced for the other services in this study, in two significant respects. First, they have a strong prescriptive element: that is they assess performance in terms of desired objectives, instead of merely comparing the activities of different authorities. Second, they alone include a qualitative dimension: that is they measure performance against explicit standards of what the product should be like.

So in the case of water supply, there are indicators both of the adequacy of the service being offered to consumers and of the quality of the product being delivered. If there is a breakdown in the supply of water to the consumer, a good response time is defined to be three hours, and an adequate response time is taken to be five hours. Further, water authorities have to report the number of customers suffering from inadequate water pressure (adequacy being defined as water being available at a pressure sufficient to reach the top storey of every building) or supply failure for twelve hours or more (defined as 'suffering complete loss of piped supply') in any one year. Equally there is a battery of quality standards for drinking water, reflecting international standards as laid down by the World Health Organisation and the European Economic Commission. For example limits are set on the acceptable concentration of substances like lead, nitrate, iron, chloride, and copper, among others. Similarly there is a set of bacteriological standards. In each case, water authorities are required to take routine samples and report on the proportion that fail to comply with the required standards. Lastly, and least amenable to precise measurement, water has to be of an acceptable quality to consumers: water authorities are required to show how many customers receive water which, although chemically and bacteriologically sound, gives rise to 'sustained complaints on colour, taste, smell or presence of "vehicle" animals (daphnae, shrimps, worms, etc.)'.

There is a similar set of indicators for the other activities for which water authorities are responsible. In the case of sewerage, authorities have to report on the number of premises flooded by foul sewerage, the number of sewer collapses, and the number of unsatisfactory storm overflows. In the case of sewage treatment and disposal, there is an elaborate system for classifying the quality of water in rivers and estuaries. Thus, rivers are classified in a variety of categories, ranging from those which have a high amenity value and can be used for 'game and high-class fisheries' to those which are 'grossly polluted and likely to cause a nuisance'. In the case of land drainage and flood protection, water authorities are required to set their own 'target standards' and to report on the extent to which these have been achieved.

All this might suggest that accountability for the achievement of most quantitative and qualitative standards of service in the water industry could be left to computers: that there is no area of discretion left for members of water authorities in the exercise of their role. But this would be misleading. Even though there is an explicit and clear language of accountability, its application to specific circumstances may still leave scope for argument. As stressed in the discussion of financial accountability, water authorities differ in the physical environment in which they operate. The achievement of particular targets may therefore not be equally feasible for all of them. Similarly climatic conditions may vary from year to year: a drought, for example, may cause a dip in performance. Lastly, relating investment decisions to desired outputs involves, as the earlier quotation from Sir Peter Harrop's evidence to the Public Accounts Committee suggests, more than applying neutral technical methods of appraisal. They involve judgements about just how much extra investment is justified to improve, say, the quality of water. They involve judgements about the life-span of improvements: the trade-off between relatively cheap but short-term alleviations and longer-term but more expensive ones. They involve judgements, further-more, about the geographical distribution of investment funds within the area of each authority: given that capital resources have to be rationed, it may be a matter of controversy about who should get what – which coastal resort, for example, should get the new sewage outfall that will make its beaches more attractive.

The accountability of water authority members is therefore no different from the accountability of other authority members in that they have to justify their actions: that they have to find good arguments for explaining why they have not achieved particular standards or targets, or why they have preferred to give priority to one target over another. But they are different in two crucial respects. First, they have to justify their performance against clear criteria and objectives. There is no doubt about what their performance should be (in contrast to the other services being studied, where it is precisely the notion of performance itself that is problematic and contestable). Second, the criteria and objectives which define their collective performance also define the currency of accountability *within* the organization. In other words, they have criteria for judging the performance of those responsible for the actual delivery of the service. A water engineer who fails to carry out an emergency repair within three hours is clearly failing to achieve the target standards. He has failed to get to Marathon on time. No doubt he may be able to plead justification for his failure, such as other calls on his time or a breakdown in communication. But in answering for his conduct, the onus on him is to justify his actions in terms of concrete and specific aims: unlike the policeman, the doctor, the teacher, or the social worker, he cannot plead that defining the aim is a professional judgement (and that running to Marathon was an unprofessional activity, anyway). There may well be scope for discretion among the service-providers, but it is not discretion about defining the nature of the service being produced.[14] There is, furthermore, a hierarchy of command, untroubled by claims to professional autonomy or answerability to professional peers. In a service dominated by pipes rather than people, there is at least no dispute about the lines of accountability.

All this would suggest that the exercise of accountability should be less problematic for members of water authorities than for members of other authorities, and this indeed turns out to be the case when we examine the evidence of our interviews. But to make this point is also to underline a paradoxical feature of the 1973 legislation which created water authorities. As noted at the start of this chapter, this provided that the majority of the membership should be nominated by local authorities. In this respect, water authorities were similar to both police and, to a lesser degree, to health authorities. They were, in effect, a hybrid model, part nationalized industry, part local authority. Their membership represented, as it were, a general, if vague, nod in the direction of local as well as central accountability. Further, as the Public Accounts Committee pointed out:[15] 'a measure of local accountability' was introduced by the provision in the 1973 Act that authority meetings should conduct their business in public.

However, in contrast to the experience of health authorities, the potential for conflict between central and local accountability has been defused since 1973 by the ever-greater assertion of the former. It is central government which, if in discussion with the water industry, has evolved the ever-more rigorous and precise financial and performance targets criteria discussed above. And in determining the currency of accountability to central government, in limiting the scope of authority members for defining what is meant by good performance, they have effectively also limited the scope for local accountability. As the National Water Authority, the voice of the industry, complained in its 1980–81 annual report when reviewing the government's financial targets:[16]

> 'The most important reservation of the industry about the changes arises from the feeling that the degree of control now exercised by government through fine tuning of target-setting and the remainder of the battery of financial controls is clouding the accountability of water authority members and executives as managers of their enterprise.'

The wording is odd, but the meaning would seem to be clear. In specifying more rigorously the currency of accountability, the government was effectively narrowing the autonomy of members and managers. In reacting with hostility to this process, members and managers were behaving rather like professionals whose freedom to set their own criteria of performance was being questioned.

The trend of government policy in the 1980s was therefore undermining whatever conceptual justification, political expediency apart, underlay the constitution of water authorities. By 1981 the Monopolies and Mergers Commission was already questioning the need for local authority representation:[17]

> 'Despite its historical origins, the authority is not an instrument of local government, and does not therefore have to be controlled by a body which is largely composed of people who derive their membership from the electoral process of local government. Its policies and activities are in no way dependent on political issues within its particular boundaries. It is one of the ten similar bodies which are virtually nationalised industries organised on a regional basis, responsible to Ministers.'

Moreover, the Commission argued:

> 'When the rights of local authorities to nominate a majority of the members of the authority were established under the 1973 legislation it was hoped that this would enable consumer interests to be adequately taken into account when the policies of the authority were being determined. It is clear to us that

these hopes have not been satisfactorily fulfilled; and that better arrangements need to be made to enable the views of consumers to be properly considered.'

Accordingly the Commission recommended that water authorities should be smaller, more managerial bodies with no local government representation, and that the role of consumer representation should be vested in separate consultative bodies. This in effect became government policy and was reflected in the Water Act, 1983. The Act provided that water authorities should consist of between nine and fifteen members, 'all appointed by Ministers',[18] although of course, ministers are free to appoint councillors with special expertise if they wish to do so. In addition, consumer consultative committees were to be set up. 'We want the way in which this very important basic industry is managed to take another step towards the business management ethos with which we run other basic industries', the minister responsible explained.[19]

The new legislation came into effect just as our interviewing of water authority members came to an end. The interviews with members reflect the situation as it was before 1984. But in interpreting our findings, it is important to note that the water authority in our study already had many of the post-1983 characteristics rather than being representative of the original 1973 mould. It had a membership of only fifteen. It deliberately fostered an ethos of corporate managerial responsibility, for both managers and officers. It had earlier set up an elaborate network of consumer consultative committees, and could thus comment that the government's 1983 changes simply generalized what it had already done. So, although in what follows we are reporting on an historical case study, it is also a study of an authority which helped to provide the model for the system that is now in place, unless and until the nationalized industries model is replaced by the privatized industry model.

The experience and perceptions of members

It is tempting to imagine that not only the nature of water but also the very language associated with it has profoundly influenced its organization and production as a service and in particular, the distinctive style of its authority members. The duties and objectives of members are largely straightforward and clear, as we have seen, and this was reflected in interviews with members of the water authority in the study. These members exhibited an enthusiasm for their task not apparent in other public services where ambiguous roles and unclear objectives were muddying if not polluting members' assessment of their own activities.

In contrast to all the other services in our study, the members of the water authority impressed by their collective cohesion. There was no obvious difference between those nominated by ministers and those representing local authorities. They shared many common characteristics, even in terms of their previous experience. Most of them, even those from local authorities, had experience of water or water-related activities. All eight of the party political members were on local planning and resources or environmental committees for their authorities, two of them being expert on water engineering and sewage disposal. In all, ten members had direct water experience, and four others had management and business experience. Only one member, a county councillor, gave his trade as horse breeder and confessed to no relevant experience. Yet even he was a member of the county planning committee. The others included company directors, a retired naval officer, a landowner with fishing interests, a planning consultant, a farmer expert on land drainage, and an academic.

The Ogden Committee had in 1973 expressed some doubts about the mixed membership and relationships between members, in particular where local authority representatives 'may find it difficult to repress that instinctive response to geographical constituency considerations and where ministry-appointed members' interests may or may not coincide with the interests of the local authority members and considerable care will be needed by both members and officers to avoid conflicts deepening.'[20] In the event, members interviewed, whether ministerial or local authority nominees, were unanimous that elected representatives were neither too parochial nor party political. All said that there was no real difference between them in their enthusiasm and concern for the service. Two county council members added that too much politics in the water service would be a nonsense although both said it didn't happen anyway in their authority:

'Water is different, somehow. The members make a concerted effort for water. The ministry and local appointees don't have any particular constituency apart from water.'

(councillor member)

'Water is different . . . we know what we want, both officers and members, and we are almost totally united on the means of achieving these ends.'

(councillor member)

Members pooh-poohed the idea, put forward in justification of the 1983 reorganization, that elected councillors were bringing the less efficient style and attitude of local government services to the water services. They were emphatic that the reverse of this had actually happened and the style of the water authority had rubbed off on to local authority services. Councillors found the smaller size and business-like methods more satisfying. All the local government representatives, Labour and Conservative, stressed the advantages of the water authority over the public service committees, and how much less frustrating the experience was for them as members: in particular they appreciated the absence of politics and confrontational debate. In the words of one councillor member: 'If I had to choose between my membership of the council and of the water authority, I would choose the latter.'

If there was cohesion between the different kinds of members on the authority, equally there was cohesion between members and officers. This was based on mutual trust, respect, and a sense of partnership in an exciting venture:

'Full support and open house provided by officers to new members. It takes a while to learn the trade but eventually members get hooked. Water is absolutely fascinating.'

(ministry appointee)

'I felt initially, when I first became a member, that the chief officers were operating on a personal pride basis and I had confidence in the chief officers.'

(councillor member)

Members particularly praised the quality of the information supplied by chief officers to the authority, emphasizing the clarity and sharpness of documents prepared on sometimes very highly specialized and technically complicated subjects. They saw no attempts by officers to obscure issues with unnecessary detail or to assert a superior expertise. One possible explanation for this might be that, as noted above, water authority members themselves had considerable and varied expertise, whether about land drainage or finance. But the same was true of other services. In the case of the health authorities, as we have seen, there were medical members; in the case of the education committee, as we shall see, there were teacher members. However, in these services mutual expertise did not lead to the kind of mutual admiration between officers and members found in the water authority. Indeed, in other services, it created a sense of rivalry, conspicuous by its absence in the water authority where the expertise of members (whether financial or technical) was seen as making a valuable contribution to the authority and to the service as a whole.

This absence of rivalry, this sense of being involved in a common enterprise, in turn meant that members did not distinguish between their own roles and those of officers. In contrast to other services, they described themselves as working together with officers towards a common end. They referred to the authority as a co-ordinated group with a high level of solidarity and with no 'them' and 'us' attitude among either officers or members:

> 'Most decision-making comes from a think tank made up of officers and members. This feeling of solidarity comes from corporate planning ideology which makes everyone feel responsible for the whole organization. It gives more scope for long-term planning.'
>
> (councillor member)

> 'We all, officers and members, act together for the good of the water service . . . and expertise in finance and engineering is apparent in both officers and members.'
>
> (councillor member)

> 'There is a concerted effort between officers and members to give a service.'
>
> (ministry appointee)

'Authority members are unified and concerted in their authority interests.'

(councillor member)

Members were happy to leave the day-to-day management of the service to officers, acknowledging that it was a service which depended very much on operational efficiency. All members were at pains to emphasize the co-ordinated nature of the authority and the joint efforts of officers and members to produce the best possible service. In practice, the net result was that officers alone were concerned with operations, while both members and officers were involved in policy making.

All members attributed much of the success of the water service to a combination of clear aims and objectives, agreed methods of achieving them, and appropriate performance aims. Again, contrasts were made with other public services:

'We can work in the water authority in a way that is not possible in social services or education, as in these services there are no standard agreements on either the aims or methods of achieving them.'

(councillor member)

The degree of consensus on objectives cut across all members in spite of their very different backgrounds. So both local authority councillors and businessmen included considerations of costs and consumers in their objectives:

'Water is my objective – purity and quantity – all measurable and the right price for it.'

(councillor member)

'Schemes completed on time and in the right order of priority is what we are aiming for – this is the quality of the service.'

(councillor member)

'We would like to provide water to the user as cheaply as possible.'

(ministry appointee)

'My role as a member is to make water more efficient for the general public.'

(ministry appointee)

'Maintaining the top quality of water, I do know that our water service is the top quality although I know only about water and sewage.'

(councillor member)

Not only were members agreed on the overall objectives, but also they were agreed about the means of measuring and monitoring the performance of the service, that is progress towards the achievement of the objectives. Unlike any of the other sets of members in our study, they used and relied upon the standard indicators of performance. They were particularly impressed with water industry league tables comparing regional activities and costs. Unlike the others, too, they relied on ministry auditors as well as external consultants. And in all this, there was total trust in the information provided by chief officers whose reports were seen to be 'right to the point' and 'not too little, and not too much'.

Central to the system of evaluation, and an important indicator of the quality of the service, was the satisfaction of the consumer. Problems and enquiries as such were not considered by members to be complaints unless they had failed to be resolved by the departments at the appropriate levels. Members were only concerned with actual complaints which had reached them via this sifting system, and had therefore become a concern of the authority itself. To this end the water service had been organized to solve problems operationally with members making 'last resort' interventions. Having said this, all members, both ministry appointed and local councillors, said they received very few complaints and assumed that this indicated a high level of performance of the service. This attitude of water members followed the Ogden Committee's suggested ideal situation. The committee had envisaged the operational divisions as being the appropriate place for consumers to direct queries and complaints in the expectation that most of them would and should be solved at this level.

When it came to the subject of accountability, almost all the members said that both their accountability and responsibility was to the consumers and users of water in the region as a whole. Only two mentioned a specific accountability to the minister, both as a second place accountability after that to consumers; and only two said that their accountability was mainly to themselves. Most interesting, though, was the generally low priority members gave to accountability when discussing their role. They saw the act of being accountable as their routine pursuit of a good quality service rather than the act of answering to consumers.

The water authority members' version of downward accountability to the consumers was therefore crucially different from the way in which this was seen in other services. What they meant by this was a duty to ensure an efficient, responsive service, not a duty to be answerable directly to the consumer. In other services, while members stressed this answerability, in practice they had little contact with consumers. In the water authority, members probably had as much contact (indeed, they stressed the importance of local contacts and their own part in local networks of interests) but, as noted, they relied on the organization's own system for handling consumer complaints. Members saw it as their responsibility to ensure that the service was to the satisfaction of the consumer, and in doing so could draw on a battery of statistics showing the number of complaints and the way in which breakdowns were coped with, rather than relying on their own hands-on experience.

In short, most members did not see the need for any fuss about accountability. It was something routine, visible, and integral to the organization of the service:

> 'Accountability – probably too grand a word to apply to the role of members. Our job is to make water more efficient for the general public. There is a pride in doing something properly for its own sake and looking for efficiency for its own sake. There must be a large part of this in the measure of accountability.'
>
> (ministry appointee)

Summary

The members of the water authority were, quite simply, different in their perceptions from members of other services in this study. This was not because they were different kinds of people; quite apart from the local authority members, some of the ministry appointees had experience of the other services being studied. Nor was it because, in general terms, they saw their role in a different way from the members of other authorities; like the latter, they saw their objective as being to produce the best service for the community. The real difference lay in their high consensus, high morale, and the high level of trust between all members and officers. Uniquely, they gave the impression of a set of people who knew what they were doing, enjoyed doing it, and who were convinced that they were doing a good job for the community. There was none of the agonized hand-wringing about their own effectiveness and ability to control the service displayed by the members of other authorities.

In short, the water authority would suggest that the way in which members see their role reflects the characteristics of the service, rather than the characteristics of its constitutional status (that is whether or not it is elected). If they gave the impression of being depoliticized, it was not so much because they were dealing exclusively with technical issues which do not lend themselves to partisan divisions or horse trading: there is plenty of scope for politics, both local and party, about such issues as the siting of new plant and the metering of water. It was because the nature of the service, and in particular the clear relationship between inputs and objectives, gave members a sense of purpose and achievement. Trust and confidence were based on the absence of ambiguity and uncertainty. At least some members wistfully wanted to export the same style to other service committees on which they sat. If they saw accountability in a matter of fact, unproblematic way, it was because they saw the water service in the same fashion.

REFERENCES

1 This chapter was written just as the Conservative government announced its intention of privatizing the Water Industry (February 1986). In what follows, however, the analysis ignores possible future developments and concentrates on the existing situation.

2 Department of the Environment and Welsh Office (1973) *A Background to Water Reorganisation in England and Wales*. London: HSMO.

3 R. Klein (1983) *The Politics of the NHS*. London: Longman.

4 Department of the Environment and Welsh Office (1973) *A Background to Water Reorganisation in England and Wales.* London: HMSO: 8.
5 *The Water Industry in Figures* (1984) London: Water Authorities Association, November.
6 D. A. Okun (1977) *Regionalisation of Water Management.* London: Applied Science Publishers.
7 Department of the Environment, Welsh Office, Ministry of Agriculture, Fisheries and Food (1976) *Review of the Water Industry in England and Wales: A Consultative Document.* London: DoE: 16.
8 Management Structure Committee (Chairman: Sir George Ogden) (1973) *The New Water Industry.* London: HMSO.
9 Committee of Public Accounts (1985) *Eighteenth Report, Session 1984–85, Monitoring and Control of the Water Authorities.* London: HMSO HC 249, Q. 1089.
10 Committee of Public Accounts (1985) *Eighteenth Report, Session 1984–85, Monitoring and Control of the Water Authorities.* London: HMSO HC 249, Q. 1089: para. 12.
11 Monopolies and Mergers Commission (1981) *Severn–Trent Water Authority.* London: HMSO HC 339: paras 2.35–2.36.
12 Committee of Public Accounts (1985) *Eighteenth Report, Session 1984–85, Monitoring and Control of the Water Authorities.* London: HMSO HC 249, Q. 1085.
13 Committee of Public Accounts (1985) *Eighteenth Report, Session 1984–85, Monitoring and Control of the Water Authorities.* London: HMSO HC 249: 31–54. Also, Monopolies and Mergers Commission (1981) *Severn–Trent Water Authority.* London: HMSO HC 339: 34–58. The details that follow are drawn from these sources.
14 For a case study of pollution control, see K. Hawkins (1984) *Environment and Enforcement.* Oxford: Clarendon Press.
15 Committee of Public Accounts (1985) *Eighteenth Report, Session 1984–85, Monitoring and Control of the Water Authorities.* London: HMSO HC 249: para. 7.
16 National Water Council (1981) *Annual Report and Accounts 1980–81.* London: NWC.
17 Monopolies and Mergers Commission (1981) *Severn–Trent Water Authority.* London: HMSO HC 339: paras 11.156 and 11.161.
18 Department of the Environment Circular 16/83 (1983) *Water Act 1983.* 30 June. London: DoE.
19 W. Waldegrave (1983) One More Step Forward for the Water Industry. *Water Bulletin* 77, 30 September.
20 Management Structure Committee (Chairman: Sir George Ogden) (1973) *The New Water Industry.* London: HMSO.

7

Accountability and the education committee

In this chapter and in the following, we deal with the two services in our study which, in theory, conform most nearly to the traditional model of direct accountability to the people: education and social services. Both are local authority services, controlled by elected representatives answerable to the voters for what they do in that they may be turned out of office if the people don't like what they are doing. They would, therefore, seem to offer examples of accountability in the strict definition: answerability with sanctions if the answers fail to satisfy. Indeed, they are often cited as the paradigms to which the other services in our study – in particular police and health authorities – should conform. If only police and health authorities were directly elected, it is often argued, then the problems of accountability examined in the previous chapters would disappear: the role of members would be clear, unambiguous, and effective.

This particular thesis ignores, as we argued in the earlier chapters, the possibility that problems of accountability may derive as much from the nature of the services being delivered as from the institutions of political accountability. But before turning to examine the particular characteristics of education as a service (and to social services in the next chapter), we consider some of the general factors which make the notion of accountability problematic in the context of local government as a whole. In doing so, we elaborate and widen out some of the points already touched on in Chapter 2, without attempting to summarize the proliferating literature on the problems of local government. Specifically, we concentrate on the general implications for accountability of four themes which emerge from this literature, before exploring them in detail in the particular context of education. First, we consider the relationship between local and central government, and what this means for the accountability of elected members to the voters. Second, we consider the nature of the linkage between the members and the voters. Third, we consider the circumstances under which members actually exercise their responsibilities. Fourth, we consider the nature of the linkage between members and the services for which they are responsible.

To be accountable for one's actions or performance implies a certain measure of autonomy: a freedom to do otherwise than one has actually done. Thus, it would be a nonsense to talk about the accountability, as distinct from the reliability, of a robot whose actions are programmed by someone else. But the history of local government in the twentieth century has largely been the history also of diminishing autonomy. In part this reflects a trend towards national standards and models, determined by central government. In part, also, it reflects the increasing dependence of local government on central government finance, and the growing insistence by the centre on controlling the total amount spent by local authorities. It is a process which culminated in the 1980s when central government took the power to control the spending levels of individual local authorities. But already in 1976, long before this point was reached, the Layfield Committee was arguing that financial dependence was undermining accountability:[1]

'The effect of increases in local expenditure, whether arising from improvements in services or increased costs of maintaining services, being regularly met to a large extent from national taxation, and of local authorities coming to count on this aid, is to weaken accountability to local electorates. The sharp changes in the level of taxation unrelated to local expenditure decisions which can occur with comparatively small changes in grant distribution when grants are high, have the same consequences. Under these conditions the decisions on the amount of the grant and the distribution formulae come to assume crucial importance. At the same time, the government seeks to secure a total level of local government expenditure in line with its economic planning objectives and to restrain the rise in rate poundages. It is easy, therefore, to see how local authorities come to request, and the government to provide increasingly detailed specifications of the extent to which expenditure on individual services, and the components of services, should be varied – and how Ministers, local authorities and the public come to regard this guidance as having overriding importance. But, continued over a period, the process destroys local accountability.'

In other words, as local autonomy diminishes, as members 'own' fewer of their decisions, so does accountability to the voters, as distinct from accountability to central government. Furthermore, it is not only central government which constrains the autonomy of local authorities. To a large extent, decisions about how much they should pay their employees, and about conditions of work, have been taken out of their hands. It is national agreements which determine wage and salary levels and conditions of employment, thus inhibiting the ability of individual local authorities to control their budgets and to deploy their staff as they wish.[2] Once again, therefore, local autonomy is constrained and diminished.

Public perceptions of this process of diminishing autonomy may be one of the factors in explaining, to turn to the second of our themes, why linkages betwen elected members and voters appear to be fraying, as already noted in Chapter 3. Apathy rules in local elections; low turn-outs are the rule. Why bother to call elected members to account if the latter can make only incremental, marginal decisions about the services for which they are nominally responsible? It is therefore not surprising that the outcome of local elections seems to be determined by national voting trends and national negotiations rather than local issues, if it is the perform-ance of the national government rather than that of the local authority which is called to account. 'For the councillor', it has been argued, 'electoral defeat is not so much a vehicle of accountability as a visitation akin to death – a phenomenon whose possible occurrence must be acknowledged but whose incidence cannot be planned against, and which is therefore rarely a factor in decision taking.'[3] The problem of the councillor's accountability to his or her electors is further compounded by the growing emphasis, particularly evident in the Labour Movement in recent years, on accountability to the party. If decisions are increasingly taken in party caucuses,[4] and if the individual councillor is seen to be answerable for his or her actions, either to the caucus or to the local party, then it is once again unclear to what extent he or she can be seen to 'own' those actions, that is to be an autonomous actor, responsible for what is done. While it may well be argued that a system of binding party decisions strengthens collective party accountability to the electorate, the price may be to weaken the linkage between the individual councillor and the voters.

The point is all the more important because, to turn to our third theme, the environment of accountability in local government is very different from that in central government. In contrast to central government, the distinction between ministers and members of parliament – between those accountable for performance and those who hold them accountable – is blurred. Local government is government by committee. Thus it has been argued that: 'Where many are responsible, no one is responsible. How can we find out where authority and responsibility lies, so that we may initiate proposals or apportion praise or blame?'[5] Given the lack of a highly visible executive, given the diffusion of responsibility, it has been argued further that accountability is not 'a major concern' to individual councillors.[6]

In effect, then, the councillor combines the roles of a minister and that of a backbencher if he or she is a member of a ruling party. In the former role, he or she is responsible for overall policy or performance; in the latter role he or she is responsible to his or her constituents for the impact of policy or performance. It is precisely this tension which helps to explain both the emphasis of successive committee reports on focusing the councillor's role on policy issues, as noted in Chapter 2, and their failure to transform the actual patterns of local government: to establish a clear demarcation between the role of members (setting policy objectives) and that of officers (policy implementation). In the academic literature, councillors tend to be divided between those who see themselves as delegates, the voice of their constituents, and those who see themselves as trustees, following their own judgement.[7] But even if the councillors do not see themselves as being answerable to their constituents, they may well be dependent on maintaining local support if they are to keep their seats; taking up constituency grievances, doing case work on behalf of their voters, may be a necessary condition for retaining the support of their local ward party.[8]

If the need for political survival helps to explain the reluctance of councillors to give up their backbench role in favour of adopting an exclusively 'ministerial' stance, so may the problems faced by part-timers in trying to keeping a grip on large and complex organizations faced, increasingly in the 1980s, with a turbulent financial environment. Despite the recommendations for stream-lining the work of councils, made in the 1960s, the actual workload of councillors has increased. Whereas the average councillor spent twenty-nine hours a month on committee work in 1964, by 1977 this had risen to fifty-four hours. Whereas the average councillor spent eight hours a month on dealing with the problems of electors, by 1977 this had risen to thirteen hours.[9] Averages may be deceptive; some councillors have become, in effect, full-timers. But the conclusion drawn in 1969 by Heclo, in his study of councillors, would seem to be as applicable today as it was then:[10]

'The basic source of many difficulties in the councillor's job lies in the tension between the assumed nature of the councillor as a voluntary amateur and the facts of life in a complex local authority. It is valid to say that the councillor is meant to represent the public's ordinary, non-specialist view, but this does not mean that the councillor can do so simply by being an ordinary non-specialist himself. Such representation is not likely to be meaningful unless the councillor has the time and resources to study and comprehend what is going on around him.'

From this perspective the preoccupation of councillors with detail, rather than policy or performance, represents an under-standable psychological strategy for coping with the conflicting expectations held of them. Thus Heclo argues that: 'the trivial details may not be something which are forced on councillors but something which they seize upon almost with desperation in what is otherwise an unmanageable situation'.

There is little evidence that the trend in local government towards a more managerial, corporate style of decision-making has resolved this tension. Indeed, it may have introduced some new problems, particularly in respect of the linkage between the members and the services for which they are responsible (to turn to our fourth and last theme). If members are to be accountable for the services for which they are responsible, then in turn the services have to be accountable to them, that is they have to exercise control over what is happening. In turn, this line of accountability runs through the chief officers in charge of these services. But the role of the chief officers has been subtly affected by the development of a corporate style of management in local government. This stresses the concentrated co-ordination of decision-making both at the chief officer and the member level: hence, the development of chief officer teams and policy committees. Whatever the advantages of such a system, one effect may be to blur lines of accountability. If a chief officer is part of a management team, responsible for collective decisions, he or she can no longer be exclusively accountable to the committee charged with running his or her particular service. Moreover, the development of key policy committees, often explicitly charged with developing a coherent *party* strategy for all the council services, may also call into question what has been called the traditional local government model of officer/member accountability.[11] This sees the officers serving the council as a whole, treating all members as equal. In contrast, what has been called the civil service model sees the officers accountable to the majority party. To the extent that local government has moved towards a centralized style of decision-making about major issues of policy, as determined by the majority party, so there also appears to have been a shift in the way some officers perceive the locus of their own accountability.[12]

The role of chief officers, and their relationship to members, will be further explored in the context of the two services, education and social services, which we examine in the rest of this chapter and the next. But two related general developments, crucial to the linkage between members and the services for which they are responsible, need first to be noted. They are well illustrated by a discussion of the problems of accountability as seen by a local authority member, with long experience of the role, Margaret Simey.[13] To talk of accountability, she argues, is to talk of control. But the control of local authority members has been eroded by two trends. First, in Margaret Simey's view:

'the administration of public services now amounts to a system of workers' control by those employed in them so far reaching as to be beyond the dreams of the most idealistic of revolutionaries. Selection and entry, training and qualifications, conditions of employment and the deployment of manpower and resources – all these are to a large extent controlled by those who are themselves employed in the service. Less evidently, but even more effectively, it is in reality they who decide what sort of facilities would best meet the needs of the community the service is intended to benefit.'

Second, Simey points out, the officers' perception of themselves as professionals or experts has increased their sensitivity to what is seen as political meddling. It is they, in effect, who claim to determine how accountability is to be exercised:

'Theirs is thought to be the active role. It is for them to provide information and write reports, to justify their existence and defend their activities. By implication, although this is never stated, the elected members sit passively at the receiving end. How they are supposed to audit the "accounts" rendered to them is a matter on which little guidance is available; and it is perhaps for this reason that many members settle for officer-knocking or drift into the actual running of the services.'

To translate this conclusion into the language of our own analysis, the power of the service-providers – their ability to evade the control of elected members – would seem to rest on their power also to determine the currency of accountability. There is no agreed language of evaluation for, as Margaret Simey further argues, while efficiency may be relatively easy to measure, it is questions of effectiveness which are crucial to members: 'Facts and figures cannot measure the "value" of a foster parent as against that of an ambulance driver or a teacher. The cynicism with which crime statistics are coming to be regarded illustrates the difficulty of pinning on paper the effectiveness of a service.' It may, of course, be argued that it is precisely the role of politics to create through dialogue and discussion such a language of evaluation. In what follows, however, we adopt a more limited perspective (leaving the wider issues for the concluding chapter) and concentate on the attempts to provide a technical input of evaluation into local government and the effects, if any, on the way in which members perceive their role. In particular, we examine the extent to which members are influenced in their role by the work of the Audit Commission, with its general remit to examine not only the propriety of expenditure decisions but also value-for-money issues,[14] and the specialized inspectorates concerned with education and the social services.

Education, the profession, central and local government

Of all the services directly provided by local authorities, education is by far the biggest. Expenditure on education represented about 45 per cent of all current spending by local authorities in England in 1984/85: four times the proportion devoted to either the police or to social services.[15] It is a local authority service, moreover, in the strict sense. In contrast to the police, education is wholly funded out of the local authority budget; there is no central goverment block grant. Equally, it is a service which is the responsibility of elected local authority members. Under the Education Act, 1944, local authorities are required to set up education committees with a majority of elected members, although there is also provision for the co-option of representatives of the teaching profession (who have voting rights; an interesting example of worker representation), the main religious denominations and industrial, commercial, and agricultural interests. It is the statutory responsibility of those local education committees (LEAs), in turn, to execute national policies. In exploring the practice of accountability in education, we are therefore examining the way in which members perceive their role in being answerable both for executing national policies and using their discretion in those areas where they have autonomy or at least scope for manoeuvre.

For national policies in the case of education are a mixture of the very general and the very particular.[16] Thus Section 7 of the Education Act, 1944, requires LEAs 'to contribute towards the spiritual, moral, mental and physical development of the community by securing that efficient education' shall be available to meet the needs of their areas. They are further required to ensure that schools in their area are sufficient in number, character, and equipment and that they offer such a variety of instruction and training as may be desirable in view of the different ages, abilities, and aptitudes of the pupils. So far, so general. But LEAs are also required to 'make arrangements for enabling the parent of a child to express a preference as to the school at which he wishes education to be provided for his child' (under the Education Act, 1980) and to set up an appeals committee for parents who have been refused their preferred school. They are further required to carry out a series of very specific duties, such as securing 'that the person or clothing of any pupil found to be infested with vermin or in foul condition shall be cleansed at suitable premises with suitable appliances'. The legislation also enshrines the power of the secretary of state for education to determine the overall pattern of school provision. Thus, the Education Act, 1976 (partially repealed by the 1979 Act) imposed a duty on local authorities to submit plans for a system of comprehensive schools. And no school can be opened or closed or changed in character without the approval of the secretary of state.

In their exercise of accountability, members of LEAs are therefore operating in conditions of constrained freedom. While LEAs have a statutory obligation to provide a school place for every child below the statutory school-leaving age, lacking the freedom of either health or police authorities or indeed social services to determine the demands made on them, they have considerable discretion about the resources which will be invested in each place. One set of figures will illustrate this point. In 1985/86 unit costs per child varied in metropolitan LEAs from £661 to £881 in primary schools, and from £981 to £1,411 in secondary schools; in county LEAs the variations were from £647 to £823 and from £1,007 to £1,163 respectively.[17] These figures may exaggerate the extent to which LEAs have freedom at any one point in time to determine the inputs (and may therefore be held accountable for them) to the extent that spending levels tend to be a function of historical trends, local social conditions, and lags in adjusting to changes in the size of the school age cohort: given central government restrictions on the overall level of local authority spending, the scope for affecting inputs is thus at best marginally incremental. However, the element of discretion is real, if narrow.

If LEA members can be thought to be answerable, if only to a limited extent, for the inputs into the education system, in that they have a degree of discretion in determining the resources for any given level of demand, the problems of accountability become more confused and complex when we turn to processes and outcomes: to what happens in schools, and what comes out of them. But before analysing these in detail, it is important to put them into context. For education is unique among our services in that, for the best part of a decade, its very purpose has been questioned in a national debate that still goes one. It is a debate about what the aims of education should be, and who should determine them; a debate, moreover, which reflects deep-rooted differences not only about what the role of education should be in shaping society but also about what kind of society it should be shaping. It was launched in 1976 by James Callaghan, the then Labour Prime Minister, in his Ruskin College speech, when he called for a national discussion about the 'subject matter and purpose of education', stressing that 'parents, teachers, learned and professional bodies, representatives of higher education and both sides of industry, together with the government, all have an important part to play in formulating and expressing the purposes of education and the standards that we need.'[18] It has simmered on ever since. Although there were signs by the mid-1980s of a similar if minor key reappraisal of the role of the police and the social services, education remains unique for the length and intensity of this painful experience. It is an experience which has spawned a large literature on accountability in education and which provides the essential backcloth for our own analysis. Perhaps the most significant aspect of Callaghan's 1976 speech, from the perspective of this chapter at any rate, is the omission of the LEAs from his list of those who should be involved in the 'great debate' about education. If accountability is dialogue about what should be done, and what the currency of evaluation should be in assessing progress towards the achievement of agreed aims, then LEAs were conspicuously absent from his cast list of those taking part.

In contrast to the United States of America, the main concern of the accountability debate (in Britain) has been with 'schools and the teaching profession rather than with the government system', it has been argued.[19] It is central government which has challenged the right of teachers to determine what goes on in schools, the nature of the curriculum taught, and the standards achieved, bypassing LEAs. In doing so, it has also by implication challenged the traditional interpretation of their statutory duties by LEAs, which have tended to view their responsibility for providing education 'as a matter of administering resources rather than prescribing their use. The latter has largely been the prerogative of headteachers and their professional staff in schools.'[20] In short, the 'great debate' in education has made explicit a problem which is common to all labour-intensive public services: how can service-providers (whether or not they are seen as professionals) be called to account for the way in which they use resources? In what follows, we shall explore some of the main issues raised before returning to the role of LEAs.

A number of competing models of accountability have been put forward in this debate by academic theorists.[21] They fall into three main groups. First, there is the traditional public model of accountability, which sees teachers as having a contractual relationship with the State, that is a contract which specifies what they should be doing, and lays down criteria for measuring the products of schools. Second, there is the professional accountability model. In this model, 'teachers become, in effect, an elite, protected from accountability to the elected political leadership. They sustain, however, their moral position by explicit modes of self-account and by the requirement to establish procedures through which processes will be explicit.' Lastly, there is what might be called the explanatory model of accountability (to use the phrase coined by Marshall in his analysis of the role of the chief constable; see Chapter 5). This is seen to involve dialogue or a 'partnership' with parents; the accountability of teachers is seen to reside in their duty to explain what they are doing, in particular to parents. To oversimplify, these might be classified as models of upward managerial accountability, professional accountability, and downward accountability. Each raises questions about the locus of control (who determines the aims of education?) and the currency of evaluation to be used.

The model of public accountability is implicit in many of the policies pursued by central government since 1976, especially since the Conservatives took office in 1979 (although there has also been a flirtation with the idea of downward accountability: see pp. 170–73). A variety of strategies have been pursued in an attempt to specify the nature of the 'contract' with teachers. For contrary to the requirements of a contractual theory of accountability, the actual contract with teachers (as in other occupations) is fuzzy when it comes to defining positive duties and the nature of the job – a vagueness that has generated contention, strife, and legal disputes. The Department of Education has produced a series of documents which seek to develop objectives for the curriculum.[22] It also set up an Assessment of Performance Unit, designed to develop criteria for assessing outcomes. More recently, it has directly attacked the notion of professional self-regulation by proposing a system for grading the classroom performance of teachers; the aim, in the words of the secretary of state for education, was to apply 'to the teaching force standards of management which have become common elsewhere'.[23] In short, the public accountability model has been developed in a way which stresses the role of central government, rather than that of LEAs.

However, there is little sign as yet of an agreed language or currency of evaluation. The concern about accountability in education largely reflects anxiety about the products of schools, that is the children leaving them. Shaping much of the discussion was the widespread belief that children were leaving schools without the appropriate skills, at an adequate standard, required in the labour market. This would suggest an outcome approach to the assessment of performance, that is measuring whether school-leavers have the appropriate skills at an adequate standard required to find employment. But such an approach depends, crucially, on social consensus about the objectives and conceptual tools for measuring progress towards their achievement. Neither exists. The notion of performance in education is contestable precisely because there are multiple aims,[24] and because of the conceptual perplexities involved in trying to devise tools of assessment. The two are linked. Producing school-leavers with particular sets of skills is only one aim of education. Assessing the performance of schools in terms of the skills (or examination results) of their products, therefore, encounters two difficulties. The first is that if the definition of performance is too narrow, the perverse result may be high performance but poor education. The point was made over a century ago by that most famous of all Her Majesty's Inspectors, Matthew Arnold, when protesting against the system which made grants to schools dependent on the performance of their pupils in three examinations: reading, writing, and arithmetic. Denouncing the change, Arnold wrote:[25]

'In a country where everyone is prone to rely too much on mechanical processes, and too little on intelligence, a change in the Education Department's regulations, which by making two thirds of the Government grant depend upon a mechanical examination, inevitably gives a mechanical turn to the school teaching, a mechanical turn to the inspection, is and must be trying to the intellectual life of a school. . . . Meanwhile, the matters of language, geography and history, by which, in general, instruction first gets hold of a child's mind and becomes stimulating and interesting to him, have in the great majority of schools fallen into disuse and neglect.'

Furthermore, Arnold argues, the problem would not be overcome by changing the incentives:

'In the game of mechanical contrivances, the teachers will in the end beat us; and as it is now found possible, by ingenious preparation, to get children through the Revised Code examination in reading, writing and ciphering, without their really knowing how to read, write or cipher, so it will, with practice, no doubt be found possible to get children . . . through the examination in grammar, geography and history, without their really knowing any one of these three matters.'

The second difficulty in trying to measure the performance of schools is that (as in the case of health and the police) the level of inputs is only one factor – and by no means the most important – in determining outcomes. Overwhelmingly the evidence suggests that it is the social background of the children which explains most of the variations of outcomes measured by examination results. For example, a statistical analysis carried out by the DES, in an attempt to explain variations in the examination performance of pupils in different LEAs, found that results were strongly associated with socio-economic variables but not with the input of resources.[26] This is not to claim that schools make no difference; there is indeed evidence that school style is linked to performance.[27] But it is to argue that performance indicators, based on examination results, are shot through with ambiguity. They do not speak for themselves but need interpretation; most members of LEAs (or parents, for that matter) are not, after all, experts in regression analysis, capable of teasing out the contribution of the school and its teachers to measures of performance influenced by a variety of other factors.

As against the results-based, public-control-based model of accountability, there is opposed the process-based, professional model of accountability.[28] The proponents of this model argue that the focus of accountability should be not on results ('the mere testing of results assumes that a teacher has greater control than is possible') but on the schooling process ('within which much more sophisticated judgements may be made about a teacher's effectiveness'). The emphasis is on self-assessment by schools: the production of 'accounts', or explanations of their conduct, by the schools themselves.[29] It is further argued that if changed be needed, it should be in the direction of professional self-government by the teachers themselves: the development of professional bodies and professional codes (on the medical model) which would lay down principles of syllabus construction, assessment, and styles of teaching, as well as providing for disciplinary procedures and the redress of grievances.

Perhaps the most significant aspect of this approach, from the perspective of analysing the role of LEAs, is the justification given for arguing against the hierarchic, managerial public control model of accountability. Not only is this criticized as excessively 'mechanistic', a word which stalks through the literature produced by educationalists (starting, of course, with Matthew Arnold), but also it is attacked as failing to capture all the various dimensions of accountability. Thus it is argued that teachers are accountable, if only in the weak sense of having to explain themselves, to a variety of groups. For example the headmaster of a secondary school, in a discussion of accountability, has listed the government of the day, the LEA, the governing body, parents, and employers as the agencies and groups to which he sees himself as accountable.[30] To stress managerial accountability is, in this view, to subvert the teacher's wider accountability to society and to his or her clients, that is the children and their parents. Conversely, of course, to stress multiple accountability is to subvert the principle of hierarchical managerial accountability, to advocate the replacement of a system where the duty to explain is backed by sanctions (in theory, at least) by one in which the obligation to give an account to a variety of audiences becomes part of the professional ethos; a means, furthermore, of legitimizing the claims of teachers to professional status.

Leaving aside the prescriptive arguments of the professional model, it seems clear that descriptively it gives a more convincing picture of how schools and teachers perceive their own accountability than the public control model. This emerges clearly from a study of how, and to whom, teachers in practice see themselves accountable.[31] This found that a majority of teachers 'feel primarily accountable to one another and collectively accountable to clients'. But they 'lack any strong sense of contractual obligation to their LEA or its representatives. It was rare indeed to come across staff, even heads, who felt hierarchically accountable in this way.' Furthermore, the study concluded:

> 'Faced with a choice between greater contractual accountability to the LEA and greater answerability, there is little doubt that they [teachers] would opt for the latter. In fact, there was evidence that they were consciously trying to become more answerable to parents in order to counter pressures towards greater contractual accountability already being exerted "from above".'

In short, the production of self-accounts by schools, the opening of a dialogue with parents, can be seen as a defensive strategy for creating a constituency of support designed to weaken attempts to move towards a hierarchical system of managerial accountability by LEAs (or central government). Downward accountability is invoked in order to resist upward accountability; giving an account is seen to be a way of avoiding being called to account. Teachers, like the police, are left in control of the language of evaluation.

However, it would be a mistake to see this exclusively as a strategy of expediency, designed only to stave off moves towards greater managerial accountability. Teachers, as argued in Chapter 3, are precariously perched on the ladder of professionalism. Their status is ambiguous. And one of the characteristics of a profession, seen in the most highly developed form in the case of doctors, is precisely the emphasis on individual responsibility to clients rather than collective accountability to management. To the extent that teachers aspire to recognition as professionals, that is a body of service providers which has successfully privatized the language of evaluation, so inevitably they are led to stressing their responsibility to the client. But lacking the strength of the medical profession (so far doctors have not needed to invoke their accountability to patients in order to stave off demands for public accountability) they are forced to try to form an alliance with them.

It is this which perhaps explains the growing popularity of the explanatory model of accountability, and the consequent attempts to strengthen the role of school governors and to encourage the participation of parents in the government of schools over the past decade. The irony of this is that it brings into coalition two partners with opposed interests. For the teachers it represents, as argued above, a strategy for legitimizing the professional model. For the government, and in particular the present Conservative administration, it represents a strategy for mobilizing parent power to balance teacher power, on the assumption that the former will force the latter to be more responsive to the needs of society. Add to this a more general, societal scepticism about professional claims and enthusiasm for participatory democracy (that ambiguous, versatile phase), and it is not surprising that the 'great debate' about education has coincided with growing interest in changing school government. In 1977 the Taylor Committee recommended that school governing bodies should include representatives of LEAs, school staff, parents, and the local community.[32] These bodies, the committee argued, 'should be given by the local education authority the responsibility for setting the aims of the school, for considering the means by which they are pursued, for keeping under review the school's progress towards them, and to decide upon actions to facilitate such progress', that is that accountability should be devolved. These recommendations are only now being implemented.[33] But in the 1980s the government has taken a variety of steps designed to make schools more responsive to parents, in line with the explanatory accountability model. So, for example, Section 8 of the Education Act, 1980, requires local education authorities to provide each year a range of information about their schools to parents, including admission arrangements and examination results. Furthermore, the reports of Her Majesty's Inspectorate (HMI) on individual schools have been published since 1983, and are in theory available to parents.

There are a number of problems about this approach. The assumption that strengthening school governing bodies by involving parents will make teachers more answerable is put into question by the evidence of at least one study; that of the Sheffield school system where parent representation was introduced in the 1970s.[34] This concludes that the role of the new bodies is 'likely to remain marginal and symbolic', and that parents are absorbed by the existing power structure of the education system rather than changing it:

'although most parental representatives in Sheffield had some fairly general knowledge of education, typically based upon a combination of their own experiences as school children and a smattering of the popular educational culture found in magazines, television programmes, and Sunday colour supplements, they were in the main unfamiliar with the policies, techniques, philosophies or even linguistic codes used in their child's particular school. Consequently, most parents were forced by the logic of this situation to look towards the headteacher for guidance on the policy of the school, and to the chairman or clerk for guidance on the policy of the local authority. Thus, in order to be active within their own local school system, the parental representative was forced by the logic of his structural situation to enter into a *de facto* pupil relationship with the headteacher. . . . Naturally, people entering this type of dependent social relationship were generally unlikely to want to raise general questions of aims and ends which might facilitate a greater degree of responsiveness or accountability to the client interest. . . . Consequently they mainly concerned themselves with those more tangible, if mundane matters, concerned with fund raising, maintaining the school's fabric and taking part in annual ceremonial events.'

If there is any 'partnership' with parents, it would seem, therefore, to be a very unequal one – posing little threat to teacher dominance. The findings would seem to support the view expressed in a minority dissenting note to the Taylor Committee by the chairman of a LEA, Mr P. O Fulton, who argued that its recommendations would devolve responsibility to a body 'without any accountability' and eventually lead 'to the position where what goes on in schools will become the sole province of the teacher'.[35] The problems of accountability would seem to be deeply rooted in the asymmetry of information between service providers and consumers.[36] And even when schools have statutory obligation to provide information, they still have a large degree of discretion about how to select and present it. Thus, one survey of school reports (or 'self-accounts') found that 'many schools waste a lot of time, money and effort in producing unattractive, uninformative material; the result is that a majority of schools don't produce a proper annual report at all'.[37] So the evidence would seem to support the view that a strategy of downward, explanatory accountability is indeed a strategy for teachers to make sure that any dialogue will be carried out largely on their own terms.

There is, of course, one independent source of information about the performance of schools, the reports of HMIs, as already mentioned.[38] The inspectorate, in effect, addresses two audiences. On the one hand, its role is to interpret what is happening in schools (and elsewhere in the education world) to the government. On the other hand, it is also responsible for interpreting the government's policies to schools. It reports annually on the overall performance of the schooling system, and in particular on the effects of expenditure policies. So it may criticize the level of spending of individual LEAs as inadequate or point to the

174   Accountabilities

consequences of government constraints on public expenditure;
thus a 1982 report reported that 'Many primary and secondary
schools have found themselves obliged by a combination of
resource reductions and falling rolls to concentrate on the middle
range of pupils with a consequence that the educational needs of
the most and least able are not adequately reflected in either
curriculum or organisation.'[39] Equally it reports on individual
schools. These reports review the curriculum and organization of
the school, with sections on the 'quality of classroom experience'
and the 'quality of the school community'. They may criticize in
detail the style and content of teaching as well as commenting
more generally on the school, sometimes quite severely. For
example, in the case of one school, the HMI report concludes
'Educational standards, as evidenced by classroom work and
examination results, are not high, even taking into account the
ability range represented in the school';[40] another comments:
'Some heads of department could show stronger leadership in
curricular thinking and in staff development. Standards of work
are, in the main, acceptable but limited in scope for the able pupils
who are not sufficiently challenged or encouraged to explore their
undoubted talents.'[41] But although the HMI reports offer a rich
source of information about the performance of schools, it is
information perceived through the lenses of the service-providers.
HMIs are in the business of propagating best practices as defined
by the teaching profession itself:[42]

> 'In their reports and their advice, HMIs use no blueprints, wave
> no magic wands. They offer the best professional judgements
> they can about what they see when they visit education
> institutions, administrative offices or professional bodies and
> associations. . . . Perhaps their most significant characteristics
> are their professional independence from government, local
> authorities and teachers and their obligation to report as they
> find without fear or favour.'

In other words, inspection, as with the advisers or inspectors
employed by individual LEAs, is about peer judgement by
professionals reviewing the work of their fellow professionals. It
fits, therefore, most neatly into the professional model of

accountability. The extent to which it feeds into the public model is, of course, another matter, as the inspectorate has recognized: 'The routes by which inspection reports reach those directly involved in education are fairly clear, though the process of making sure that all teachers and lecturers see the report on their institution could be improved. The routes to parents, the wider community and local councillors are less developed.'[43] In particular, the extent to which HMI reports are perceived by members of LEAs as part of the accountability process is far from clear.

Straddling the worlds of the service providers – those who see themselves, although they are not necessarily seen, as professionals – and members, is the LEA's chief education officer (CEO). He or she is the statutory link (every local authority has to appoint one) between the members and the service providers. To explore this role, which fortunately is well documented, is also to explore the problem of accountability, seen as getting a grip on or control over the service concerned as the necessary if not sufficient condition for being held answerable for it. The first point to note is that most CEOs, like teachers generally, see themselves as being accountable to a variety of audiences. Of the sixty-one CEOs interviewed by Bush and Kogan,[44] thirty-one saw themselves accountable to the council as a whole, forty-three to the education committee, twenty-eight to the chief executive, and fifteen to their professional peers (the numbers add up to more than sixty-one, since each CEO was free to give more than one answer). As one of the CEOs interviewed put it, 'accountability is a two-way process, not simply vertically hierarchical. Therefore, I feel accountable to heads of schools and colleges, to the teaching profession as a whole, to my own staff, and to the public.' Indeed, some CEOs go further than this. They see themselves both as the representatives of the professional interest – or as one put it, 'the chief education officer, in my view, is in the last resort accountable to his professional conscience'[45] – and also as best equipped to define the needs of the community as a whole. In the words of one such CEO, interviewed in the 1970s:[46]

'A CEO and other officers can be said to represent the community much more than any one individual councillor, or indeed, very often a group of councillors. A CEO knows his

area, knows its educational and other needs much better than
any individual lay councillor is likely to do.'

But if the CEO is to be an effective link between members and
service-providers in the chain of accountability, he must not only
be answerable to the former but also be able to control the latter.
For how can she or he answer for the performance of schools to
the LEA if she or he is not effectively in control of their activities?
This question raises the second important issue to emerge from
studies of the role of the CEO. As Bush and Kogan put it:[47]

'The education service differs from other local government
service in that the great majority of employees work within
institutions separate from the town or county office. Schools
and colleges are separate entities, staffed largely by professionals who expect and enjoy discretion in carrying out their
teaching role. The relationship between the CEO and head or
principal is not, therefore, that of a manager-subordinate, as is
found in the social services, or housing or other local authority
departments. Both are senior professionals yet both work
within a setting of public accountability.'

In the outcome, most CEOs appear to feel that they have
persuasive or investigatory authority, but no direct managerial
authority. While CEOs vary in the extent to which they are
prepared to contemplate intervening in the affairs of a school, and
in the last resort to remove the headmaster, they all seem agreed
that they are not in a hierarchical, managerial relationship with
them. In the words of one CEO:[48]

'I would be reluctant to be in a position of an officer trying to
enforce my conception of education on them. All I would do
was to set out the case, try to persuade them and if they didn't
accept my advice, to accept the decision.'

All this would suggest that the linkages between LEA members
and the providers, and their ability to control the performance of
the service for which they are answerable to voters, are more frail
and tenuous than the strict doctrine of local government account-

ability would require. More generally, as our necessarily brief review of developments over the past decade suggests, LEA members are in a somewhat anomalous position. The 'great debate' about the aims and content of education, and the consequent implications for accountability, has largely excluded them. They find themselves in a kind of no-man's land, caught between those who wish to strengthen upward accountability to central government and those who want to strengthen downward accountability to individual schools, their governing bodies, and parents. At the same time, LEA members are exhorted to direct a more efficient management of education at a time where there are also populist pressures for devolving responsibility to the community. They are constrained by national public expenditure policies and national agreements about salaries and conditions of work, while yet being urged to be more responsive to the preferences of parents. It is against this background of tensions, and conflicting expectations, that we now turn to the perceptions of accountability of the members of the LEA in our study.

The experience and perceptions of members

Providing adequate facilities for all compulsory-school-age children, making primary, secondary, and further education efficient and sufficient to meet the needs of their area and through this provision, making 'a contribution towards the spiritual, moral, mental and physical development of the community' has to be a huge and complex task for members of local education committees. Add to this the traditional autonomy and remoteness enjoyed by educational establishments and the decision-making partnership between parents, local authorities, governors, and schools urged by the Education Act, 1980, as discussed in the previous section, then this complex task becomes positively daunting. So how do members, elected and co-opted, deal with this situation and how do they see their role? Nowhere in legislation, either ancient or modern, does it say what kind of skill or expertise is best suited to education membership, only that most members should be local, elected councillors with a small number of co-opted trade union, religious, and community representatives as voting members.

As already noted, education is different from other public services in as much as the policy and operations tug of war involves consumers as well as officers, members, and professionals. Further, how things are done in schools appears to be as crucial as what is done, with the not unexpected consequence of fudged distinctions between inputs, process, and outcomes.

The analysis of the perceptions of education committee members shows that the short answer to how they define and execute their role within this complex situation is – with difficulty. In an educational service racked by debate about its purpose, beset by falling rolls and years of inconsistent central government instructions on comprehensive education, most councillors were uncertain about the objectives of the service in their area, except for the very general aim of 'producing the best education service for the county with the best possible use of resources'. The litany of general aims also included improving the quality of education, enabling children to achieve their potential and meeting the statutory duties for the education of 5- to 16-year-olds. Surprisingly even those Labour councillors who saw their objectives as being defined by their party tended to make this point in general terms rather than spelling out the specific commitments (to introducing peace studies, abolishing corporal punishment in schools, and providing more facilities for under-fives). The following quotations provide a sample of the generalities produced by councillors of all parties:

> 'My aim is to improve the quality of education in county schools.'
>
> > (Liberal member)
>
> 'My priority aim is always the best use of resources.'
>
> > (Conservative member)
>
> 'Basically, the objective of the Education Service is contained in the policy document of the Labour Party.'
>
> > (Labour member)

Given the vague generality of most of the objectives, it is not surprising that members found it difficult to specify the language of evaluation, or currency of accountability, which they were using or which, in their opinion, could be used. Thus, as we have seen,

they talked about the 'best use of resources' as one of their
objectives: which would suggest a hard-nosed approach to
analysing services in terms of the relationship between inputs and
outputs. In fact, there was little evidence of this. Half the members
were emphatic that public services in general and education in
particular could not be examined in precise, quantitative terms.
So, for example, the councillors split down the middle in their
views as to whether or not it was possible to assess value for
money; a division which, as the following two quotations make
clear, did not reflect differences between parties:

'Most local authority services cannot be looked at in terms of
value for money. It can't be seen. All members can do is to be a
watchdog.'

(Labour member)

'You can measure value for money in education in pupil/teacher
ratios, capital works, and three-year infant education in
schools.'

(Labour member)

The scepticism about the possibility of using 'value for money' as
the tool of evaluation tapped a deeper sense of unease. There was
widespread doubt as to whether it was possible to measure the
outputs of the education system: whether, in particular, examination results could be used as an indicator of either efficiency in
the use of resources or of quality:

'The quality of education cannot be measured by examination
results, in schools most certainly. However, the committee can
look at the correct provision of physical and manpower resources.
In addition, the organization of education in the county can be
monitored. That is the changing over to comprehensive
education.'

(Labour member)

'Education results are not very useful as an indicator of
education service performance.'

(Conservative member)

But if it is impossible to use examination results or other measures
of outputs, then it follows that it is also impossible to adopt a

strict value-for-money approach by measuring efficiency (since this is concerned with the relationship between inputs and outputs). Perhaps even more important, the logic of rejecting output indicators is to put exclusive emphasis on inputs: to make the quantity of inputs the language of evaluation. Indeed, some members appeared to take this line, and to think that the only real measure of performance was the growth of resources put into the system. But other members clearly felt uneasy about looking only at inputs and were beginning to feel that it might be necessary to examine the connection between resources going into the system and what was coming out at the other end. Only one councillor was able to articulate this point clearly, stressing that examination results could actually be used as an indication of quality and effectiveness:

'Assessing the service for the majority of members and officers and the teaching profession is about inputs into the service. There is little regard or discussion about the outputs. There is a general reluctance to assess the outcomes of the service for three main reasons:

1 Reluctance to change.
2 Profession sees itself in danger of being evaluated and does not want to be accountable.
3 Neither officers nor members like comparisons between authorities.

We know that across the county 40 per cent of children leave school with no qualifications at all, and it should be possible with some weighting factors to make comparisons countrywide between authorities on 'A' level and 'O' level and CSE results. We could compare the top 20 per cent of pupils in each LEA to see how the quality of our product rates with other authorities. The DES has not provided the service with any performance aims, so "value for money" is missing from the educational service aims. What we are left with in the education committee are quasi-political aims and quasi-emotional aims. This attitude is strong in education. It is a thinking that has dominated education for a long time.'

(Conservative member)

But this confidence in statistics was not shared by most of the other members, who rejected the 'precise' statistical measures in favour of a hands-on strategy of visiting schools and talking to teachers. They felt strongly that the statistics produced did not help them to evaluate the service, and in particular, they did not like the statistics produced by officers which, they felt, were designed to obscure rather than reveal facts:

'You can measure achievement by visiting and parent demand. Statistics you can twist to prove any case you want but if you go to see for yourself, it's different.'

(Conservative member)

'Unless you are at ground level, you don't know what is going on and how your county policy is working. We do use statistics but again, it has to be done school-by-school and as a councillor I have to ask officers to disaggregate totals for the county.'

(Labour member)

'Real monitoring involves talking to teachers and talking to schools, departments and advisers; statistics are not really useful.'

(Labour member)

None of the members had used the reports of Her Majesty's Inspectors as a means of assessing the performance of education although a few had seen them as school governors. Most of them had not even considered that they might be used in this way. However, at the time of the study, these reports had not long been freely available. The problem, according to members, was that the reports took a mysterious route around schools, first to heads and chairmen/chairwomen of governors and the administrative staff of the director of education. The net result was that they most often bypassed councillors. Several members speculated that it might be possible to look at reports if the chairman or chairwoman of the committee and the director of education took the initiative.

'HMI reports are given directly to the director of education and the chairman of the committee. It is then up to these two to report to the authority if they think it really necessary.'

(Conservative member)

'HMI reports have stopped circulating even to school governors.
I believe that they were not provided in a quantity sufficient for
circulation. The problem has always been that if directors and
chairmen of governors wanted to keep anything quiet, they just
didn't circulate HMI reports.'

(Labour member)

Apart from the difficulties of getting HMI reports, members did
not really know how these could be used for evaluation in schools
even if obtainable. Rather, members tended once again to stress
the importance of actually visiting schools and inspecting them as
being the best way of assessing the service. Almost all gave this a
greater priority over other methods including internal and external
reports and statistical analysis.

Yet while stressing that monitoring performance in education
means seeing what schools and teachers are doing, members also
reported an inability actually to get into schools except as school
governors: this would suggest a weakness, if not a break, in the
chain of accountability. Three-quarters said that it had become
routine for councillors to take up school governorships as the only
way of getting into school premises. Although for some this was
mainly a political expedient, to ensure the party's representation
at school level, all emphasized this activity as a way of getting in on
decision-making in schools where teachers would otherwise carry
out their own autonomous policies. Getting into schools was no
easier for councillors who had been or were teachers themselves:

'Within most professions now there is a degree of cynicism
about control, since the grass-roots people just get on with the
job anyway. We don't know what goes on in schools. The only
means of regulation we have over the profession is through the
budget. Every school should be a cost centre, then councillors
would be able to monitor their performance.'

(Labour ex-teacher member)

'Members' role does not extend to visiting schools but most
members are school governors in one or two schools. In this
way all schools in the county have the scrutiny of county

councillors (albeit disguised as school governors). In this way
members are responsible for education down to school level.
However, it is very difficult to get rid of a bad teacher in a
school, and that is usually left to the Head to cope with, either
by redirecting the teacher, advising them, or containing their
unsuitability in some way.'

(Conservative ex-teacher member)

'The main problem of judging effectiveness of schools locally is
that only governors at school level are in a position to know
what goes on in individual schools, and the head of a school is
totally responsible for the teaching in his school.'

(Labour member)

'We don't get intimate knowledge of schools as county
councillors but we get the basis of involvement as governors.'

(Labour member)

If the elected members of the education committee found it
difficult to know what the service was doing and were uncertain
about its objectives, how did they feel about their own accountability for the service? Contrary to what one might expect, given
all the difficulties of getting a grip on the service and knowing
where it was supposed to be going, most councillors saw their
accountability as unproblematic. Two did see some problems,
but these were limited to their own lack of time. For the rest,
accountability was something taken for granted rather than
discussed: as a self-evident fact of life stemming from the nature of
the councillor's job. The word did not trigger off any great
reflections or introspective questioning about their own ability to
be accountable: no real distinction was drawn by members, even
when prompted, between accountability to and for. Indeed, the
only point repeatedly stressed by members was that they saw
themselves accountable to the county as a whole for the
performance of education as a whole, rather than to particular
localities for particular schools. They wanted explicitly to repudiate
the traditional parish-pump style of accountability in education:

'Decisions we take on the education committee have to be taken on the broad spectrum of education in the county: that is, available resources, equity and the best possible service.'

(Labour ex-teacher member)

'I feel accountable for the whole of the educational structure in the county.'

(Conservative member)

One variation on this central theme of accountability to the county came from some Labour members. These saw themselves accountable to their own party, though this was not necessarily to the exclusion of other audiences:

'I see myself as accountable to the party, and then to the county as a whole. I am ultimately responsible to the ballot box but if we did anything against party policy we would be in dead trouble before that.'

(Labour member)

'The Labour Group is accountable to the party and individual councillors are accountable to the ward party organization.'

(Labour member)

'At the end of the day, Labour councillors should implement party policy. I feel accountable to my electorate. I have to explain what I am doing.'

(Labour member)

So most members found neither the concept of accountability nor its direction in any way problematic. They were, as they saw it, automatically accountable to the county or electorate (whether or not via the party). But they did not appear to translate this to mean direct answerability to the voters. Some said that, once elected, they had been given a mandate to act on behalf of the electorate, without having to refer back to them except at elections: they saw themselves, in other words, as trustees, not delegates. A few also felt that they were accountable to their own consciences; a couple saw themselves to be responsible for staff. But even among the majority who declared themselves to be accountable to the electorate, the stress was rather on story-telling and explanation than justification. Their contacts with individual voters tended to be limited; although a number of members did deal with education queries at surgeries or at their own homes, half of them said that the bulk of such queries were about local authority housing. In addition, of course, they were involved in addressing public meetings about educational changes and re-organization. But again, they saw this mainly as an opportunity to explain *their* policy decisions rather than getting the views of the voters about what ought to be done. Indeed, some were positively suspicious of contacts with the public, individual or collective, since they saw the views expressed as being representative only of the vocal middle classes.

If there was not much evidence of any systematic dialogue between members and public, there was considerable evidence of a perceived barrier between members and service deliverers, both officers and teachers. This sense of separateness was not of the positive kind, associated with clarity of roles, but rather a demarcation of activities devised and controlled by the officers. Although two councillors said that their own role ought to be a policy-making one, and two others thought that a partnership between officers and members should be producing an education policy, most others stressed that there was no positive policy emerging generally from the education service. Rather the status quo was being maintained at a physical distance within schools and being consolidated by the psychological distance maintained by senior officers. There was no indication from the interviews that the traditional distinction between operations and policy was even being considered or that anyone was controlling operations or policy in the education service. Members' overwhelming impression of their relationship with senior officers was one of being kept away from vital information about what was going on:

'Officers exercise power by drawing up agendas – giving some items priority, others little, and missing some items altogether. Members have to rely on officers to produce a full account of what is going on so that members can consider priorities. This never happens. Priorities are already selected by officers and presented accordingly.'

(Liberal member)

'Officers can prevent some policy-making by withholding information or just presenting reports that aren't satisfactory. They can present options unsatisfactorily by leaving out items or giving some items less prominence than others. Officers control everything in this way.'

(Labour member)

'Officers are the most powerful group in the education committee. Members do not have this "expertise" by which I mean:

1 Amount of time to devote to the task.
2 Most important, access to information about the county as a whole and the service in general.'

(Conservative member)

Both the doubt and the ambivalence about the circulation of information and about the roles that the different actors in the system ought to be playing were summed up by one member:

'I am a teacher but have been fobbed off by the director of education when I have asked for agenda items and these have not appeared meeting after meeting. In truth, I sometimes get glimpses of what he is getting at and the teacher in me says that only teachers ought to be making decisions about some of the items on the agenda. I know that I would not really expect or welcome non-teachers making curriculum decisions or assessing the performance of teachers.'

(Labour member)

The majority of members did see officers as all-powerful but were not so certain about their expertise:

'Members have to rely on the services of officers but I would not say they have the same professional expertise as heads of schools.'

(Conservative member)

'Officers are trained professionals but they have vested interests. But really their main advantage is that they have information at their fingertips – members don't.'

(Labour member)

When it came to members' opinions about professionals, experts, and others in the education service, they talked of teachers, particularly head teachers, as a profession in the sense of being an autonomous body of people carrying out an activity exclusive of advice and scrutiny from others. The emphasis was on the ability of teachers to keep councillors out of schools, so preventing them from having any direct oversight of service provision. They felt themselves excluded from both information and control by the professionals. There was little reference to the positive aspects of professionalism. Even the teacher and ex-teacher members claimed a limited influence in both education policy and operations when confronted by the power of the professional:

'Heads of schools have a tremendous influence on the subjects, both in range and type, taught in their schools. We, as members, can recommend and urge but only put a limited amount of pressure on schools. Even when we have the backing of educational advisers, we are limited, and we need the backing of the governing body; if the governing body doesn't agree with us members, then we have no authority on the curriculum. Governors themselves do have curriculum authority but either don't realize it or rarely use it. Traditionally, heads of schools have assumed total power of curriculum responsibility. Even the inspectorate has limited influence on schools and heads, although this may increase as schools are named in published reports.'

(Labour ex-teacher member)

'The curriculum is not and never has been a political decision, neither is it an officer decision. It is a professional decision and up to school themselves.'

(Conservative member)

'No one tells a teacher how to teach – we certainly can't – that is left to teachers themselves at school level with headmasters supervising.'

(Labour member)

Even the power of a political party was seen to fade in the eyes of some members when confronted by the realities of professional power:

'In terms of broad policy, there is an awful lot of heed paid to teachers and teaching; although policy is developed by the Labour party it is teachers as party members who develop the educational policy.'

(Labour member)

'Professionals have a clear advantage over members and governors in the education authority. They have a lot more power and influence over their own areas than either a member or a senior officer. We as members should be building up expertise to combat professional dominance over teaching.'

(Conservative member)

If teachers and the profession have all the power, what did members see as a way of distributing it more evenly, more fairly and more rationally?

'Teachers should be assessed; their performance assessed every year. This is not possible at present because the profession would not allow non-teachers to make the assessment.'

(Conservative member)

If the profession is powerful, and officers are part of the profession, what are members' chances of asserting themselves?

'Members have to rely on the services of officers who, although they do not have the same professional power as heads of schools are nevertheless of the profession.'

(Conservative member)

'Particularly in education, there is a tendency for officers to give specific guidance to members arising out of officers being part of the teaching profession.'

(Conservative member)

The overall impression that emerged was that the members saw themselves enmeshed in a web of powerlessness spun by the professionals actually running the service. Even those Labour members who stressed the importance of the party manifesto as an instrument of accountability – that is of having a set of politically determined objectives – shared this general pessimism. Indeed, there was a general rejection of the view that sharpening up politics, in the sense of having a set of party politicians with a clear mandate, would allow councillors to assert their control over the service. On the contrary, councillors of all parties saw politics often as an obstacle to greater control: the divisions of local politics were simply exploited, as they saw it, by officers and teachers pursuing national professional ends. Members were critical of what they saw as the past and present excessive 'politicization' of the service. This was seen as a negative activity by councillors of all parties but particularly by Conservatives:

'Education is becoming more and more politically divided along party lines. I have been increasingly disillusioned by the paucity of intellect in educational policy-making at county level.'

(Conservative member)

'In county services there is more political care taken by officers who feel constrained by the political parties and are therefore more cagey about what they actually feel. I think this stops them from giving proper guidance and advice to members on policy.'

(Labour member)

'The whole education service is, and always has been, compounded by party stands'.

(Liberal member)

The best prospects of getting a grip on the service, some members thought, lay in professionalizing themselves more. While they rejected the view that they should become more expert about education as such, as we have seen, they argued that councillors should become less amateurish in their capacity as elected members, in particular, by getting more independent support and advice:

'I would rather not have councillors as experts, neither do I want to rely on officers alone. I would rather see a paid consultant – an expert adviser to develop policy. A place like the Greater London Council has managed to afford policy advisers. It is hard for members to turn down professional policy suggestions on staff matters. A third party expert and outsider would be the answer. They could write policy papers to be circulated to the profession, officers and members. Expertise is needed to deal with professional experts.'

(Labour member)

'I believe it is more important to be elected than appointed. I believe in changing rules frequently rather than the absolute power of the corporate state. This flexibility can be achieved only through the democratic system. However, members ought to treat membership a little more professionally. They should receive at least secretarial assistance. After all, they spend more money than central government.'

(Conservative member)

Summary

With only a marginal control over the spending of a budget of about £250 million, with a history of hotly disputed objectives and radically changing ideas about education, it is not surprising that the members of committee felt powerless and frustrated. Unlike health authority members, however, they did not translate this powerlessness and frustration into any doubts about their accountability. Like the water service, this was unproblematic, if for very different reasons. Accountability was automatically invested in their role by virtue of being elected. The fact that they did not in any real sense perceive themselves to be in control of the service and that their linkages with the voters were tenuous did not shake them in this faith. They were, as we have seen, quite clear about the inhibitions on their role. They saw themselves excluded by an autonomous and remote labour force, and forced to spy on schools by disguising themselves as governors. They were uncertain about their objectives and sceptical about their ability to measure performance as distinct from going to see for themselves (which is why, of course, they resented their exclusion from the coal-face of service-delivery all the more). Yet even this accumulation of doubts and grievances did not lead to any self-questioning about their role.

This conclusion cuts across all parties. In this chapter we have deliberately attached party labels to our quotations, since the explicitly political nature of local government (in contrast to the other services) might show up partisan differences. In fact, however, members were unanimous about their powerlessness and lack of control. Generally no systematic party patterns emerged from the interviews; about the only exception was the insistence by some Labour councillors that their party manifesto provided them with both policies and a focus of accountability – even though they conceded that it did not necessarily allow them to implement these policies.

One explanation for this apparently schizophrenic attitude might be that members find it too painful to contemplate that there can be no accountability without control. Another move likely explanation is simply that, as discussed in Chapter 1, accountability as a word and a concept mean different things to different people. The members of the education committee overwhelmingly defined their accountability to the public as giving a retrospective account, or telling a story about their decisions. Although they were all for accountability, and were committed to their version of what it meant, they put little emphasis on interpreting this to mean a duty to justify their actions by engaging in a public dialogue. Such justification, as they saw it, was contained in the mandate given to them by virtue of their election which, as it were, provided them with a moral seal of approval.

REFERENCES

1 F. Layfield (Chairman) (1976) *Report of the Committee of Inquiry on Local Government Finance*. London: HMSO.
2 D. M. Hill (1974) *Democratic Theory and Local Government*. London: Allen & Unwin.
3 J. Gyford (1976) *Local Politics in Britain*. London: Croom Helm: 142.
4 J. Gyford (1976) *Local Politics in Britain*. London: Croom Helm: 70–1.
5 K. C. Wheare (1955) *Government by Committee*. Oxford: Clarendon Press: 192.
6 D. E. Regan (1980) *A Headless State: The Unaccountable Executive in British Local Government*. Nottingham: University of Nottingham: 15.
7 K. Newton (1976) *Second City Politics*. Oxford: Clarendon Press: 118–19.

8 H. Heclo (1969) The Councillor's Job. *Public Administration* 47, Summer: 185–202.

9 D. Robinson (Chairman) (1977) *Report of the Committee of Inquiry into the System of Remuneration of Members of Local Authorities*, vol. I. London: HMSO Cmnd 7010.

10 H. Heclo (1969) The Councillor's Job. *Public Administration* 47, Summer: 185–202.

11 R. Greenwood, K. Walsh, C. R. Hinings, and S. Ranson (1980) *Patterns of Management in Local Government.* Oxford: Martin Robertson: 72–5.

12 M. Laffin and K. Young (1985) The Changing Roles and Responsibilities of Local Authority Chief Officers. *Public Administration* 63, Spring: 41–59.

13 M. Simey (1985) *Government by Consent: The Principle and Practice of Local Government.* London: Bedford Square Press.

14 Audit Commission (1983) *Code of Local Government Audit Practice for England and Wales.* London: Audit Commission.

15 HM Treasury (1986) *The Government's Expenditure Plans 1986–87 to 1988–89.* London: HMSO Cmnd 9702, vol. II, Table 4.1

16 Labour Party (1981) *Local Government Handbook.* London: Labour Party: 6/5–6/30.

17 T. Travers (1985) LEAs, Other LEAs and Statistics. *Guardian* 3 September: 11.

18 Quoted in T. Becher and S. Maclure (1978) *Accountability in Education.* London: NFER Publishing: 10.

19 J. Welton (1980) Accountability in Educational Organisations, Part 1. *Educational Administration* 9, 1, Autumn: 25–41.

20 J. Elliott (1981) Introduction: In J. Elliott, D. Bridges, D. Ebbott, R. Gibson, and J. Nias, *School Accountability.* London: Grant McIntyre: x.

21 M. Kogan (1984) Different Definitions of Accountability in Education. *ESRC Newsletter* 53, Supplement: xiii–xiv.

22 Department of Education and Science (1980) *A View of the Curriculum.* London: HMSO. DES (1981) *The School Curriculum.* London: HMSO. DES (1985) *Better Schools.* London: HMSO Cmnd 9469.

23 D. Walker (1985) Performance, Competence and Professional Autonomy: Teachers on the Rack. *Public Money* 5, 1, June: 23–5.

24 See the chapters by W. Taylor, T. Pateman, M. Kogan, and E. R. House. In T. Becher and S. Maclure (1978) *Accountability in Education.* London: NFER Publishing.

25 M. Arnold (1908) *Reports on Elementary Schools, 1852–1882.* London: HMSO: 112–16.

26 Department of Education and Science (1983) School Standards and Spending. *Statistical Bulletin* 16/83. London: DES December.

27 M. Rutter, B. Maughan, P. Mortimore, and J. Ouston (1979) *Fifteen Thousand Hours*. London: Open Books.

28 For an exposition of this approach by various educationalists, see H. Socket (ed.) (1979) *Accountability in the English Educational System*. Sevenoaks, Kent: Hodder & Stoughton, especially the editor's introductory chapter.

29 T. Becher, M. Eraut, and J. Knight (1981) *Policies for Educational Accountability*. London: Heinemann Educational.

30 M. Smith (1979) A Secondary Head in a Maintained School. In J. Lello (ed.) *Accountability in Education*. London: Ward Lock Educational.

31 T. Becher, M. Eraut, and J. Knight (1981) *Policies for Educational Accountability*. London: Heinemann Educational.

32 Committee of Inquiry (Chairman: Tom Taylor) (1977) *A New Partnership for our Schools*. London: HMSO.

33 At the time of the study, legislation was before parliament designed to strengthen school governing bodies.

34 W. Bacon (1978) *Public Accountability and the Schooling System*. London: Harper & Row.

35 Committee of Inquiry (Chairman: Tom Taylor) (1977) *A New Partnership for our Schools*. London: HMSO: 125.

36 R. Klein (1984) The Politics of Participation. In R. Maxwell and N. Weaver (eds) *Public Participation in Health*. London: King Edward's Hospital Fund for London.

37 R. Rogers (1983) Schools' Reports to Parents. Where To Find Out More About Education, no. 193, November/December, Advisory Centre for Education: 19–22.

38 For a general survey of the work of HMIs, see S. Browne (1979) The Accountability of H.M. Inspectorate. In J. Lello (ed.) *Accountability in Education*. London: Ward Lock Educational.

39 *Report by Her Majesty's Inspectors on the Effects of Local Authority Expenditure Policies on the Service in England, 1982* (1983) London: DES, July.

40 Department of Education and Science (1985) *Report by HM Inspectors on St. Philip Howard School, Tower Hamlets*. London: DES: 13.

41 Department of Education and Science (1985) *Report by HM Inspectors on Liskeard School, Cornwall*. London: DES: 15.

42 Department of Education and Science (1983) *HM Inspectors Today*. London: DES: 3.

43 Department of Education and Science (1983) *HM Inspectors Today*. London: DES: 11.

44 T. Bush and M. Kogan (1982) *Directors of Education.* London: Allen & Unwin.
45 E. Briault (1979) The Chief Education Officers. In J. Lello (ed.) *Accountability in Education.* London: Ward Lock Educational: 60.
46 M. Kogan and W. van der Eyken (1973) *County Hall LEA: The Role of the Chief Education Officer.* Harmondsworth: Penguin Education: 46.
47 T. Bush and M. Kogan (1982) *Directors of Education.* London: Allen & Unwin: 57.
48 T. Bush and M. Kogan (1982) *Directors of Education.* London: Allen & Unwin: 117.

8

Accountability and the social services committee

If constitutional theory were the only determinant of how accountability is defined and exercised in practice, this chapter would be redundant – as indeed would be the previous one. The social services, like education, are a local government agency. Again, like education, they are financed out of the local authority budget with the exception of some fairly marginal charges to consumers. They are, once more like education, run by a statutory committee of local councillors: the elected representatives accountable, in theory at any rate, to the voters. They share, with all other local government services, the problems of constrained autonomy posed by the twin pressures of national public expenditure policies and national agreements on pay and conditions of work. But just as in education, it is the nature of the service itself which blurs and confounds the simple model of accountability assumed in textbook theories, as shown in the last chapter, so the special characteristics of the social services provide the context and shape the practice of accountability.

One characteristic, in particular, sharply distinguishes the social services from education. In the case of education, local authorities have to respond to demands largely and clearly defined for them by legislation. They have to provide school places for all children who are of an appropriate age. They may, as we saw in the last chapter, have some marginal discretion about how they meet this demand; they may, in addition, have other, more vaguely defined duties and scope for extending their activities. But their main task is given. The social services, in contrast, are (to exaggerate only a little) defining demand by their own activities. In this respect, they are more similar, perhaps, to the health service or to the police than to education inasmuch as it is the service providers who define who the customer is, what his or her 'needs' are, and how they should be met. It is a service dominated, indeed, by the language of needs rather than that of rights. While children have rights to a school place, the users of social services have needs. If the consumer of the NHS is a patient (a person to whom 'something is done', in the definition of the Oxford English Dictionary) the user of the social services is a client (a person who is 'under the protection or patronage of another, a dependant').

In part, this reflects the history of the social services: their origins in the Poor Law and its tradition of providing succour for the less eligible.[1] While the principle of lesser eligibility has been repudiated, the language of need is embodied in the statutes which define the role of the social services.[2] Indeed, the legislation also underlines the heterogeneity of the social services, since it consists of a series of Acts which spell out the powers or responsibilities of local authorities towards particular groups of the population, ranging from the elderly to children, from blind and deaf people to physically and mentally handicapped people. Under Part III of the National Assistance Act, 1948, local authorities are required to 'provide residential accommodation for persons who by reason of age, infirmity or any other circumstances are in need of care and attention which would otherwise not be available to them', and to provide home-helps 'on such a scale as is adequate for the needs of their area'. The Chronically Sick and Disabled Act, 1970, requires local authorities to obtain information on the numbers and needs of disabled people who are permanently and substantially handi-capped by illness, injury, congenital deformity, or old age. The Child Care Act, 1980, imposes on local authorities a duty not only to make provision for children in need of care, but also to 'diminish the need to receive children into care'. And the legislation, apart from imposing a general duty on local authorities to meet the needs of specific groups, also empowers social services committees to provide a host of different services: from residential homes to training centres, from meals on wheels to home aids, from community homes for children to intermediate treatment.

The most striking aspect of the legislation, apart from its sheer extent and heterogeneity, is the wide scope left to local authorities in interpreting their duties. With the significant exception of some of the statutory provisions for children, where decisions about demands on services are made by the courts, it is local authorities who are left to determine which needs are to be met and how. Social services are all about rationing scarce resources according to criteria set by the service providers;[3] in this respect they are similar to the NHS. It is therefore not surprising that local authorities vary considerably both in their total level of expenditure on social services and in the mix of individual services provided. Despite floods of guidance from central government, despite circulars and advice about desirable practices and levels of provision, they remain stubbornly and idiosyncratically local. They may be constrained by national policies and agreements, as in the case of education, but they appear to enjoy a larger degree of autonomy. Of all the services in our study, they would seem to be the most local in character, in part perhaps because they are also among the smallest. Social services account for about 10 per cent of all local government expenditure, compared to education's 45 per cent share. A decision by a social services committee to increase spending, therefore, has less impact on the total budget and rate demand than a similar decision by the education committee. Add to this the rapid expansion in total expenditure, in line with government policy until the 1980s, and it is clear that members of social services committees have had more opportunity than most councillors to put their imprint on the services for which they are responsible – at least as far as resource inputs are concerned.

Local variations in the level of total resource provision are dramatically illustrated by the expenditure figures.[4] In 1983/84 spending estimates per head of population varied from £88 to £162 among the Inner London Boroughs, from £42 to £112 in the Outer London boroughs, from £28 to £48 in the counties, and from £34 to £92 in the metropolitan districts. Nor are these variations explained by differences in need, in so far as these can be defined by such measurable factors as the demographic composition of the population. When actual expenditure is compared to the spending level appropriate to local needs, as calculated by the government's formula for determining the grant to individual local authorities, large variations remain. Some social services committees spend over 70 per cent more than would be expected; others spend up to 28 per cent less. This may, of course, simply demonstrate the difficulties of determining need by the statistical manipulation of social data. But if need is such an elusive and ambiguous concept, if it is so difficult to determine by means of 'objective' evidence, then this would in turn appear to underline the scope for local discretion. The scope for such discretion is, once more, demonstrated by the reaction of local authorities to the expenditure constraints imposed by central government in the 1980s. In 1983/ 84, for example, eleven authorities cut their expenditure in response to central government constraints, while forty increased spending by more than 5 per cent, variations which were not explained by demographic change.[5]

If there is great scope for local decision-making about the level of total spending on the social services, equally there is scope for local variation in the mix of services produced. Just about every study ever produced on the specific services provided by local authorities has emphasized the variations in the level of provision for particular groups and differences in the kinds of services provided.[6] For example, an inquiry by the Audit Commission showed that residential provision for the elderly, by far the single biggest element in the total spending of social services committees, varied greatly between local authorities.[7] While the bottom 10 per cent of local authorities care for fourteen elderly people per 1,000 population over 65, the equivalent figure is twenty-three for the top 10 per cent (although importantly these figures ignore the availability of places in private or voluntary homes):[8] while the bottom 10 per cent provide four home-helps per 1,000 population over 65, the top 10 per cent provide twelve – a threefold variation. Although central government has, over the years, published a series of guidelines laying down desirable norms of provision, divergence is the real norm.[9]

All these figures are, of course, about service inputs. These are visible and measurable. The real problems of accountability emerge, as in education and some of the other services in this study, when the focus switches to the way in which social services are run (process) and their impact on society (outcomes). The problems of devising a currency of evaluation for process are considered below in the context of examining the role of the service-providers. Here we explore the ambiguous, uncertain, and tenuous nature of the relationship between what the social services do, and their impact on society; the reason why it is so difficult to assess their performance and why, in consequence, maximizing inputs is so often equated with maximizing impact (despite the lack of evidence of any direct link). These difficulties reflect two characteristics of the social services. The first is their dependence on, and interrelationship with, other services; the second, in part stemming from the first, is the difficulty of demonstrating their . effectiveness. In neither respect are the social services different from some of the other services already discussed, notably the NHS and the police. Where they are different, however, is that they have turned the problems of dependence on other services into a positive ideology, and explicitly see themselves as the service which deals with the mistakes and omissions of others.

The contingent nature of social services performance can best be illustrated with the example of the elderly who absorb more than half of the total social services budget. The objective of public policy is to enable elderly people to live as long as possible in their own homes, and to provide residential care only if this is no longer feasible.[10] To this end, as we have seen, local authorities are empowered to provide meals on wheels, home-helps, day centres, and home aids, as well as residential homes. But the achievement of this objective, itself rather vague and difficult to monitor, is dependent not only on the social structure of the community but also on a variety of other services. It will depend on the extent to which the local district health authority provides repair services – such as hip replacements – which will allow the elderly to remain physically active, and on the DHA's policies towards the provision of services in the community. It will depend on the attitudes of local general practitioners, and their willingness to support the elderly in their own homes. It will depend on the policies of the local housing department, and the extent to which it provides sheltered housing or takes the circumstances of elderly people into account when making housing allocations. It will depend on the activity of local voluntary organizations. It may even depend on attitudes in the local social security office. Much the same applies even in the case of the social services responsibilities for children and families. To the extent that it is the function of social services to cope with the symptoms of social stress, reflecting a whole variety of factors ranging from poor housing to unemployment, so it becomes difficult to disentangle their particular contribution. Not surprisingly, the literature on the effectiveness of the social services – and, in particular, the role of social workers[11] – is remarkable both for its size and its agnostic conclusions. There is no accepted currency of evaluation, no measures of outcome to set against the measures of inputs.

This is not to argue that it is totally impossible to evaluate the social services; there is a large literature, both academic and professional, on evaluation. For example, the Audit Commission, in the study already cited,[12] sought to develop a methodology for assessing the effectiveness of services for the elderly, which examines the appropriateness of the mix of community and residential services provided by different local authorities; so a high level of residential provision, drawing in elderly people with relatively mild physical or mental disabilities, might be taken as evidence of the inadequacy of services in the community. But since the local authority community services are only one factor in determining the ability of elderly people to remain in their own homes, such an approach raises questions rather than providing answers. The problem of assessing social services in terms of outcomes remains, even when the focus of attention switches from the overall effectiveness of a service to the specific effectiveness of individual institutions. So, for instance, a study of residential homes which sought to measure their effectiveness in terms of outcomes for residents, such as life expectancy and dependency, found that there appeared to be little, if any, relationship between the style and regime of particular homes and such indicators.[13]

The ambiguities of the notion of 'performance', the problems of assessing effectiveness or impact, are in no sense unique to the social services. As previous chapters have demonstrated, the same is true of the NHS, of the police and education. But their implications for the practice of accountability and the role of members are somewhat different, given the structure of the services, the status and mix of the service providers, the culture of the service, and the traditions of social services committees. In what follows, we shall examine each of these in turn.

Social services, in contrast to both the NHS and education, are organized as a bureaucratic hierarchy. There is a chain of command running from the director of social services through assistant directors to area offices (although currently most departments are in a state of chronic reorganization). There are often elaborate manuals laying down procedures; every child-care tragedy tends to lead to a tightening up of procedural rules. There is usually a requirement for certain types of decisions to be referred up the hierarchy from the coal-face of service delivery: some of these decisions may, indeed, be taken by the members of the social services committee. These, on occasion, may act as a court of appeal if a client disagrees with the decision of a social worker. For example, in the case of the committee in our study, a disgruntled client appealed against a decision to allocate a particular number of home-help hours to her – and her appeal was upheld. The director of social services, a statutory post, is responsible for the services provided. In the words of one such director:[14]

'The social services director is actually responsible for the day-to-day work that goes on in his department, unlike the area medical officer, say, whose role is more to do with planning and looking at services across the board. He has no responsibility for the daily judgements of the clinical staff as I have for my social workers.'

Not surprisingly, therefore, it has been concluded that: 'Social services departments have originated less from experience with other types of service organisation, in or out of local authorities, than from experience of industrial structures and management processes. In this system, social workers are skilled labourers not professionals.'[15]

Indeed, the debate about accountability in the social services largely revolves around the role of social workers who, while they make up only one-eighth of the total labour force, take most of the key decisions affecting the lives of clients and the allocation of resources. It is a debate which, as in the case of the police and of teachers, has in part been prompted by growing criticism of, and disillusion with, social work. The context of discussion has been provided by a series of child abuse cases over the past decade – starting with the Maria Colwell inquiry,[16] and culminating most recently with the Jasmine Beckford inquiry[17] – which have called into question the skill and judgement of social workers. The central feature of the debate has been an argument about whether, and to what extent, social workers can or should be considered as professionals accountable only to their peers as distinct from 'skilled labourers' accountable to their bureaucratic superiors: that is how far they can claim professional autonomy and assert control over the language of evaluation.

Among social workers themselves, there has been a debate about what their collective occupational strategy should be: whether they should seek full professional status, on the medical model, with a general council responsible for maintaining professional standards of performance and disciplining individual members. In this, there have been sharp divisions of opinion. These are reflected in the evidence submitted to the Barclay Committee set up in 1980 at the request of the secretary of state for social services to examine the 'role and tasks' of social workers.[18] On the one hand, the British Association of Social Workers (BASW) argued that the creation of a council 'would give reality to the concept of professional accountability (the consciousness in the mind of a practising social worker that not only has he a duty to his client and to his employer, but also as a member of a profession, to the ethics and values laid down by that profession)'. On the other hand, the National and Local Government Officers' Association maintained that social workers could not aspire to the status of a profession, on the medical model, because of 'the absence of core knowledge and the fact that the skills required have not been identified'. Furthermore, it was argued in evidence to the Barclay Committee, the professionalization of social workers would cut them off from clients and others working in the same field, whether volunteers or other social services staff. In short, social workers are perhaps the only occupational group in our study with a strong strand of anti-professional ideology: where, at least among an active minority, the view is taken that professionalization is elitist and as such undesirable. Not surprisingly, perhaps, the Barclay Committee found itself divided, and concluded that any immediate attempt to establish a general council would 'tend further to damage the public image of social workers'.

To whom, then, *are* social workers accountable for their actions? One answer has been given by a working party, representing social workers and social services directors.[19] This distinguishes between a variety of different forms of social work accountability. There is personal accountability, defined as being 'a matter of personal integrity and being true to one's own standards and values'. There is professional accountability, defined as 'a responsibility to see that colleagues remain professionals' – with the important proviso that 'professional accountability is, however, undeveloped as long as it remains no more than an allegiance to each individual's own idea of what his profession requires of him', that is lacking the formal machinery of professionalism. There is accountability to non-employing agencies, such as the courts. There is accountability to the public, and above all, there is accountability to the employer, as the same document argues:

'An employing body has objectives and policies which impose limitations, and employees have an accountability towards these objectives. Professional employees, however, should expect to have discretion delegated to them to enable them to apply their knowledge and skill, and should expect that their professional opinions will, by and large, be respected by the employer. . . . Delegation of discretion and respect for professional opinion do not, however, detract from accountability to the employer. On the contrary, they provide the conditions in which the employee can be accountable to the employer, not for following fixed rules, *but for the exercise of his professional judgement*'. [emphasis in the original]

Social work would, therefore, seem to be an example not of professional autonomy but of what has been called delegated discretion.[20] There may be a widespread perception of multiple channels of accountability – to fellow professionals and to clients (see pp. 205–10) – but the reality would seem to be that the social worker is the agent of her or his employer and as such, answerable to the latter in a way which is not true of the doctor, the police officer, or the teacher.

But before embracing this conclusion wholeheartedly, it is important to distinguish and explore further the distinction between two forms of accountability: between accountability for individual actions and for overall performance (that is the pattern of activities or the sum of decisions taken). It is clear that social workers are accountable to their employers for individual acts: that is that they may have to answer for their decisions, as in the instance of child abuse cases, not just to their professional peers or hierarchic superiors but to the social services committee. As a report published by the British Association of Social Workers puts it:[21]

'It should be open to an elected or nominated member to request a committee to examine a specific allegation against a member of its staff or to consider a specific exercise of discretion. . . . Ordinarily the response of a committee to a request for consideration of a social worker's action or decision should be to call in the first instance for a report from the chief officer, who should consult with the workers concerned and produce a report which is agreed with them. This report may well be accepted by the committee but if it is not accepted without question, the workers concerned should have the opportunity to be present and to be represented at a meeting of the committee at which the whole of the evidence upon which the committee relies for its decision should be made known to them and opportunity given for the social worker or his representative to reply.'

Moreover, this is quite clearly an example of accountability with sanctions: story-telling to justify actions. If the agent's explanation does not satisfy, she or he may be dismissed: which is precisely what happened to some of the social workers in the Beckford case.

However, it is less clear that there is effective, as distinct from formal, accountability when it comes to the social worker's overall performance: the way in which he or she routinely uses discretion. Effective accountability for performance implies, as argued throughout this study, effective control over performance. There is little evidence of this in the case of social services, and indeed the problem of control stems directly from two of the distinguishing characteristics of social work, picked out in the BASW report cited above. First:

'Much social work is done in private. In this respect it differs from that of a classteacher or a hospital nurse where unsatisfactory practice is fairly easily detected and appraised by consumers and colleagues. [Second] No two social workers would respond in exactly the same way to the same set of problems i.e. there are few precise criteria of performance.'

The lack of effective accountability for performance, seen as control over what happens, is demonstrated by the findings of a large-scale survey of social work practice.[22] Although carried out in the 1970s, this still usefully illustrates the kind of problem involved in trying to get a grip over the service. The interviews with social workers carried out in the survey showed considerable confusion about accountability, and in particular, about the role of team leaders – the NCOs of social work, who provide the crucial link between social workers in the field and the managerial hierarchy:

'To whom one was accountable, what accountability meant, particularly if "things went wrong", how team leaders could know enough to make accountability a reality, were all questions raised by social workers and their team leaders. They recognized that they could share their worries with the supervisors but were not sure what this meant. Was it just a way of receiving some psychological support in the same way that one receives support from a colleague? Or does the sharing with a supervisor in some way hand on accountability and place a responsibility on the team leader to direct the work being done? What was obvious was that even when social workers recognized these issues, few had been able to clarify their confused ideas and feelings, either by discussion within their agency or in training.'

In effect, the survey evidence suggests social workers are largely left to themselves in terms of determining their own performance, that is their priorities, their mix of cases, and their workload:

'Few team leaders organised supervision so that they were regularly informed of all the cases and projects for which their social workers were responsible; many supervision sessions were concerned only with these cases which the social workers chose to present; a minority, usually of more experienced workers, were not supervised at all, and much supervision was informal and irregular.'

A more recent study of practices in different local authorities, carried out by the Social Services Inspectorate in 1986, suggests that little has changed since the 1970s in the highly charged area of child abuse:[23]

'In all authorities there was a general assumption that supervision is necessary but no social services department had a clear and explicit written policy statement about the nature of supervision, and no authority prescribed the method of supervision in detail. . . . Although some authorities had clear guidance about the level at which certain key decisions should be made, supervisors and workers were often unclear about this guidance, and believed that they were free to make decisions which had not been delegated to them. In reality, in the absence of plans based on a sound and thorough assessment, workers sometimes drifted into making key decisions, and did not stop to take stock with the supervisor before deciding something of importance about a child's life.'

It would seem, therefore, that whether social workers enjoy a measure of professional autonomy or merely delegated discretion, in practice they are largely unaccountable for what they do routinely. But unlike doctors, for example, they can be called to account by the managerial hierarchy when their decisions are disputed or end in disaster. It is accountability for individual actions rather than for performance.

So far, the discussion has been concerned with social workers whose public profile, given recent child-care scandals, is high, even though they form only a small part of the total labour force of social services departments, as already stressed. In fact, most of the care provided is delivered by a variety of semi-skilled or unskilled people, with no pretensions to professionalism, be they home-helps, residential care assistants, or drivers delivering meals on wheels to people's homes. But even in these services, a leakage of control is apparent. The point can be illustrated by a 1985 report from the DHSS's Social Services Inspectorate, which examined the way in which residential care for the elderly and for children was run in the London Borough of Southwark.[24] This found a sharp contrast between the theory and practice of accountability. In theory, the report explains, the position was very clear:

'The formal line of accountability for the management of homes in Southwark is quite specific; it flows from the elected members to the director of social services; to the head of residential and specialist day care division; to the child care manager and then to three group managers. It is the group managers who exercise the direct management of the homes. In addition to these visits, this also involves a detailed monthly review of each home, undertaken jointly with the officer in charge who exercises the direct management of the homes. The review covers staffing, the progress and behaviour of the children, their health care, education and employment arrangements, the furnishings and fabric of the premises and an overall assessment of the home's performance.'

There could hardly be a more clear-cut example of a hierarchical, managerial system of control and accountability. Yet in practice, the SSI team of inspectors found, in the case of homes for the elderly in particular, (operating under the same system), that styles of care and standards varied widely between homes: 'In every home there are certain custom and practice arrangements that have become traditional.' Furthermore, these 'custom and practice arrangements' often reflected the needs of staff rather than those of the residents. Commenting on the habit of waking residents by 6 am in order to allow the night staff to complete their duties before the end of their shift at 7.30, the report comments:

'The unsatisfactory early morning routine in the homes inspected
does not reflect on the caring attitudes of the staff. It follows
directly from the institutional and management arrangements
that require as much work to be done before breakfast, and
before the change of shift. The waking of residents so early in
the morning was not endorsed by management, neither was
there a total awareness by officers in charge just how early night
staff were commencing their duty.'

The report not only underlines the problems of asserting effective
accountability, in the sense of control over performance, in self-
contained institutions, but also provides an example of the
challenge to accountability posed by 'workers' control', to use
Margaret Simey's phrase quoted in the previous chapter, in public
services:

'Trade union activity maintains a high profile amongst staff in
the majority of the homes and *tends to permeate most of the
practices* [emphasis added]. In every home apart from one,
there was a shop steward, and it is to that person that staff
frequently turned when they had a grievance. The shop steward
would then negotiate with the officer in charge and the majority
of issues were resolved within the work place. There had been
examples where shop stewards had gone direct to their union
official, bypassing the officer in charge, which created tensions
between the officer group and staff. Feelings were expressed by
officers that shop stewards attended meetings with elected
members and senior management and were informed about
new practices, prior to the officers in charge receiving the
information.'

Given a highly unionized labour force and given also a social
services committee with a membership drawn in part from union
officials, it would seem, therefore, that lines of political communication may cut across and break links of managerial accountability
(a phenomenon not unique to social services: in the case of
education, as noted, teachers have voting representatives on
LEAs).

The report of the SSI has been quoted at some length, not only because of the particular insights offered, but also because it illustrates the work of the inspectorate dealing with social services. The creation of this inspectorate itself represents a move towards greater accountability to the centre. The SSI, set up in 1985, replaced the DHSS's Social Work Service, which traditionally saw its role as being primarily to promote good professional practices rather than to monitor performance formally.[25] In contrast the SSI, whose reports are now publicly available, appears to be taking a more managerial approach, in that it reviews the overall performance and standards of the services provided if still largely from the perspective of best practices as defined by the professionals.[26] It differs from the work of the Audit Commission, whose remit covers local authority services as a whole and whose emphasis chiefly is on efficiency in the use of resources rather than the promulgation of professionally defined standards. It overlaps, to an extent, however, with the role of the third body concerned with social services: the Health Advisory Service which stresses that it should not be regarded as an inspectorate, but that it exists 'to stimulate development and improvement of services'. The HAS's remit covers elderly and mentally ill people, and concentrates in particular on the relationships between NHS services and social services. For example, its reports, now also published, may criticize standards in a particular hospital or residential home, or the inadequacy of expenditure on particular services: 'The social services committee should seek to increase the level of expenditure on services for the mentally ill as a matter of urgency', it commented in one case.[27]

The development of these inspectorates offers a sporadic searchlight on the performance of the social services. It is sporadic in the sense that the visits or inquiries may be widely spaced over time, and that not all the services provided will necessarily be reviewed at any one time. Whether the inspectorates should be seen as an instrument of central control, or as a means for enabling local authorities to assess their own services, is perhaps an open question. To answer it would mean being able to establish who uses the information generated by the process, and how. At present, the evidence needed to answer this question is lacking, as is the evidence about the compatibility of the three inspectorates. But if accountability is at all about increasing the visibility of services – if it can be assumed that more information means more effective accountability by giving a picture of performance – then, in theory at least, the growth of inspectorates in the social services field should lead to greater transparency for their activities.

Whether or not the development of inspectorates will lead to greater accountability to central or to local government eventually may be an open question. But in the social services, as in education, it is already clear that there are strong pressures for promoting downward accountability. These mirror the anxieties of social workers, already noted, about distancing themselves from their clients by seeking full-blown professional status. This Seebohm Committee, whose recommendations led to the creation of social services departments in their present form,[28] argued for 'citizen participation in the running of services'.[29] Such participation, it is argued, would both 'reduce the distinction between the givers and takers of social services' and provide 'a means by which further consumer control can be exercised over professional and bureaucratic power'. More recently, the Barclay Committee, whose report has already been quoted, took up the same theme in its recommendations for the setting up of local welfare advisory committees. These, it argued, should be designed 'to provide a forum in which representatives of clients, employers and social workers could discuss agency policies with respect to the rights of clients, including such issues as confidentiality, access to information, and criteria for resource allocation'.[30] In short, the same kind of pressure for the development of a machinery of downward, explanatory accountability is evident in the social services, as in education and the police. However, at present it has not moved beyond rhetoric; social services committees do not, at present, have any institutional or other rivals challenging their monopoly of formal accountability.

This brings the argument full circle, back to the role of members of social services committees. There has been no full-scale study of this role. But the evidence, such as it is, once again underlines the chasm between theory and practice. The Seebohm Committee wholeheartedly embraced the doctrine of the separation of functions between members and officers, as set out in the Maud Committee recommendations (see Chapter 2), quoting with approval the distinction between the 'deliberative and representative' role of members, and the 'directing and controlling' role of officers.[31] It endorsed the argument that members should not be involved in case work or the routine processes of inspection. It further argued:

'Mutual trust and confidence between members and officers, and respect for the contribution of each to the cause they both seek to serve will be the key to success in the development of the personal social services. The delicate balance of this relationship must not be upset on the one hand by unnecessary interference on the part of the members with day-to-day administration and case work, or on the other hand, by insensitivity on the part of officers in identifying what the Maud Committee describe as the particular problem or case which in their view and from their understanding of the minds of the members, has such implications that members must consider and decide on it.'

As in other services, this neat distinction appears to break down in practice. In part, this may reflect the problems of defining that elusive concept, performance. In part, it may reflect the pre-Seebohm tradition with its roots in the nineteenth century of welfare services being seen as patronage in the hands of councillors. Whatever the explanation, councillors do not necessarily perform as required under the Maud formula. An extreme example illustrates the general point in this description of a chairman of a social services committee given in a 1980 inquiry report:[32]

'He assumed a highly eccentric role. He was not merely interventionist, he interfered in the actual detailed running of the Department. He made excessive demands on senior management in the referral of individual cases.'

However extreme, the example underlines the tension between the member's accountability for the performance of the service for which she or he is responsible, and their accountability for how that performance impinges on particular people. And if the notion of performance is so elusive, is it inevitable that members should seek to generalize from the particular? It is against the background of this question that we now turn to examining how the members of the social services committee in our study perceived their accountability role.

The experience and perceptions of members

Members of social services committees operate in an environment, to summarize the arguments of the previous section, which sharply differs in some crucial respects from that of the other services discussed in this study. The parameters of the social services' role are established by the activities of society as a whole, and by other service agencies. Many of their clients are individuals excluded from adequate education, housing, and health care and often from employment, and others who find themselves marginal to the 'good life'. Social services' traditional culture has been one of taking up where other agencies left off, filling the gaps, and making do and mending where possible. This culture has been fully endorsed by the service itself, particularly those service-providers who have seen their role as righting society's wrongs. Like the health service, the statutory responsibilities are vague and the definition of duties very general. But medical service providers, in contrast to social workers, have never interpreted health care as mainly a response to society's ills. The culture of health services has been traditionally less humble, less contingent on other services, and has had a more positive association with autonomous activity.

Like the service itself, the members of the committee had some distinctive characteristics. The committee was made up of roughly equal numbers of men and women and it had the most polarized age structure of any of the authorities in our study as well as the largest proportion of members over 60 years of age. More than half the councillors were 60 years and more, while most of the rest were 40 or under. Two-thirds of all the members were new to the committee and many of these were newly elected councillors also. This composition can be explained to a large extent by the culture and traditions of the county council itself which has its own status hierarchy of committees, and where the social services committee has tended to provide the political training ground for new councillors and the resting place for older members. Two-thirds of the members were Labour, one was Liberal, and the rest were Conservative.

When talking about their objectives, the members of the social services committee again did so in a distinctive tone of voice. Like the members of most other authorities, they tended to have rather vague and generalized aims. But, unlike the others, they particularized these aims in terms of specific client groups. Three-quarters said that their objectives for the social services were to meet the needs of the poorest in society and the underprivileged, especially children and the elderly:

'Helping the weakest members of society and trying hard to supply services to more people in their own homes. Keeping children with the family, and keeping the family group together.'

(Labour member)

'The welfare and well-being of those in the community who cannot look after themselves.'

(Conservative member)

'The maintenance of the quality of life for those receiving social services.'

(Labour member)

Two members said that their aims were to fulfil the Labour Party Manifesto for all services in the county, while two others said that they did not know what the end product of the service was. Only one had as a priority aim the best use of resources since he had come to believe that efficiency is not incompatible with care. He had learnt this style from being a water authority member, and this was now his aim for all the services he helped to produce as an elected member. Although not emphasized as much as this, the use of resources was beginning to interest other members who confessed that efficiency had not been high on the social services agenda until recently. Indeed, there were more general signs of changing attitudes in the way members were thinking about the purpose of the service. Most of them did stress that their concern was about the underprivileged in society, however defined, but it was also apparent that many of them were beginning to consider the appropriateness and calibre of the services they were providing. Across the political spectrum, members were beginning to translate vague and general objectives into more specific quality of life and quality of services issues, and to relate these to the best use of resources. The differences between the councillors appeared to be more an age and experience split rather than a political one. It was the older members of both parties who stuck to the old platitudes; it was the new intake of younger councillors (mainly Labour) who questioned the organization and set the pace of change:

> 'Members are aware of how they should be thinking about changing social services policy but staff reaction to change is to dig in their heels – staff are reluctant to change their patterns of work. Having said that, social services have rejigged dramatically in the county in recent times. As a member, I want to use all our facilities more appropriately.'

> (Labour member)

Given the broad and general aims, it was not surprising that there was a high level of uncertainty about monitoring the performance of the service – as in health and education. Almost half the members, including the new wave, said that it was difficult if not impossible to assess the performance of social services:

> 'Performance aims are not possible in social services as there are no standard agreements on either aims or methods of achieving them. This means that there is no way of measuring the efficiency of social services.'

> (Labour member)

Several members said that statistics were of limited value in assessing the services. Statistics did not provide any kind of insight in their view, and inter-county comparisons were seen as highly dubious:

> 'Officers provide statistics on all kinds of things, but it is up to members to say how meaningful they are. Figures on total

referrals of children to social services are interesting but it is
what happens to these people after referral that is difficult to
monitor and assess. Further, one can see changes in social
services but cannot see the bulge this change might be creating
in other services. For example, I would like to compare social
services figures on children referred and taken into care with
Home Office statistics on children sent to Borstal or reforma-
tories by courts.'

(Conservative member)

'I don't use statistics very much to look at performance. They
are a good guide to what is actually happening, a rough guide to
the organization of a service but performance and value for
money have to be looked at using different methods.'

(Liberal member)

'I don't use inter-county statistics. I don't see the value of
looking at successful areas because it is mainly political success
you would be looking at.'

(Labour member)

Those councillors who did think it was possible to assess
performance did not do so because they had greater faith in
statistics than their agnostic colleagues. The scepticism about
statistics was near-universal and was, to a large measure, shared by
the officers. What distinguished the optimists, that is those who
had no doubts about their ability to evaluate the service, was their
faith in a hands-on approach. They believed in going out to look
for themselves at the results of the service, and being on watch for
warning signals from the field. In short, they were assessing success
in terms not so much of achieving positive objectives, as in
avoiding mistakes:

'Efficiency is measured by the end results of an adopted policy.
This can be measured by visiting residents in homes. So it is
retrospective appraisal of a policy. Really, only if things go
wrong are policies rethought. If everything goes smoothly, then
it is assumed that policies are being carried out successfully. It is
a question of alarms ringing in the system, to which councillors
are always alert.'

(Labour member)

Overwhelmingly, members of all parties and ages wanted to visit and see for themselves what was going on in their service. Sometimes visits to staff might provide the right information:

'I get vibrations from people who work in the system. A social worker that I trust told me that it is the first winter without a queue for old people's homes in the county. This, I think, shows that we have good domiciliary care services in the county.'

(Conservative member)

Others felt that visits to both providers and consumers of the service were essential:

'Effective evaluation needs client visits, talking to staff and looking at what is going on in the service.'

(Labour member)

'The only way to monitor the quality of the service is to talk to consumers and those who provide it. Members visit residential establishments and talk to staff and consumers.'

(Labour member)

'I find it useful to go around old people's homes and handicapped homes to see what provision is actually made and how it matches our policy.'

(Conservative member)

Interestingly the 'looking around' method of evaluation was almost totally confined to the residential parts of the service. Members reported very little contact with the domiciliary services except for special cases brought before the committee. Even in a service said to be working towards more community and home care, they still felt more comfortable inspecting residential services as a method of evaluation. Oddly only one member suggested that looking around the service as a whole would give more realistic clues about the state of social care being provided at a time when the objective was to release as many clients as possible from residential care. In doing so he also underlined the problems of evaluation in so complex a service:

'One should be able to see ways of monitoring the service and assessing value for money, but right now, I would find it difficult. Although I feel basically that the services are doing a good thing, for example, if we compare ourselves with other authorities, we come out reasonably well, but if we want to see if we are getting value for money, we have to do a more sophisticated exercise, e.g. not accepting certain premises we accept at the moment; this is the hard bit. Overall, in the county we could say that the budgeting system does not work towards value for money. Effective evaluation needs client visits, talking to staff and looking at county and comparative statistics with care – nothing on its own is very good.'

(Labour member)

Another member moved from scepticism to nihilism about the problems of evaluation in the social services:

'Social services organization makes evaluation very difficult. It is too big, too complex, and too centralized.'

(Conservative member)

Despite such lone voices, the great majority of committee members had no doubts about their own accountability role. With very general aims and objectives, but with a fairly open access to the residential part of the services, they were confident and clear about their ability to be accountable for the service. Most did not differentiate between responsibility and accountability when asked, but a constant theme in the interviews was their sense of responsibility downwards in the direction of clients and consumers. Three-quarters of members said that their accountability was primarily to the recipients and clients of social services. Most were at pains to emphasize the county-wide nature of their accountability rather than a narrow political constituency. This was presented, particularly by the older members, as something exciting that they had just learned from the younger, newer county councillors. Almost all felt that the constituency for the service were consumers and clients in the county as a whole. But the complexity of the service did remind some members of the many facets of accountability:

'Staff are an important part of members' responsibility and one has to weigh their welfare and employment conditions with their ability to provide a flexible service. The interests of the staff at the working level are particularly important to members who are providing a face-to-face service with the community.'

(Labour member)

There were also one or two older members who felt accountable to their consciences, while voicing a sense of paternal responsibility for the interests of the community:

'Being answerable to the people keeps a member on his toes, but the personal moral responsibility still operates without this.'

(Labour member)

'I am accountable to myself since I have served the public since 1936. But I take the view that once you are elected, you must represent all the views of the people, and represent their interests.'

(Conservative member)

One or two Labour councillors also felt accountable to the party:

'Accountability to the people really equals accountability to the Party Manifesto. It is much more difficult to be accountable directly to clients, for example, to get someone an adequate home help service.'

(Labour member)

'The Labour Group has a manifesto for the county, and we use this to be accountable to the people in the county. If we fulfil our manifesto, then we are accountable.'

(Labour member)

Only one member, the same one whose scepticism about evaluation has already been quoted, cast doubt on the ability of elected members actually to be accountable for complex public services:

'Like other services, social services members are expected to be responsible and accountable but are not given the power to be accountable. Accountability is about total responsibility and access to information, i.e. manpower levels, performance, and finances. We have very little access to information, and very little control over manpower.'

(Conservative member)

Overall, though, the dominant impression given by the members was that of a set of people who were comfortable with their own role and cushioned from doubt by a sense of doing good. This sense of being at ease with themselves spilled over into their relationship with officers. As in the case of water, and in contrast to education and health, there was also a sense of trust between members and officers and of being involved in a common enterprise. This extended to policy-making, that is the setting of objectives. Three-quarters of members saw a great deal of overlap in the roles of officers and members in policy-making for the service. Only three were convinced that policy-making should be exclusive to members whereas the others did not expect or see a clearly defined policy role for themselves:

'There is no true separation between officers and members in roles and activities. Even in the making up of the Party Manifesto, the officers took part and gave advice.'

(Labour member)

'In theory, there is a simple, basic principle – that councillors make policy but that officers carry out policy. But in reality, the working system is different. A good officer gives alternatives which are used as the basis of policy.'

(Conservative member)

But if officers are involved in policy-making, members also get involved in the day-to-day running of social services:

'I think that in social services, county officers feel a bit hamstrung because they have to keep returning to committee to get every detail of management and operations agreed – and all the nitty gritty that officers would normally expect to carry out unaided and unsupervised.'

(Conservative member)

'Officers' traditional domain is carrying out policy directives of members, but in practice there are grey areas where members may get involved, e.g.:

1 Children going into care.
2 Appeals on registration and de-registration of private residential care.
3 Some staff dismissals where staff feelings against dismissal are strong and where the case is serious.'

(Labour member)

The sharing of responsibility between officers and members was seen to be necessary by one councillor for the successful implementation of policies:

'The problem is that if technical policy decisions are made by members, it can go badly wrong for officers unless they are all involved in what is substantially a co-operative. It can go badly wrong in terms of staff relations and staff co-operation. When policy decisions are made that staff don't like, then both officers and staff can undermine the policy at the working level: that is, where the policy is put (or not put) into practice. For example, staff can refuse to carry out policy or they can agree to carry it out but in practice not carry it out, or they can carry it out in such a way that the net result is unsatisfactory for clients and consumers.'

(Labour member)

This quotation underlines a crucial difference between social services and the water authority. These two were similar in so far as members shared responsibilities, but very different in so far as the former involved the management of people rather than the management of pipes. The greater involvement of social services members in details therefore reflected an attempt, perhaps unconscious, to assert control: to get a grip over the service by looking at the way in which it was delivered at the coal-face. Thus, not only did members put a lot of emphasis on visiting old people's homes and so on, as we have already seen, but also they claimed some routine involvement at the provision of service level, occasionally overturning the decisions of social workers and other staff in committee.

With this level of intervention in production and delivery, it was not surprising that some of the members were sceptical about the expertise of social services staff. While they respected the expertise of their chief officers, they did not think of the service deliverers as either experts or professionals:

'Really there is no "expert" opinion as one voice out of the social work body. If all social workers joined together they could not produce a definitive expert opinion or method of dealing with a particular aspect of the service. Anyone is an expert. Everyone is an expert.'

(Labour member)

'You take account of social workers' expertise, but you don't take it as the last word as you would with a surgeon or a lawyer.'

(Conservative member)

'I think that large numbers of social services staff, like teachers and nurses have tended to promote themselves out of the working job and are therefore no longer experts on the job.'

(Labour member)

One member explained the low position of social services staff in the professional status hierarchy as follows:

'People have an assumption that social workers have less expertise and professionalism in the sense of a body of knowledge than doctors and medical practitioners. The impression of lay people is made worse because the range of workers in the social services is huge and so many of them are untrained. There are people dispensing services to clients who are classified as manual workers. In social services posts are classified as professional only when headquarters staff are professionals.'

(Labour member)

But members did not necessarily accept the expertise even of those who were classified as professionals. In contrast to the NHS, where it would be unthinkable to question the professional judgement of doctors, councillors did not think that social workers should necessarily have the last word as decision-makers or as the authoritative interpreters of information about clients:

> 'At present, it is under review whether or not councillors can see case records of social service clients. I have an actual case where a social services officer has said that under no circumstances are we showing case records to councillors. I don't know how I feel about this; I feel I don't know whose information I should rely on to make a decision as a councillor.'
>
> (Labour member)

Another member was even more uncertain as to the expertise of social workers, particularly where the question of clients' legal rights was concerned and called for another expertise to be brought into the service in certain circumstances:

> 'We receive children into care based on statements received from field social workers and I feel that children and parents are almost better protected by judicial procedures. Councillors are expected to accept that the evidence has already been weighed and that all they are required to do is to nod approval to the director's decision. The advantage of the involvement of the law is that a neutral body/person/agency would be listening to both sides of the case and these proceedings would then be brought to councillors. You cannot rely solely on professional judgement when people's rights may be taken away.'
>
> (Labour member)

In contrast, as already indicated, most councillors held the expertise of senior officers in high regard:

> 'Officers are full time and they should be professionals. The non-expert members like myself rely on officers for assessment of the service.'
>
> (Labour member)

> 'Officers are the experts. We have top officers in the social services.'
>
> (Conservative member)

But the overriding impression left by the interviews was that, in contrast to all the other services in the study, councillors regarded themselves as experts, although some would contribute more expertise than others on the basis of their career involvement in the social services. In effect, the councillors saw their own expertise as great as that of the service deliverers.

Summary

Most members of the social services committee, as we have seen, were both confident about, and comfortable with, their own accountability role. Like their counterparts on the education committee, they saw this as largely unproblematic and nothing to agonize about. But it would be misleading to conclude from this that the fact of election produces a uniform perception, let alone practice of accountability. For there were some significant differences between the two sets of councillors. While the members of the education committee mostly saw themselves accountable to the community, the members of the social services committee saw themselves predominantly accountable to their clients. In neither instance, however, was there much stress on the textbook form of accountability by elected members to the voters. Perhaps this is not surprising in the case of social services since these, unlike most public services, exist largely to deal with people who either cannot, or do not, vote, that is children, the very elderly, and society's casualties.

The two sets of members also differed in another crucial respect. In education, as we saw in the previous chapter, there was a divorce between perceptions of accountability and control. Councillors saw nothing incongruous about stressing both their accountability and powerlessness. In the social services, there was congruity between the perceptions of accountability and control. The members felt both accountable and to a large degree in control. In this respect, they were very similar to the *non-elected* members of the water authority. But again, a distinction needs to be drawn. For the apparent similarity in the perceptions of social services and water authority members about their own ability to exercise control conceals important differences.

Among water authority members, the perception of effective

control derived from the relationship between inputs and outputs: there were clear objectives, and ways of measuring progress towards them. None of these conditions held in the social services, a clear example of a service where objectives of members were vague and generalized, where there was a high degree of uncertainty about the relationship between inputs and outputs and little use of measures of performance. If most members of the social services committee were nevertheless confident about their ability to exercise control, this was because they put the emphasis primarily on control of process. They perceived control in terms of a hands-on, bricks and mortar approach: they looked at what was happening in the council's own homes and institutions. And unlike the members of the education committee, who were effectively barred from schools by the teaching profession, they had no problems about getting access.

This last point stresses yet another crucial difference between education and social services in our study, overriding the fact that both are run by elected members. This is that in the former, the service providers have successfully asserted many of their claims to professional autonomy – however resented it may be by the elected members. In the latter, as we have seen, the service providers have failed to achieve the position, and elected members concede them neither special expertise nor professional autonomy. It is because of this that the social services councillors feel able to call individual service providers to account for their actions. Whether their own confidence about their ability to control what was happening was actually justified is, of course, another matter. The control of people is very different from the control of pipes, and there is almost certainly a seepage of councillor control when it comes to the more diffuse, non-institutional, and therefore non-visible, activities of the social services. Indeed, at the heart of this confidence found among most members, there was also evidence of a nagging doubt. If control is all about the personal involvement of councillors in service delivery – what we have called the hands-on approach – then what happens when the councillors are not around? To the extent that even low-status service providers can make themselves invisible, they can make their activities as immune from scrutiny as if they were high-status professionals with formal autonomy.

REFERENCES

1 M. Payne (1979) *Power, Authority and Responsibility in Social Services.* London: Macmillan: 20.
2 Labour Party (1981) *Local Government Handbook.* London: Labour Party.
3 K. Judge (1978) *Rationing Social Services.* London: Heinemann.
4 Social Services Committee Session 1982–83 (1983) *Public Expenditure on the Social Services*, Minutes of Evidence. London: HMSO HC 321–I and II: 64–7. More recent figures, which do not change the pattern, can be found in the annual statistical series published by the Chartered Institute of Public Finance and Accountancy.
5 M. O'Higgins (1984) Local Variations in Social Services Spending and Demographic Changes. Memorandum in Social Services Committee Session 1983–84. Fourth Report, *Public Expenditure on the Social Services.* London: HMSO HC 395.
6 See, for example, K. Judge (1978) *Rationing Social Services.* London: Heinemann Table 2.6.
7 Audit Commission (1983) *Social Services: Provision of Care for the Elderly.* London: HMSO.
8 D. Larder, P. Day, and R. Klein (1986) *Institutional Care for the Elderly: The Geographical Distribution of the Public/Private Mix in England.* Bath Social Policy Paper no. 10. Bath: Centre for the Analysis of Social Policy.
9 See, for example, Department of Health and Social Security (1977) *The Way Forward.* London: HMSO.
10 Department of Health and Social Security (1978) *A Happier Old Age.* London: HMSO.
11 T. Bamford (1982) *Managing Social Work.* London: Tavistock: 158–61.
12 *Audit Commission (1983) Social Services: Provision of Care for the Elderly.* London: HMSO. See also the following report, Audit Commission (1985) *Managing Social Services for the Elderly More Effectively.* London: HMSO.
13 T. Booth (1985) *Home Truths.* Aldershot: Gower.
14 W. Harbert (1978) Interview: *Health and Social Service Journal* LXXXVIII, 4615, 3 November: 1,242–244.
15 B. Glastonbury, D. M. Cooper, and P. Hawkins (1980) *Social Work in Conflict.* London: Croom Helm.
16 T. G. Field-Fisher (Chairman) (1974) *Report of the Committee of Inquiry into the Care and Supervision Provided in Relation to Maria Colwell* London: HMSO.

17 L. Blom-Cooper (Chairman) (1985) *Report of the Panel of Inquiry into the Circumstances surrounding the Death of Jasmine Beckford.* London: Borough of Brent.

18 Working Party (Chairman: P. M. Barclay) (1984) *Social Workers: Their Role and Tasks.* London: Bedford Square Press.

19 Joint Steering Group (1980) Accreditation in Social Work: Second and Final Report. January, Appendix C in British Association of Social Workers, *Social Workers and Employers.* London: BASW.

20 D. Billis, G. Bromley, A. Hey, and R. Rowbottom (1980) *Organising Social Services Departments.* London: Heinemann.

21 Joint Steering Group (1980) Accreditation in Social Work: Second and Final Report. January, Appendix C in British Association of Social Workers, *Social Workers and Employers.* London: BASW.

22 P. Parsloe and M. Hill (1978) Supervision and Accountability. In O. Stevenson and P. Parsloe (eds) *Social Service Teams: The Practitioner's View.* London: HMSO.

23 Social Services Inspectorate (1986) *Inspection of the Supervision of Social Workers in the Assessment and Monitoring of Cases of Child Abuse.* London: DHSS, March.

24 Social Services Inspectorate (1985) *Inspection of Residential Care for Elderly People and for Children in the London Borough of Southwark.* London: DHSS, December.

25 R. Klein and P. Hall (1975) *Caring for Quality in the Caring Services.* London: Bedford Square Press.

26 See, for example, Social Services Inspectorate (1985) *Inspection of Local Authority Care for Elderly Mentally Disordered People.* London: DHSS. September.

27 See, for example, NHS Health Advisory Service (1986) *Report on Services for Mentally Ill People Provided by the East Surrey Health Authority and the Social Services Department of Surrey County Council.* Sutton: HAS, February.

28 P. Hall (1976) *Reforming the Welfare.* London: Heinemann.

29 F. Seebohm (Chairman) (1968) *Report of the Committee on Local Authority and Allied Personal Social Services.* London: HMSO Cmnd 3703: paras 491–94.

30 Working Party (Chairman: P. M. Barclay) (1984) *Social Workers: Their Role and Tasks.* London: Bedford Square Press: para. 12.60.

31 F. Seebohm (Chairman) (1968) *Report of the Committee on Local Authority and Allied Personal Social Services.* London: HMSO Cmnd 3703: paras 605–27.

32 Quoted in T. Bamford (1982) *Managing Social Work.* London: Tavistock: 133.

9

Interpretations and implications

In trying to reflect on our exploration of how members of different authorities perceive and define their own role in accountability, we found ourselves attempting to tease out a puzzle. Our starting-point, anchored in the logic of the academic literature on the theory of accountability and the assumptions of public policy pronouncements, was that to be fully accountable implies the ability to exercise control. If service providers are not accountable to authority members, that is if the links in the chain are broken, then how can authority members be accountable, be it to voters or to a secretary of state? In our study, however, we found that members of some authorities saw no incompatibility between perceiving themselves as accountable, while yet lamenting their own lack of control. The difference between the authorities made up of directly elected members and those made up, to varying degrees, of nominated members, did not stem from different perceptions of their own role. It reflected, rather, differences in the way in which they responded to and interpreted the tensions inherent in that role.

Consider first the non-elected members of the health and police authorities. In both cases members were worried about their ability to control the services for which they were responsible. And, in line with our expectations, they were also worried about their own ability to be accountable for those services. In short, their attitudes were consistent in that they were aware of the tension between the requirements of formal accountability and the reality of lack of effective control. Consider next, however, the directly elected members of the education and social services committees. In the former case, as we saw in Chapter 7, the members expressed considerable doubts about their ability to control the service; in the latter case, as we saw in Chapter 8, they had far fewer doubts. But both sets of authority members, to a remarkable degree, saw the exercise of their accountability as unproblematic. This would, in turn, suggest that directly elected members differ from nominated members not so much in their perceptions of accountability but in their ability to convince themselves that accountability is unproblematical and to ignore the relationship between accountability and control. From their perspective, the fact of election, the constitutional myth that election *ipso facto* makes members accountable, washes away the contradictions involved in the role. Accountability is taken for granted.

The contrary does not follow, however. Here, the case of the non-elected members of the water authority is instructive. These were unique among the members of the non-elected authorities in our study in that they saw neither the exercise of accountability nor that of control as problematic. They were as confident about their role as the local authority members, despite lacking the imprimatur of elections. Their confidence stemmed from their perceptions of congruity between practice and theory in their exercise of their own role, inasmuch as accountability and control marched hand in hand.

The evidence therefore suggests that the distinction, in much of public discussion between elected members as being accountable by definition and non-elected members being non-accountable by definition, is oversimple. And it is oversimple because it ignores the link between control and accountability. Our findings would suggest that the real distinction is in the perceptions of members. It is between those elected members who perceive themselves to be accountable, even when the requirement of effective control is lacking, and those non-elected members who feel themselves to be accountable only when the necessary condition of effective control is met. The paradox would seem to be that the rhetoric of election as synonymous with accountability may, in fact, divert attention from the conditions that have to be met if accountability in the full sense is to be achieved; in contrast, members who lack the legitimacy of election appear to be more conscious of their need for control.

All this is, however, to assume that accountability itself is an unproblematic concept. Again, our findings would suggest the need for a more finely shaded interpretation, as well as providing a warning against assuming that members of authorities necessarily read the textbooks which tell them what their accountability role is. The different ways in which the authority members thought aloud about their role, in response to our questions, in themselves illustrate the ambiguities of the concept. They often tended to use a clutch of words – accountability, answerability, and responsibility – as though they were interchangeable. Few appeared to use accountability in the strict sense, that is the revocability of a mandate. There was little sense, either among the members of nominated authorities (whose mandate could, in theory, be revoked by the secretary of state or his agents) or among the members of elected bodies (whose mandate could, in theory, be revoked by the voters) of sanctions if their justification failed to satisfy. More frequently their implicit definition of accountability seemed to shade into answerability: the duty to provide explanations or to give visibility to their actions. Lastly, many members tended to define accountability in terms of their responsibility, either to the community being served or to use their own sense of what was sensible or proper: they internalized accountability, as it were, as a general duty to pursue the public good according to their own criteria of what was right. As they saw it, their mandate also imposed a duty on them: the real sanction was not revocability of the mandate, but their own civic super-ego. They saw themselves as trustees or tribunes rather than delegates.

It is this perhaps which helps to explain a pattern running right across our services: the emphasis among members on seeing accountability, answerability, or responsibility as being directed *to* the 'community' at large, rather than following the lines of constitutional accountability. Whether nominated members of health, police, or water authorities or elected members of education or social service committees, it was this emphasis which provided a common thread through the responses. The nominated members did not, for the most part, see themselves directly accountable to a secretary of state, as they are in theory (the main exception being the chairmen of the authorities concerned). The elected members did not, for their part, see themselves directly accountable to the voters, as they are in theory. Some Labour councillors saw themselves accountable to the party; but interestingly the Conservatives did not. This indeed was one of the very few issues where there was even a hint of consistent differences between political parties: going through the notes of the interviews, it was often impossible to tell the political allegiance of the respondents.

In adopting a 'community' view of accountability, members may in fact have been reflecting the actual pattern of their day-to-day linkages, which have little to do with such remote abstractions as the secretary of state or voters. The duty to explain and justify, the interviews would suggest, was part of the texture of members' lives, deriving less from their formal position than from their informal contacts with a network of local or occupational interest groups, (contacts which may, in the first place, have been instrumental in getting them nominated or elected). They rarely discussed their services with individual citizens or voters: as we have seen, even in the case of councillors, most of the issues raised by members of the public were, in fact, to do with public housing. They were, however, involved as active citizens themselves in a variety of contacts, responding to pressures and demands and thus forced to justify the actions of the authorities of which they were members. This would suggest that the way in which members of authorities define their accountability – as a general, diffuse duty to justify or explain to that nebulous notion, the 'community' – reflects their position as public persons, rather than the route (nomination or election) by which they arrived at that position. It is because they are publicly exposed to scrutiny that they feel themselves accountable, in one or other meanings of that concept. It is their own, personal visibility – whether as magistrates on a police authority or councillors on a local authority committee – which makes them sensitive to the need to explain and justify themselves in face-to-face encounters. In other words, the subjective sense of accountability of authority members has its roots – our evidence would imply – as much in the social context in which they operate, as in constitutional doctrine.

Performance, policies, and actions

But for what do authority members see themselves accountable? What is their language of evaluation? Again, our discussion must start with a puzzle, this time stemming from the discrepancy between the conventional doctrine of accountability and our own findings. The drift of public policy, as we saw in our earlier chapters, has been towards conceiving accountability as being responsible for the overall performance of a service and using what might be termed managerial tools of analysis as the language of evaluation. However, our interviews provide little evidence that the members of the five authorities in our study – with one significant exception – saw their own role in the way assumed in public policy and much academic discussion. Moreover, they also suggest that many of the assumptions made are unrealistic – given the characteristics of the services themselves.

First, our use of the notion of performance in public services needs some explanation. This encompasses two concepts which stalk the literature: policy-making and policy implementation.[1] To talk about the performance of a service is to combine these into one concept: to convey the idea that a service is to be evaluated by what it does, which will inevitably be a combination of what policy decisions have been taken, often over a very long period of time, and the processes whereby those policies are translated into action. To be accountable for the performance of a service, in our definition, is thus to be answerable for the achievement of multiple objectives (which may or may not be expressed in terms of explicit policy decisions of either policy-makers or service providers). It is from these objectives that the language of evaluation is derived, since there can be no criteria of assessment without a sense of what is desirable. The objectives may be about ends or about means. To return to a distinction drawn in our first chapter, they may involve either political accountability or managerial accountability: argument about what should be done and argument about whether what is being done is being done efficiently and effectively. The notion of performance thus embraces the various dimensions of accountability in that it assumes that members of authorities will be answerable not just for the different strands of service delivery

but for the way in which these combine to form a total tapestry of
service provision. Using this wide sense of the term there is little
evidence that members of the various authorities in our study –
with the single exception of the water authority – had any sense of
being accountable for the performance of their services. They may
have perceived themselves as 'owning' particular policy strands:
that is for being accountable for pursuing specific policies (perhaps
because these were in the party manifesto; for example, in the case
of the education committee members, abolishing corporal punishment, and introducing peace studies in schools). But our interviews
provided scant evidence of the members consciously striving to
achieve particular performance goals: Marathon, for them, tended
to be a vague platitude – such as peace in the community or
realizing the full potential of children. Other than that, members
tended to see good performance in terms of higher inputs. Where
members of the various authorities tended to differ was chiefly in
whether or not they found their inability to set some overarching
set of goals bothersome. Again, the members of the elected
authorities tended to find this issue unproblematic, while others
(notably the members of health authorities) were worried about
their inability to define performance in terms of the efficient and
effective pursuit of specific objectives. Even in the case of the
elected members, there were signs of a dawning interest in the
notion of performance among the young councillors: in this
respect, as in some others, there were signs of a generational
split.

   There are a number of reasons for the apparent lack of interest
in the overall performance, that is outcomes of their services, by
most members. First and foremost, the notion of performance is
genuinely difficult and elusive in the case of most of the services in
our study, as we have seen in the chapters dealing with them. The
relationship between inputs and outcomes is often difficult to
discern, which might explain the traditional preoccupation of
members with their accountability for inputs only; the contribution
of any particular service is often difficult to isolate from the wider
social environment. All this is self-evidently so in the case of
health, the police, education, and social services. In the one
instance where there is a clearly defined concept of performance,
that of the water authority, the members had indeed a confident

sense of knowing where they were going and how to check the achievement against objectives.

The second set of reasons stem from the complexity of the concept of accountability itself. This has, as argued in the first chapter, a number of different dimensions. If accountability for achieving goals is not possible, it may still be possible to be accountable for process: the way in which services are run as judged by the competence of individual actions. But process is, as we have seen, largely the domain of the service providers. It is they who claim to determine the language of evaluating the process of service-delivery, be they surgeons, police, or teachers. Where members of the authorities in our study did not perceive their accountability as responsibility for the performance of their services, seen in terms of process, they were only being realistic. They were, in fact, largely excluded from this domain by the service-providers.

The point is brought out by the two services in our studies where, if for very different reasons the members *did* see themselves to be accountable for process. In the case of the water authority, this was because the criteria for assessing process directly followed from those defining objectives: a failure in process could be deduced from a failure to achieve such objectives as an adequate supply of water or of the efficient disposal of water. There was no doubt about causality. More interesting, because more unexpected, the members of the social services not only saw themselves as accountable for process but also appeared to be reasonably confident that they were successfully carrying out their role. They were the only members responsible for labour intensive services (as distinct from those delivered by pipes) who seemed remarkably free from doubts about their own ability to know what is going on in their service. Nor is this surprising, perhaps, given that social services are different – as we have seen – in that the service-providers have failed fully to assert their claim to the language of evaluation: witness the ability of the members of the social service committee to review and reverse the decisions of service-providers (to underline the uniqueness of this, only imagine a health authority telling a surgeon what operations he or she should carry out or an education committee telling a headteacher how to score examination papers).

The third reason why members lack interest in outcomes is that they tend to be suspicious of managerial tools and techniques for assessing performance with the exception, as always, of the water authority. Across services they are, as we have seen, at best agnostic about the use of comparative information or performance indicators. Statistics invite immediate scepticism. In part this reflects the ambiguities of the statistics, and the real problems involved in using them (as noted in the service chapters). But there is also a sense of being in a hostile territory, where there is a risk of being manipulated by the natives: in particular, by chief officers. The pattern is not entirely consistent, and there were once again signs of a generational divide. The sense of being manipulated by the gatekeepers of information and data was particularly strong among members of the health and education committees who both complained about the lack of relevant information. It was less evident in the case of the police and social services. The differences seem to reflect less variations in the adequacy or quality of the information being supplied (on reading some of the interview material, officers of the council concerned commented indignantly that members had all the information they wanted) than variations in the degree of trust between members and their chief officers. The paradox would seem to be that if a chief officer is not trusted, he or she will be asked for ever more information – yet never satisfy her or his audience. Conversely, if he or she is trusted, so his or her rendering of accounts – in terms of the information provided – is likely to be accepted. Moreover, given trust, it is the chief officer who interprets the meaning of the information: significantly the scepticism of the members in our study mirrored the scepticism of the chief officers interviewed about statistics and performance indicators (who, it may be argued, have a self-interest in denigrating information which may reflect on the performance of the services for which they are responsible: to the extent that there are 'objective' measures of the efficiency and effectiveness of their services, so their own realm of discretion is narrowed).

It is this wariness towards official information, and particularly statistical data, which helps to explain the lack of the use made by the members in our study of the kind of comparative analyses of performance provided by the Audit Commission or by inspectorates. Independent managerial accountability and political accountability do not appear to mesh: the former, contrary to our own expectations, and that of the policy-makers, does not link with and reinforce the latter. Partly this may reflect the timing of our study: when the members were interviewed, the system of audit and inspection was only beginning to get off the ground. Partly, however, it also reflects an underlying antipathy towards technical tools of accountability (qualified by generational differences, once more). Our interviews suggested considerable suspicion of a value-for-money approach as somehow being incompatible with services dedicated to the public good and perhaps also threatening qualitative and professional objectives. Matthew Arnold's hostility to a 'mechanistic' approach to evaluating education is clearly shared by many members responsible for delivering human services.

In line with this wariness about statistical information and hostility to 'mechanistic' methods of evaluation, members tended to see the performance of their services in terms of what they could see or learn for themselves. They were most comfortable for being accountable for service provision which they could inspect for themselves, or about which they could get information through their social networks; a kind of 'hands on' view of accountability. It is this which explains the high degree of satisfaction felt by members of the social services committee, who actually could visit residential homes (to the neglect, as we have seen, of diffuse and less visible services provided in people's own homes). It is this, equally, which explains the frustration of members of the education committee who felt themselves to be excluded from schools and their anxiety to gain entry by becoming governors. This would suggest that, in addition to the complexity, heterogeneity, and uncertainty, dimensions of services discussed in Chapter 3, the degree of institutionalized visibility is also an important factor in the exercise of accountability. To the extent that services vary in their concentration or diffusion of provision, so the exercise of accountability becomes more problematic, with the police perhaps offering the most extreme example of a service delivered on the hoof.

The example of the social services committee brings out a further dimension of accountability. The members of this committee, as we have seen, were able to review decisions taken by service providers; many of them, furthermore saw themselves as responding to individual needs and problems – on a case-by-case basis – rather than providing a coherent, planned service. They stressed, therefore, a dimension of accountability which can all too easily be overlooked when the emphasis is on the efficiency and effectiveness of the overall performance of a service. That is accountability in the traditional sense of being answerable for the individual actions of service providers. Thus it may be argued that the performance of a service is no more than the sum of the actions performed, and if these are done conscientiously and competently, then all is well with the service as a whole. Conversely dissatisfaction with individual actions can be seen as evidence of inadequacy or failure. Indeed, this view seemed to underly the emphasis put by many of the authority members on using individual complaints or cases as their criterion for evaluating the performance of services: if there were no such complaints or problems, they often seemed to assume, then there was no cause to worry about the performance of the service. Accountability, on this interpretation, revolves around the ability to call service providers retrospectively to account for their actions, and good performance can be deduced from the absence of noise.

This view of accountability presents some difficulties. First, individual competence is no guarantee of collective competence. If the wrong service is being provided to the wrong people, then the ability to call individual service providers to account will do nothing to ensure that they are meeting the appropriate objectives of the service. In other words, accountability for individual actions cannot substitute for, only complement, accountability for setting the appropriate objectives, that is for the framework within which individual decisions are taken, and which provides the criteria for justifying those decisions. Second, to bring the argument back to the thesis developed in our opening chapters, accountability is problematic precisely because of the assertion by many service providers that only they can define and evaluate competence. The social services committee is unique, as we have seen, among our services precisely because members do not concede this monopoly of evaluation to the service providers, just as the water authority is unique in that competence can be deduced from outcomes because the service providers are pipes, to exaggerate only a little: that is it is about the meeting of specific objectives, with little uncertainty about the relationship between inputs and outputs. In other words, even if the ability to make service providers answerable for their actions is an important dimension of accountability, albeit only one dimension, it is one which the members of many authorities cannot, in practice, exercise. And it is precisely this inability, cutting across members of elected and nominated bodies, which explains the kind of baffled frustrations which our interviews uncovered among members of health authorities and of the education committee. To make this point is to turn to our next puzzle, which is the extent to which the success of service providers in appropriating the language of evaluation depends on their professional status.

Members, experts, and professionals

One clear conclusion emerges from our evidence. This is that professional status, in the strict sense, has nothing to do with the occupational power of service providers to determine the language of evaluation. The argument that the problems of accountability in the NHS, and the consequent frustrations of authority members, stem from the professional status of doctors, does not survive our comparative approach. Many of the same problems, and many of the same frustrations, were evident in the case of the police authority, despite the fact that the police lack all the attributes of a profession as traditionally derived from the medical model. So, whatever the reasons why a particular occupation manages to appropriate the language of evaluation, they would appear to have little to do with high social status, esoteric knowledge, and the other characteristics of the medical profession which are usually invoked to explain its power.

Nor does the explanation lie in the fact that members of authorities perceive their service providers as professionals even when the latter lack such defining characteristics; that is their subjective definitions differ from textbook definitions. Despite the rhetoric of professionalism adopted by the police, as documented in Chapter 5, the authority members were not at all inclined to subscribe to it. On the contrary, they were assertively sceptical about such claims, as they were to a lesser extent in the case of teachers and social workers. Equally, they tended to be doubtful about the degree of 'expertise' of the service providers: emphatically so in the case of social workers, but hardly less so in the case of teachers and the police. This scepticism was shared by elected and non-elected members and cut across political parties. So it would be difficult to argue that the power of the service providers to appropriate the language of evaluation rests on the recognition by authority members that they have a monopoly of expertise inaccessible to the laymen.

The reasons why some occupations manage to assert their ability to define the language of evaluation, while others don't, seem to be complex. A possible explanation might run along the following lines. First, this ability seems to reflect the differential capacity of service providers to make their own activities invisible. Thus, our interviews suggest that many service providers were seen not as professionals or experts but rather as members of a 'mystery' in the dual sense of that word: that is as belonging to a guild or engaged in secret, enigmatic rituals (OED). In turn, this would indicate that the service characteristics, the environment in which work is carried out, may be as important as producer characteristics. For example, in the health services, authority members found the activities of ancillary workers as mysterious (in the sense of being difficult to control, assess, and get to grips with) as those of doctors. Second, this ability also seems to reflect service characteristics in one key respect. If the service ranks high on certainty, as in the case of the water authority, then members may impute a high degree of expertise or professionalism to the service managers, and yet feel that they are in command of the language of evaluation: this is because, to return to a point already made, there are clearly defined objectives and the effective and efficient performance of the service can be assessed in terms of outputs.

While these explanations help to make sense of our findings, they still leave some puzzles. In particular, there remains the contrast between social workers, on the one hand, and teachers and the police on the other. In terms of both service and producer characteristics, social workers do not seem to be so very different from the other two groups. They are relatively low-status, would-be professional. They all work in services with a high degree of uncertainty and complexity (Table 1 in Chapter 3). Yet social workers are very much the exception among the three occupational groups when it comes to being held accountable by authority members for their actions. One reason may be – to return to our classification of services – that social services, unlike the other two, rank high on heterogeneity: that is social workers are only a minority of the total labour force. In short, we may be getting a hint that where a particular occupational group dominates a service, its ability to appropriate the language of evaluation may derive from its power as an organized interest group or trade-union: the one common element shared by teachers and the police. And where a particular occupational group is only one of many contributing to the productions of service, its power may (as in the case of the medical profession) reflect either status or a key role in that service, that is the ability to bring it to a standstill. When a group has neither status nor the ability to bring the service to a standstill or to chaos, then it may also lack the ability to function as a mystery: precisely the case of social work.[2]

These explanations are necessarily tentative and perhaps incomplete. It may be that a historical dimension would help to solve our puzzle: for example the peculiar experience of social work may reflect the fact that the managerial structure for delivering services (the Poor Law system) evolved before the occupation itself gained an identity – precisely the opposite of what happened in the case of the medical profession. However, while our findings may not yield a full explanation, they do generate some firm if negative conclusions. In summary, these are: first, that the problems of accountability cut across elected and nominated authorities; second, that professional status as such does not provide an adequate explanation of the differences and similarities found across services; third, that the way in which authority members perceive their accountability role does not fit neatly with the current policy emphasis on managerial accountability for the efficient and effective performance of services. It is to the implications of these findings for policy and ways of thinking about accountability to which we turn in our final section.

Thinking about accountability

In drawing out the implications of our study, we do so in full awareness of the fact that the members of our authorities were not necessarily representative and that, furthermore, they were studied at one point in time. Studies of authorities in different political environments might have yielded a different picture of the perceptions and performances of members; an inquiry into the authorities in our study carried out now might also have produced a different picture of the perception of members. With changes in the management structure of the NHS, with police forces and authorities in the process of adopting a more managerial style and with a shifting political scene in local government, we are dealing with a turbulent environment. What follows therefore is based on a minimalist strategy. We draw out those implications which help to identify the various dimensions and problems of accountability: that is where we do not necessarily have to claim that our findings are generalizable in order to identify specific issues. It is a strategy which, furthermore, emphasizes our negative findings on the assumption that if there is only one 'Black Swan',[3] then certain theories or conventionally held ideas about accountability may be put into question.

The first, and perhaps strongest, conclusion generated by our study is that the widespread assumption that direct election can somehow be equated with the effective practice of accountability does not hold water. If member accountability to the public (or to a secretary of state) logically entails the ability of members to call service deliverers to account, then the education committee in our study is a 'Black Swan'. While members saw themselves as accountable, they also complained about their inability to control the service. Conversely the equally widespread assumption that nominated bodies can be equated with the absence of effective accountability is not sustained by our evidence. If members' perceptions of accountability are largely shaped by internalized feelings of a duty and an ability to explain and justify, as suggested by our evidence, election is not a necessary condition for bringing this about. Nor is election a sufficient condition for ensuring control. This finding should come as no surprise; it is in line with much of the literature on local government, reviewed in Chapter 8, which suggests that members often feel frustrated in their role and by their inability to get a grip on their services. What should come as a surprise is the persistence and durability of the myth that elected status equals accountability: a myth which seems to ignore what is actually involved in the practice of accountability.

The first implication of this conclusion is that problems of accountability in services like the NHS, now run by nominated authorities, would not disappear if these were to be put under the control of elected members. This would introduce 'democracy' only in a formal sense, if it is conceded that accountability in the full sense depends on the ability to establish control over the service concerned. The second implication is that, whatever one's view of the desirability or otherwise of having services run by elected bodies, if the purpose is to bring about effective account-ability to the public, then it is crucial to bring about effective control over the service concerned. This is the missing link, and the necessary condition for completing the circle of accountability.

If the negative conclusion is strong, the positive implications are less clear. If, as our findings indicate, the problems of control reflect service characteristics – and, in particular, the ability of service providers either to appropriate the language of evaluation or to make their activities invisible (and perhaps both) – then the problems of asserting effective accountability are deep rooted. Developing tools for assessing the performance of service providers not only is a conceptually difficult, though not imposs-ible, task, but also is likely to encounter resistance from organized service providers who will, quite rightly, see any such attempt as a challenge to their autonomy. Developing such tools is an intel-lectual challenge; introducing them is a political challenge – as the recent case of the teachers has demonstrated. Again, the charac-teristics of individual services may be decisive, as we have argued previously. Partly this is because they vary in the extent to which they lend themselves to the specification of clear objectives, against which the performance of service providers may be assessed. In this respect, the water authority provides the extreme paradigm case of the conditions necessary for moving in this direction. To the extent that other services resemble the water authority in terms of the ability to define the relationship between inputs and outputs, and to equate outputs with outcomes, so it may be possible to move in this direction. But the converse is also true; given unclear objectives and ambiguity about the contribution of a specific service to the achievement of a particular goal, so it will be more difficult.

Our findings also suggest strongly the need to bring together managerial and political concepts of accountability. To discuss accountability in terms of setting objectives, and monitoring progress towards them, is to adopt a managerial approach. Our finding that, with the exception of the water authority where such an approach is appropriate, members see such managerial techniques as inadequate or inapplicable, suggests that yet another link in the chain of accountability is missing. This is the link between members and technicians in the design of tools of accountability. The suspicion of members may reflect, with some reason, the fear that technical tools are usurping their own function: that auditors and inspectors are either explicitly or implicitly setting their objectives and standards which should be generated by political debate. Similarly, and with equal reason, members may feel that these objectives and standards are an incomplete and partial way of looking at performance: that the result may be to introduce hidden biases and, for example, tilt performance towards cutting costs rather than achieving quality as defined by members or professionals. The example of performance indicators, such as those used in the NHS, is a case in point. Ostensibly these are neutral, technical exercises: the objective products of experts. Yet implicit in them is a set of values or assumptions about what counts as good performance, and what therefore the language of evaluation should be. The fact that 'good performance' is itself a contestable notion tends, all too easily, to be overlooked. Even in services like water, where the notion of 'good performance' is largely unproblematic at present, this may change if there is increased conflict over competing priorities. Accountability for following a set of *rules* (whether devised by accountants, economists, or lawyers) is only one dimension of accountability; it cannot be divorced from the wider context of accountability for *conduct* (which includes the way in which rules are devised and applied).

This would in turn imply that the process of producing technical tools of accountability needs to be 'politicized' if such tools are not to be seen as a threat or irrelevance by authority members. In other words, the production of such tools should be seen for what is it: not just as a neutral exercise in the application of objective expertise but as an argument about what should count as good performance. If our concern is about improving the practice of political accountability, whether by elected members or ministers, then the politics of producing the necessary tools should be made explicit. This means opening up a dialogue between all actors in the political arena and the technocrats of accountability: a dialogue which is all the more essential given that the definition of accountability, as noted in Chapter 2, has widened out beyond such traditional concerns as financial or process regularity and propriety to encompass more difficult and contentious dimensions of accountability such as efficiency and effectiveness. If definitions of efficiency and effectiveness are seen to be imposed by the technicians of accountability then, as our evidence confirms, they are also likely to be rejected; if, however, they are seen as the product of a joint debate, they may be accepted and used.

For accountability depends, as argued in Chapter 1, on an agreed framework of meaning. If there is no such framework, if information about actions or statistical data is meaningless to one or other of the actors in the accountability arena (whether as citizens, authority members, or service providers) then the result will be a dialogue of the deaf. Information, the life-blood of accountability, will be literally meaningless; of no significance in judging actions or performance. This, indeed, is precisely what seems to have happened. As we have seen, government policy has been to promote accountability through greater visibility for the public services by the requirement to publish information about performance. There is, however, little evidence that either authority members or the public at large respond to or use such information. The only thing which has been made more visible is ambiguity, in the absence of agreement as to what meaning (if any) should be attached to the information that is published. Again, the need would seem to be for the construction of an agreed and common vocabularly, both between central and local government, and between authority members and service providers through engagement in argument.

The need to move to an agreed vocabulary is reinforced by the fact that, in local government, in contrast to central government, the machinery of audit is seen not as the servant of the elected representatives but as a check on them. In the case of central government (because of the division of responsibility between the executive and the legislature), auditors and ombudsmen are accountable to parliament; in the case of local government, there is no such link – logically enough, given the fact that councillors have both executive and representative roles. So, for example, auditors are responsible for enforcing the law about what local authorities may or may not do: they are the critics, not the servants of councillors. Like professional bodies, auditors are semi-free floating bodies (see *Figure 1*, Chapter 2) instead of being integrated into the system. They are both dead ends instead of links in the chain of accountability. It is therefore not surprising that the technicians of accountability may be viewed with suspicion by local authority members, instead of being seen as an essential part of the practice of accountability. And further compounding the difficulties, different instruments of accountability may use different criteria.[4] Thus, while the Audit Commission may be arguing that the inadequate management of falling rolls by local authorities is wasting resources, HM Inspectorate may be drawing attention to the effects of inadequate or poor professional practices: the managerial and professional approaches may be appearing to pull in opposite directions and giving very different signals.

From this perspective, accountability is brought about not only by institutions or techniques but also by dialogue. The question to put about institutions is whether or not they promote the process of argument about what should be the criteria of judgement and about the relationship between them: it is political deliberation – 'the medium wherein men make sense of their common situation in discourse with one another'[5] – which is at the heart of accountability. It was precisely this realization which, to return to our point of departure in Chapter 1, lay at the root of the Athenian concept of democracy that still tends to shape our ways of thinking about accountability. The point emerges clearly from Aristotle's discussion of the relationship between the people and the experts.[6] On the one hand, Aristotle conceded, it may well be that:

'the function of judging whether medical attendance has been properly given should belong to those whose profession it is to attend patients and cure the complaints from which they suffer – in a word, to members of the medical profession. The same may be held to be true of all other professions and arts; and just as doctors should have their conduct examined before a body of doctors, so too should those who follow other professions have theirs examined before a body of their own profession.'

On the other hand he argued:

'In the first place, . . . each individual may, indeed be a worse judge than the experts; but all, when they meet together, are either better than experts or at any rate no worse. In the second place, there are a number of arts in which the creative artist is not the only, or even the best, judge. These are the arts whose *products* [our emphasis] can be understood and judged, even by those who do not possess any skill in the art. A house, for instance, is something which can be understood by others besides the builder; indeed, the user of a house – or in other words, the householder – will judge it even better than he does.'

In short, to translate Aristotle's point into the context of the modern debate about accountability, while experts may indeed be the best judges of the technical process of service-delivery, they can – and indeed should – be called to account for the end-product or outputs. If accountability is seen exclusively in terms of process, then the experts' language of service evaluation is likely to prevail, (whether it is the expertise of the service providers themselves or that of the technicians of accountability). If, however, accountability is seen in terms of being responsible for outputs, then the language of service evaluation will be that of political argument.

To draw this conclusion is to suggest a criterion for assessing institutional arrangements for service delivery rather than to indicate a particular form. To argue for seeing accountability in terms of political *argument* is not to argue, necessarily, for political *control* in the sense of making directly elected bodies or members responsible for service delivery. The irony would seem to be, as our findings hint, that the fact of election may have the paradoxical effect of weakening the pressure on members to justify their actions in terms of the service performance, seen as the achievement of desired objectives or outputs, rather than strengthening it. Accountability, in these circumstances, tends to be taken as axiomatic – an article of religious faith – rather than as something which emerges from the process of argument. If elected members see themselves as accountable, it is either for the achievement of objectives set out in party manifestos (which often have only a tenuous relationship with the objectives of specific services, and tend to be concerned with particular inputs or policies rather than overall performance) or for the achievement of such very general ends as the good of the community.

It is also possible to draw out a number of more specific, though conflicting implications for institutional design from our analysis of accountability. One of the problems complicating the practice of accountability stems, as we have seen throughout, from the difficulty of assigning responsibility for outputs or outcomes to any single service. The converse of the contemporary emphasis on the interrelationship between different services and social factors is to blur the focus of accountability. This has given new meaning to Mill's phrase (quoted in Chapter 1) that 'responsibility is null when nobody knows who is responsible'. The logic of this would argue for moving towards all-purpose local authorities, responsible for *all* the services whose activities bear on each other.[7] But such an approach generates as many problems as it promises to solve. It does not encompass responsibility for the social and economic environment which influences all services; if we were to take a 'holistic' view of accountability, we would be driven to ever-increasing centralization (the model would be not elected local authorities, but central government agencies like health authorities). Equally all-embracing accountability might all too easily become meaningless accountability. If our analysis is at all correct in stressing that the problems of accountability reflect the heterogeneity, complexity, and uncertainty about the relationship between means and ends within individual services, then they would be compounded if the focus of accountability were to become the end-product of the sum of the performance of different services. The result might be to make the notion of performance even more vacuous and the process of service delivery even less permeable. To quote the conclusions of a study of Swedish local government:[8]

'The ideal of representative democracy with an open and direct interplay between voters and elected representatives is replaced by a process of negotiation which is difficult to penetrate and in which responsibility for the final outcome is often unclear.'

This is not only an apt summary of the contemporary problems of accountability, but also a reminder that these problems stem not from the particular nature of British institutions (although they may be aggravated by them) but from the nature of modern services and that they appear to persist even in systems, like Sweden's, where elected authorities control services which are the responsibility of central government agencies here.

The alternative implication to be drawn is that the direction of change should be towards unpackaging, rather than aggregating, individual services: in particular, towards unpackaging them geographically in order to recreate the circumstances in which an Athenian-type face-to-face accountability becomes possible. This would chime with the growing emphasis, remarkably consistent across the services in our study, on downward accountability (and, indeed, with the personal perceptions of the members in our survey who overwhelmingly saw themselves as being downwardly accountable to the community and who tended to use their hands-on experience of the services concerned as their language of evaluation). It would suggest that the direction of movement should be toward strengthening local forums in which service providers would be directly answerable for their conduct to the community being served. Again, some possible difficulties must be noted. The first is that a particular definition of accountability is implicit in such developments. It is accountability seen as explanation or justification, but without formal sanctions. But what happens if an explanation or justification fails to satisfy or, indeed, what leverage is there to compel a full rendering of accounts? It may be that informal social sanctions exercised in a face to face setting can be as strong (or possibly even stronger) than formal political or legal sanctions exercised in a larger context. The second is that it may be difficult to reconcile

downward accountability, even if only in a restricted sense, with
hierarchical upward accountability; or to put it somewhat differ-
ently, accountability for the performance of a service in a
particular locality with the overall performance of the service in a
wider geographical setting. Different forums may generate different criteria, or evaluative languages. While it may be argued
that multiple criteria should indeed be generated, since services
inevitably have multiple objectives, the result could be a Babel of
evaluative languages: the problem of reconciliation or agreeing on
a shared vocabulary of authoritative judgement would remain.

Yet a different set of implications follows if the problems of
accountability are seen to derive not from institutional design, or
lack of opportunity for engaging in argument, but from the
organizational power of service deliverers, whether these claim to
be professionals or not. If this power is taken as a given, if it is
argued that service providers will inevitably subvert any attempt at
setting criteria for the outputs of services, then two very different
approaches might be advocated. The first might be to substitute
market provision for public services: to make service providers
responsive (or accountable) to consumers by marketing their
goods. But creating a true market may be politically impossible.
Even if it were feasible, however, this model would not fit those
services like the police and parts of the social services whose
function is social control. Also, this approach fails to address the
problems of asymmetry of knowledge between providers and
consumers, that is precisely the problem which stalks the whole
discussion of accountability. The second, alternative approach
would be to strengthen the internal mechanisms of accountability
within the professions or bodies of service deliverers.[9] If peer
judgement is the inevitable coinage of accountability, given the
nature of particular services and the power of the providers, then
let it be an effective coinage. In other words, this is an argument
for opening up and making more visible both the mechanisms of,
and the criteria used in, peer accountability: forcing, as it were,
the service providers to explain how they police their performance.
Even if this were feasible, this approach still implies a particular –
and restricted – definition of accountability: it is accountability
seen in terms of the quality of the processes involved in delivering
services. It fails to deal with the question of whether a good overall

performance can be deduced from the technical quality of individual actions.

To stress the problems involved in various approaches to accountability is not to come to a negative conclusion. These problems derive from the ambiguities of the notion of account-ability itself, which it has been the purpose of this book to explore. No one approach to accountability can be satisfactory *precisely* because the concept itself has many meanings and dimensions. From this flows our positive conclusion: that accountability must be seen in terms not of individual institutions but as a system which is woven into the fabric of political and social life as a whole. Different institutions or techniques will be appropriate to the different dimensions of accountability; in turn, the emphasis on the role of individual institutions or techniques will differ depending on whether one's concern is primarily about traditional political accountability, seen in terms of individual actions or about technical accountability for the efficient and effective performance of a service. What matters, though, is that the system should be seen as a whole in recognition of the interdependence of the different forms of accountability, and the linkages between them. The challenge of modern accountability is all about responding to the complexity by repairing linkages which have snapped or frayed and inventing new ones where they do not exist, and creating a framework which brings together politics and techniques in a new dialogue. So far, the emphasis of public policy has been to respond to complexity chiefly by setting up new institutions of accountability. Our analysis suggests that this may, in turn, bring about excessive complexity in the machinery of accountability and at the same time create dead-ends. So, why not concentrate less on formal links or institutions and engage more in a civic dialogue to recreate at least something of the high visibility and directness of the face-to-face accountability with which the story of the word began.

REFERENCES

1 S. Barrett and C. Fudge (eds) (1981) *Policy and Action*. London: Methuen.
2 Note, for example, the view that the 1979 social workers' strike in

Tower Hamlets 'provided some evidence that the jobs social workers did were either unnecessary or could as well be done by others with less pretentious training and objectives', C. Brewer and J. Lait (1980) *Can Social Work Survive?* London: Temple Smith: 84.

3 K. Popper (1976) *Unended Quest.* Glasgow: Fontana: 43. Our use of the 'Black Swan' concept represents, of course, a loose application of Popper's theory of falsification. It is merely to suggest that case studies like ours are useful in raising questions about conventional assumptions, not to imply that these can be falsified (one of the problems in the social sciences being that 'theories' tend to be bundles of vaguely specified assumptions which survive precisely because they are too vague to be tested by rigorous analysis).

4 R. Beiner (1983) *Political Judgement.* Chicago, Ill: University of Chicago Press. This section owes much to Beiner's analysis (which draws on Habermas as well as Aristotle).

5 Compare two reports published within a week of each other: Audit Commission (1986) *Towards Better Management of Secondary Education.* London: HMSO; and Her Majesty's Inspectorate (1986) *Report on the Effects of Local Authority Expenditure Policies on Education Provision in England and Wales 1985.* London: DES. The messages of the two reports are not incompatible but their impact in terms of newspaper headlines was very different.

6 Aristotle, *The Politics* (trans. 1948 Sir Ernest Barker). Oxford: Clarendon Press: 145–47.

7 See, for example, the arguments in M. Goldsmith (ed.) (1986) *Essays in the Future of Local Government.* Salford: University of Salford.

8 L. Stromberg and J. Westerstahl (1984) *The New Swedish Communes.* Goteborg: Department of Political Science, University of Goteborg.

9 R. Klein (1973) *Complaints Against Doctors.* London: Charles Knight. P. Wilding (1982) *Professional Power and Social Welfare.* London: Routledge & Kegan Paul.

Appendix 1: Survey methods: the conceptual framework

The eighteenth-month-long study addressed itself to an examination of the notion of accountability as defined by the members of different kinds of committees and authorities: that is to the question of how members of such bodies interpret and perform the task of achieving control over the activities of the services for which they are statutorily accountable. The bodies studied were a water authority, a police authority, the social services and education committees of a county council, and three district health authorities.

The overall response rate is shown in *Table 2*. From this it can be seen that the response rate varied between 88 per cent and 60 per cent for those committees and authorities where it was possible to interview members personally but plunged for the two district health authorities (nos 2 and 3) where a postal questionnaire was used. Somewhat complicating the picture is the fact that during the course of our project the total membership of each committee varied from time to time as members left and others were recruited. One or two members became too ill to participate in the study and one member died. Most of the members approached were happy to give of their time; those who refused did so usually because they were too busy or because they were ill. Only a few members refused to participate because of dislike or suspicion of the project.

As a preliminary to approaching members, the chief executives or officers and the chairmen or chairwomen of all the five bodies

Table 2 *Response rate*

	water authority	police authority	social services committee	education committee	district health authorities		
total membership	17	38	25	30	18	18	18
number interviewed	15	27	21	22	13	10	6
response rate (%)	88	71	84	60	72	55	33

were interviewed. In part, the intention was to get their seal of approval for the research project and their co-operation in encouraging their members to participate (although in all cases it was left to the individual members to make their own decisions). In part too, the intention was to collect background information about the services under study. In both respects this strategy proved very successful. The chief officers and chairman/chairwomen were helpful in guiding us as to how best to recruit members: for example, they suggested that we interview members in outlying rural areas first, while the good weather lasted. Equally important, these interviews provided insights into the relationship between chief officers and chairmen/chairwomen – an important aspect of the study, as we came to realize during our work.

Following this preliminary stage, the committee members were contacted in three batches, first by letter (with a full explanation of the nature of the project) and then by telephone to arrange precise appointment details. While the first batch was being interviewed, the second wave of letters was sent out – and so forth.

In developing the line of questioning, great care had to be taken to allow members to set out their ideas in their own words. As already mentioned, the formal concept of 'accountability' did not have much resonance with most members, and the interviewing technique therefore had to be largely open-ended, pursuing in each case the same themes but avoiding leading questions. This strategy proved more time-consuming than anticipated but also provided very rich information.

In each interview the following themes, reflecting issues raised by government policy or the academic literature were explored: How did the members define the aims and objectives of the services for which they were responsible and their own role in achieving them? What did the members perceive to be the outputs or outcomes of the services? How far did members see themselves accountable for achieving value for money, and how did they attempt to achieve this? How did members monitor performance, what statistics did they use as performance indicators, and did they use advice provided by outside bodies such as auditors and inspectorates? How did members see their own roles *vis-à-vis* those of their officers? How, if at all, did members define the professional domain – or expertise – of the service providers, and what implications did they draw for their own role? To whom did members see themselves as being accountable, and in what way? What constituency did members see themselves serving?

In addition to the interviews and questionnaires, a collection and analysis of agendas and minutes was made for each of the authorities or committees throughout the eighteen months of the study. The regular supply of these items was negotiated at the beginning of the study with the chief officers, some of whom also arranged for a supply of back copies. During the study, regular searches of local papers were also carried out for news items covering the five bodies. This part of the study provided valuable information both about the service and its committee structure as well as a feeling for individual and collective membership activities.

Attendance at authority and committee meetings had, of necessity, to be selective. These were interesting chiefly for the insights they provided into the ritualistic aspects of membership activity, and what this implied for accountability. However, the greatest part of the study period was taken up by the interviewing and the focus of the research remained an examination of the perceived and practised accountability in a variety of service environments and statutorily defined roles.

Index